高职高专旅游专业"互联网+"创新规划教材

酒店服务与管理实训英语
Practical Training of English for Hotel Service and Function

主 编 王艳萍 郭丽辉 刘 艳

内 容 简 介

本书主要针对酒店服务业中的主要服务岗位展开论述，全书共包括 6 个模块，即前厅服务、客房服务、餐饮部、商务中心、康乐中心、其他酒店服务，每个模块涵盖工作流程介绍、岗位对话、岗位用语、延展阅读和实操训练 5 个部分。

本书与时俱进，采用"互联网+"的形式提供了大量教学资源，读者可以通过扫描二维码进行学习。书后附录为 2017 年全国职业院校技能大赛高职组中餐主题宴会设计赛项（英语口语测试题库及参考答案），可供学生日常练习参考。

本书既可作为高职高专旅游管理类和酒店管理类专业的教材，也可作为广大酒店管理人员、服务人员培训和学习参考用书。

图书在版编目（CIP）数据

酒店服务与管理实训英语 / 王艳萍，郭丽辉，刘艳主编. —北京：北京大学出版社，2021.1
高职高专旅游专业"互联网+"创新规划教材
ISBN 978-7-301-31655-9

Ⅰ. ①酒… Ⅱ. ①王… ②郭… ③刘… Ⅲ. ①饭店—商业服务—英语—高等职业教育—教材 ②饭店—商业管理—英语—高等职业教育—教材 Ⅳ. ① F719.2

中国版本图书馆 CIP 数据核字（2020）第 182646 号

书　　　名	酒店服务与管理实训英语 JIUDIAN FUWU YU GUANLI SHIXUN YINGYU
著作责任者	王艳萍　郭丽辉　刘　艳　主编
策划编辑	刘国明
责任编辑	李瑞芳
数字编辑	金常伟
标准书号	ISBN 978-7-301-31655-9
出版发行	北京大学出版社
地　　　址	北京市海淀区成府路 205 号　100871
网　　　址	http://www.pup.cn　新浪微博：@ 北京大学出版社
电子邮箱	编辑部 pup6@pup.cn　总编室 zpup@pup.cn
电　　　话	邮购部 010-62752015　发行部 010-62750672　编辑部 010-62750667
印刷者	北京虎彩文化传播有限公司
经销者	新华书店
	787 毫米 ×1092 毫米　16 开本　16.75 印张　396 千字 2021 年 1 月第 1 版　2025 年 1 月第 2 次印刷
定　　　价	44.00 元

未经许可，不得以任何方式复制或抄袭本书之部分或全部内容。
版权所有，侵权必究
举报电话：010-62752024　电子邮箱：fd@pup.cn
图书如有印装质量问题，请与出版部联系，电话：010-62756370

前 言

本书主要服务于高职高专旅游管理和酒店管理专业，针对酒店服务业中的主要服务岗位，如前厅服务、客房服务、餐饮部、商务中心、康乐中心等，创设语言环境，设置具体任务，使学生在工作情境下学中做、做中学，提高酒店英语服务技能。

针对"酒店服务与管理实训英语"的课程特点，为了使学生更加直观地理解本书知识点，方便教师教学讲解，本书以二维码的形式提供了大量学习资源，读者可通过手机"扫一扫"功能进行拓展学习。编者也会根据行业发展情况，及时更新二维码所链接的资源，以使书中内容与酒店服务行业发展结合更加紧密。

本书分为6个模块，24个单元，每个单元涵盖工作流程介绍、岗位对话、岗位用语、延展阅读和实操训练5个部分。第一部分系统地给出本单元的岗位流程，使教师和学生把握本单元的脉络。第二部分通过具体工作内容设置对话，按照时间顺序展开，针对实际工作岗位设计对话，用语规范简练，实用性强，每个对话提供外教录音资源，学生可以通过手机扫描二维码反复练习听力、模仿纯正英语发音；每个对话配有词语注释，便于学生理解和掌握。第三部分对每一单元的重点句型进行提炼，并带有汉语译文，学生可以在课堂和课后进行练习。第四部分是延展阅读，主要根据本单元的情景对话内容设置，作为本书的辅助阅读资料，拓宽学生知识面，开阔学生视野。第五部分是实操训练，分别针对各个岗位的实际工作需要，对工作用语、翻译技能和岗位知识等提供了切实可行的练习，帮助学生进一步巩固所学知识。同时，书后还附有2017年全国职业院校技能大赛高职组中餐主题宴会设计赛项（英语口语测试题库及参考答案），可供学生日常练习参考。

本书由王艳萍、郭丽辉、刘艳编写，其中模块一和模块二的前两个单元由王艳萍编写，共计10万字；模块二的第三、四单元和模块三、模块四的第一单元由郭丽辉编写，共计10万字；模块四的第二、三单元和模块五、模块六及书后附录由刘艳编写。全书的统稿工作由王艳萍和姜爽负责。

由于编者水平有限，加之时间仓促，疏漏之处在所难免，恳请广大读者批评指正。

【资源索引】

目录 Contents

1 Section One
Front Office 前厅服务 — 1

Topic One　Room Reservation
　　客房预订 /2

　　Introduction/2
　　Objectives/2
　　Working Procedures/3
　　Dialogues/3
　　Useful Sentences/7
　　Knowledge Extension/8
　　Section Summary/10
　　Practice/10

Topic Two　At the Airport
　　接机服务 /15

　　Introduction/15
　　Objectives/15
　　Working Procedures/16
　　Dialogues/16
　　Useful Sentences/20
　　Knowledge Extension/20
　　Section Summary/22
　　Practice/22

Topic Three　Check-in
　　登记入住 /26

　　Introduction/26
　　Objectives/26
　　Working Procedures/27
　　Dialogues/27
　　Useful Sentences/30
　　Knowledge Extension/31
　　Section Summary/34
　　Practice/34

Topic Four　Bell Service
　　行李服务 /38

　　Introduction/38
　　Objectives/38
　　Working Procedures/39
　　Dialogues/39
　　Useful Sentences/43
　　Knowledge Extension/43
　　Section Summary/45
　　Practice/46

Topic Five　Currency Exchange
　　外币兑换 /49

　　Introduction/49
　　Objectives/49
　　Working Procedures/50
　　Dialogues/50
　　Useful Sentences/53
　　Knowledge Extension /54
　　Section Summary/55
　　Practice/56

Topic Six　Check-out
　　结账离开 /59

　　Introduction/59
　　Objectives/59
　　Working Procedures/60
　　Dialogues/60
　　Useful Sentences/64
　　Knowledge Extension/64
　　Section Summary/65
　　Practice/65

2 Section Two
Housekeeping Service 客房服务 —— 68

Topic One Room Cleaning Service 客房清扫 /69
- Introduction/69
- Objectives/69
- Working Procedures/70
- Dialogues/70
- Useful Sentences/73
- Knowledge Extension/74
- Section Summary/75
- Practice/76

Topic Two Laundry Service 洗衣服务 /79
- Introduction/79
- Objectives/79
- Working Procedures/79
- Dialogues/80
- Useful Sentences/83
- Knowledge Extension/84
- Section Summary/86
- Practice/86

Topic Three Turn-down Service 夜床服务 /89
- Introduction/89
- Objectives/89
- Working Procedures/90
- Dialogues/90
- Useful Sentences/93
- Knowledge Extension/94
- Section Summary/95
- Practice/95

Topic Four Wake-up Call Service 叫醒服务 /99
- Introduction/99
- Objectives/99
- Working Procedures/100
- Dialogues/100
- Useful Sentences/104
- Knowledge Extension/105
- Section Summary/106
- Practice/107

3 Section Three
F&B Department 餐饮部 —— 110

Topic One Food and Beverage Reservation 餐饮预订 /111
- Introduction/111
- Objectives/111
- Working Procedures/112
- Dialogues/112
- Useful Sentences/115
- Knowledge Extension/116
- Section Summary/118
- Practice/118

Topic Two F&B Service in Western Style 西餐席间服务 /122
- Introduction/122
- Objectives/122
- Working Procedures/123
- Dialogues/123
- Useful Sentences/127
- Knowledge Extension/128
- Section Summary/129
- Practice/130

Topic Three　F&B Service in Chinese
　　　　　　　Style 中餐席间服务 /134

 Introduction/134

 Objectives/134

 Working Procedures/135

 Dialogues/135

 Useful Sentences/138

 Knowledge Extension/139

 Section Summary/141

 Practice/141

Topic Four　Bar Service
　　　　　　酒吧服务 /144

 Introduction/144

 Objectives/144

 Working Procedures/145

 Dialogues/145

 Useful Sentences/148

 Knowledge Extension/149

 Section Summary/150

 Practice/151

Topic Five　Settling the Bill Service
　　　　　　结账服务 /154

 Introduction/154

 Objectives/154

 Working Procedures/155

 Dialogues/155

 Useful Sentences/158

 Knowledge Extension/158

 Section Summary/159

 Practice/159

4 Section Four
Business Center 商务中心 ... 163

Topic One　Photocopy and Fax
　　　　　　Services 复印、传真服务 /164

 Introduction/164

 Objectives/164

 Working Procedures/165

 Dialogues/165

 Useful Sentences/168

 Knowledge Extension/169

 Section Summary/170

 Practice/170

Topic Two　Typing and Printing
　　　　　　Services 打字、打印服务 /173

 Introduction/173

 Objectives/173

 Working Procedures/173

 Dialogues/174

 Useful Sentences/177

 Knowledge Extension/178

 Section Summary/179

 Practice/179

Topic Three　Convention Service
　　　　　　　会议服务 /182

 Introduction/182

 Objectives/182

 Working Procedures/183

 Dialogues/183

 Useful Sentences/186

 Knowledge Extension/187

 Section Summary/189

 Practice/189

5 Section Five
Health and Recreation Center 康乐中心 — 193

Topic One   Fitness Club Service
健身俱乐部服务 /194

- Introduction/194
- Objectives/194
- Working Procedures/195
- Dialogues/195
- Useful Sentences/197
- Knowledge Extension/198
- Section Summary/199
- Practice/199

Topic Two   Swimming Pool Service
游泳馆服务 /203

- Introduction/203
- Objectives/203
- Working Procedures/204
- Dialogues/204
- Useful Sentences/206
- Knowledge Extension/207
- Section Summary/208
- Practice/208

Topic Three   Night Club Service
夜总会服务 /212

- Introduction/212
- Objectives/212
- Working Procedures/212
- Dialogues/213
- Useful Sentences/216
- Knowledge Extension/217
- Section Summary/218
- Practice/218

Topic Four   Bath Service
洗浴服务 /221

- Introduction/221
- Objectives/221
- Working Procedures/222
- Dialogues/222
- Useful Sentences/224
- Knowledge Extension/225
- Section Summary/226
- Practice/227

6 Section Six
Other Hotel Services 其他酒店服务 — 230

Topic One   Operator Service
话务服务 /231

- Introduction/231
- Objectives/231
- Working Procedures/232
- Dialogues/232
- Useful Sentences/234
- Knowledge Extension/235
- Section Summary/236
- Practice/236

Topic Two   Hotel Shopping Service
酒店购物服务 /240

- Introduction/240
- Objectives/240
- Working Procedures/241
- Dialogues/241
- Useful Sentences/244
- Knowledge Extension/244
- Section Summary/245
- Practice/245

Appendices — 248

- Appendix I   Additional Material, Resources and References/248
- Appendix II   Contest Problems for Technical Competence/249

Section One

Front Office
前厅服务

模块一

Introduction

The front office or reception is an area where visitors arrive. The members there are responsible for dealing with the visitors' questions.

The main responsibility of the front office is to receive reservations, register guests, assign rooms, distribute baggage, store guests' valuables, provide information, deliver mails and messages, exchange foreign currencies, check guests out and so on.

Front office staff are in charge of getting in touch with the guests inside the hotel, handling printing and typing tasks, sorting emails, answering phones, using the printer and fax machine and so on.

Topic One　Room Reservation 客房预订

Introduction

Reservation service offers guests a professional service in a comfortable and friendly manner.

The Front Office offers a kind of advance reservation service. The reservationist at the front desk works by the lobby, answering the questions about reservations, including types of room reservation, types of restaurants, ways of making reservation and types of hotel services, booking rooms, canceling or revising room booking and so on.

Objectives

Competence Standard	Knowledge Standard
Ability to receive or refuse a room reservation politely	Know about the working procedures of room reservation
Ability to confirm a room reservation	Learn to reserve a room, revise a reservation, change a reservation, and refuse the reservation
Ability to communicate with the guest	Know about four types of room reservation and eleven types of restaurants
Ability of listening, speaking and reading	Learn six ways of making reservation and seven types of hotel service

Working Procedures

- Greet the guest.
- Ask for the guest's name.
- Ask for the guest's time of arrival and departure, and the number of people and rooms.
- Ask for the room style.
- Check the room availability.
- Offer the room rate.
- Ask for special requests.
- Ask for the guest's e-mail address, telephone number, and way of paying.
- Confirm the reservation.
- Say good-bye.
- Express your wishes.

Dialogues

Dialogue 1

Situation Question: Do you know how to deal with FIT reservation? What kind of information should you get from guests?

FIT Reservation

R: Reservationist   G: Guest

R: Good morning. Hua Xia Hotel. How may I help you today?

G: Yes. I would like to book a room, please.

R: May I know your arrival and departure dates?

G: Yes, from Oct. 10th to Oct. 13th, for 3 nights.

R: How many people are there in your party?

G: Three, my wife, my daughter and myself.

R: What type of room would you prefer?

G: I'd like a double room.

R: Can you hold the line please? I'll check our room availabilities for those days. Thank you for your waiting, sir. We have a double room available for those days.

G: What is the room rate?

R: 1,500 *yuan* per night.

G: OK, I'll take it.

R: May I have your name, sir?

G: Yes, it's Carl May.

R: Could you spell that please?

G: Yes, Carl—C-A-R-L, May—M-A-Y.

R: Mr. May, may I have your phone number?

G: Yes, my phone number is 0044-20-5637433.

R: Would you like to guarantee your reservation, Mr. May?

G: Yes, how can I do that?

R: You may prepay, use your credit card, or make an advance deposit. Which one would you prefer?

G: I will use credit card.

R: Good. Could you tell me the type of your credit card and the number?

G: OK. It is a Master Card. The number is 5412-3320-5649-4931.

R: Thank you, Mr. May. I'd like to confirm your reservation: a double room for Mr. May from Oct. 10th to Oct. 13th, and you are guaranteeing your reservation with your Master Card, and the number is 5412-3320-5649-4931. Is that correct, sir?

G: Yes, it is correct.

R: Great. I am so glad to serve you, Mr. May. We are looking forward to your coming in October. Thank you for your calling.

Notes:

(1) FIT 散客（Foreign Independent Tourist），FIT Reservation 散客预订

(2) walk-in guest 未经预约的客人

(3) book 预订

(4) departure 离开

(5) prefer 更喜欢

(6) available 空闲的

(7) advance 预先的，先期的　advance payment 预付款　advance deposit 预付押金　by credit card 用信用卡

(8) guaranteed reservation 保证预订

Dialogue 2

Situation Question: How would you deal with group reservation? Are there any differences between group reservation and FIT reservation?

Group Reservation

【拓展音频】

R: Reservationist　　G: Guest

R: Good morning. Hua Xia Hotel. May I help you?

G: Yes, I'd like to book ten double rooms.

R: Is it a company booking?

G: Oh, yes. I'm calling from Happy Tour Travel Agency. And I want to know if you have the rooms available from September 8th to September 13th.

R: Just a moment, sir. Let me check the room reservation list and see if we have enough vacancies for the dates you required. Sorry to have kept you waiting, sir. We have the rooms available for the dates.

G: That's good. Do you have a discount for group booking?

R: Yes, we offer 15 percent discount for group reservation.

G: Great.

R: May I know how you would like to pay?

G: I'll send you a check soon.

R: May I have your name and phone number, please?

G: Mr. Johnson, my number is 69254603.

R: Mr. Johnson, let me confirm. You have booked ten double rooms from September 8th to September 13th, for 5 nights. Is that right?

G: Yes.

R: Thank you for your calling. Have a good day! Good-bye.

G: Good-bye.

Notes:

(1) company booking 团体预订，同 group booking

(2) travel agency 旅行社

(3) vacancy 空缺　vacant room 空房

(4) keep doing 一直做某事　keep sb. doing sth. 使某人一直做某事

(5) discount 折扣

Dialogue 3

Situation Question: How would you deal with the guest's request of changing a reservation? If the room the guest wants is not available, what will you do as a reservationist?

Change a Reservation

R: Reservationist　　G: Guest

R: Good morning. Hua Xia Hotel. May I help you?

G: Yes, I reserved a double room the day before in your hotel. But now something special happened. I want to change my reservation.

R: OK, sir. May I know whose name the reservation is under?

G: Yes. Dave Li. The telephone number is 46523245.

R: Mr. Li, let me have a check. Oh, yes, you have booked a double room for three nights from Oct. 9th to Oct 12th. How would you like to change it?

G: I planned to come to the city with my wife, but now she has a business trip to other city on those days. I want to change it to a single room.

R: OK, let me check. There is a single room available for the days. Will you reserve it?

G: Yes, thank you.

R: So, Mr. Li reserves a single room from Oct. 9th to Oct. 12th. Is that right?

G: Yes, thank you for your help.

R: It's my pleasure. Look forward to your coming, Mr. Li. Good-bye.

G: Good-bye.

Notes:

(1) under the name of 以……的名义

(2) business trip 公务旅行，出差

(3) look forward to 盼望，期待

Dialogue 4

Situation Question: If the hotel is fully booked, what would you do with the new reservation?

We Are Fully Booked

【拓展音频】

R: Reservationist   G: Guest

R: Good morning. Hua Xia Hotel. May I help you?

G: I'd like to reserve a room.

R: What type of room would you like, Madam?

G: I need a single room from Oct. 1st to Oct. 3rd.

R: Certainly, Madam. Allow me a few minutes to check our room availability for those days. I'm sorry, Madam. We are fully booked for those days. You know it's peak season because of the national holiday.

G: Oh, so bad.

R: Would you like us to put you on our waiting list and call you if there is a cancellation?

G: It's so kind of you. But could you recommend other hotels to me near your hotel?

R: Sorry, Madam. I'm afraid we don't have the room information of other hotels.

G: It's OK.

R: Would you like to change your reservation date?

G: No.

R: Would you like me to put you on our waiting list?

G: OK. Thank you.

R: May I have your name and telephone number? If we have the room available, we will call you.

G: OK. My name is Lily Wang and my number is 66325981.

R: OK, Mrs. Wang. We will call you as soon as we get the vacant room. Thank you for your calling. Good-bye.

G: Good-bye.

Notes:

(1) room availability 空房情况，客房预订情况
(2) fully booked 客满
(3) peak season 旺季　low season 淡季
(4) waiting list 候补名单
(5) cancel 取消　cancellation 取消

Useful Sentences

- Good morning. Great Wall Hotel, how may I help you?/ What can I do for you?/ Can I help you?/Is there anything I can do for you? 早上好，这里是长城酒店，请问您需要什么帮助？
- I'd like to reserve a room in your hotel. 我想在你们酒店订一个房间。
- May I know your arrival and departure dates? 请问您抵达和离店日期？
- What kind of room would you like to have?/What type of room would you like to reserve/book? 您想要订什么样的房间？
- Would you like a single room/ double room/ suite? 您想要订一个单人间/双人间/套房？
- I'd like a room with harbor view/front view. 我想要一个带海景/阳面的房间。
- I'd like a room with a bath tub. 我想要一个带浴缸的房间。
- How many people are there in your party? 请问您一行几人？
- How long do you intend to stay? 您准备住多久？
- For how many nights? 您准备住几个晚上？
- When do you need the room? 您什么时候入住？
- Wait a moment, please. / Could you hold the line, please? Let me check the reservation list. 请稍等，我查一下预订记录。
- I will check the availability of the room for those days. 我查一下那几天是否有空房。
- We have vacant rooms for the days you mentioned. 你说的日期我们有空房。
- The rooms are available for those days. 那几天我们有空房。
- What is the room rate? 房费多少？
- A double room is RMB1,200 *yuan* per night. 双人间每晚1200元。
- Is there any discount / preferential rate for group reservation? 团体预订是否有优惠/折扣？
- We offer a 15% discount for group reservation. 团体预订可以打八五折。
- May I have your name and telephone number? 请问您的姓名和电话号码。
- Would you like to guarantee your reservation? 您需要保证订房吗？
- How would you like to guarantee the reservation? You can choose to use credit card or pay cash in advance. 您选哪种保证订房，信用卡还是预付款？

- Does your hotel have pick-up service? 请问贵酒店有接车服务吗?
- I am sorry, sir/madam. Our rooms are fully booked. 抱歉，先生/女士。客房已订满。
- I am afraid all rooms are taken. 恐怕所有客房已订满。
- Can I take your name and number, and I will contact you if there is a cancellation? 您可以留下姓名和电话号码，如果有客人取消预订，我们会联系您。
- Please allow me to confirm your reservation. 跟您确认一下您的预订。
- You have booked a double room for three nights from Oct. 10th to Oct. 13th. Is that correct, Mr. Smith? 史密斯先生，您预订了一个双人间，从10月10日至13日共三晚，对吧?
- Thank you for your calling. 感谢您的来电。
- Thank you for your reservation. 感谢您的预订。
- Have a good day. 祝您愉快。

Knowledge Extension

◆ Hotel

A hotel is a temporary home for travelers. In a hotel, travelers can have food, have drinks and have a rest. The hotel may also offer the facilities for recreation, such as a golf course, beach or a swimming pool.

◆ Four Types of Room Reservation

Advance Reservation 提前预订
Confirmed Reservation 已确认的预订
On-waiting Reservation 等候性预订
Guaranteed Reservation 保证性预订

◆ Types of Restaurant

The restaurant industry consists of various types of establishments as follows:

Hotels

A hotel can provide accommodation, meals and other services to travelers, which have five star ratings from 1 through 5 depending on the facilities and services for guests.

Motels

A motel is a roadside hotel mainly for the motorist, with rooms in low blocks and parking lots outside. Motels can have star ratings relying on the facilities, level of service and accommodation offered.

Resorts

A resort refers to a hotel located in the place designed for the guest wanting to go to on holiday. The typical resort with several restaurants and bars offers guests all kinds of sporting and adventure activities.

Convention Centers

A convention center can hold large groups of people for stage seminars, product launches, exhibitions, banquets, cocktail parties, balls and other functions.

Convention Tourism

It refers to tourism activities arranged as a part of a convention/conference package for the partners. The package may include accommodation, travel arrangements, hiking and leisure activities.

Casinos

Some games are offered for bosses to play. If lucky, they can win money. Such games as black jack, roulette, prize wheel and two-up games are also provided. Within the casino, there are several food and beverage outlets from fine dining rooms to coffee shops and bars.

Clubs

Clubs are organizations bringing people with similar interests together and offering food, beverages and entertainments to their members and guests. Many clubs provide gaming facilities, including poker machines and keno.

Restaurants

A restaurant is a place where people pay to sit and have cooked meals. Restaurants include small casual eating places and fine dining restaurants offering silver service in the elegant surroundings. Their staff must have excellent technical skills, product knowledge and customer relations skills.

Cafes and Bistros

Both are restaurants offering meals, cakes, ice-cream, all sorts of coffees and beverages, including alcoholic beverages. There many tables and chairs are put outside on the foot path for alfresco dining.

Pubs/Taverns

A pub or tavern is a place offering beer and other beverages, as well as meals and entertainment. Different from the traditional Australian pub, especially in South Australia, Poker machines, TAB and Keno allow the customers to place bets on races or a number game. If you want to work in a pub with gaming facilities, you need to have some experiences in handling gaming machines.

Fast Food Restaurants

A fast food restaurant is an eating place with limited light meals, snacks, desserts and beverages such as soft drinks, coffee and milk shakes. Most fast food restaurants belong to chains with outlets in several countries. The staff there are efficient, well-trained and well-presented.

◆ Ways of Making Reservation

You can reserve a room in the ways of
talking at the counter 柜台预订
telephone reservation 电话预订
fax reservation 传真预订
mail/letter booking 信函预订
verbal/oral booking 口头预订
Internet reservation 网络预订

◆ Types of Hotel Services

bell service 应接服务
room service 客房服务
food service 用餐服务
hotel shop service 饭店商场服务
laundry service 洗衣服务
health and recreation service 康乐服务
operator service 电话总机服务

Section Summary

- Reservation service offers guests a professional service in a comfortable and friendly manner.
- Learn about the working procedures of room reservation.
- Know about how to reserve a room, revise the reservation, change a reservation, and refuse the reservation.
- Know something about a hotel.
- Learn four types of room reservation.
- Know about eleven types of restaurants.
- Learn six ways of making reservation.
- Learn seven types of hotel services.

Practice

Part One Dialogue

1. Fill in the blanks with correct sentences according to the context.

R: Reservationist   G: Guest

R: Good morning. Room Reservation. Can I help you?

G: Yes, I'd like to book a room.

R: _____

G: I'd like a single room with bath. What's the room rate?

R: It's RMB980 *yuan* per night. For how many nights?

G: Four days.

R: _____

G: From September 8th to 12th.

R: _____

G: Yes, how can I do that?

R: You can choose to use your credit card or pay cash in advance.

G: I'd like to use a credit card.

R: _____

G: Yes, it's 3241-8963-7661-8632, and its expiry date is June 15th, 2025.

R: OK, sir. May I have your name and telephone number?

G: Yes, my name is Harry Smith, and my telephone number is 44-4523-5632.

R: OK, sir. Just to confirm. _____. Is it correct, Mr. Smith?

G: Yes, that's right.

R: Thank you for your reservation, Mr. Smith. Good-bye.

G: Good-bye.

A. May I have your arrival and departure dates?

B. What kind of room would you prefer?

C. Would you like to guarantee your reservation?

D. You have booked a single room for four nights from Sept. 8th to 12th.

E. May I have your credit card number and the expiry date?

2. Read the following telephone numbers and dictate them to your partner.

(1) 01-4406-5643

(2) 44-7864-8967

(3) 34-7862-2845

(4) 55-6843-1245

(5) 61-8915-3047

(6) 45-9510-6813

3. Read the following time and dictate them to your partner.

(1) 8:10

(2) 8:20

(3) 7:30

(4) 6:45

(5) 12:00

(6) 16:45

(7) 19:15

(8) 22:00

(9) 15:00

(10) 10:50

4. Act in pairs to finish the following role-play activities.

(1) Student A: Act as a guest. Make a phone call to a hotel to reserve a double room for two days, leave your name and telephone number, and guaranteed reservation.

Student B: Act as the reservationist. Answer the phone call.

(2) Student A: You go to the front desk to reserve a family suite for your parents to celebrate their 50th wedding anniversary.

Student B: Act as the reservationist to serve student A.

(3) Student A: Phone the reservationist to book rooms for a tour group of 20.

Student B: Act as the reservationist. Answer the phone call.

(4) Student A: Act as a guest to make a phone call to the hotel to book a single room. But you are told by the reservationist the hotel is fully booked.

Student B: Act as the reservationist. Answer the phone call of student A, but tell him/her the hotel is fully booked.

(5) Student A: Phone the reservationist to change your original booking from a single room to two double rooms and offer reasons.

Student B: Act as the reservationist to serve student A.

5. Discussion: Suppose you are the reservationist of the hotel and you encounter the following situations.

(1) What will you do if there is no room available for the guest who has reserved in your hotel?

(2) What will you do if the guest wants to change the reservation at short notice?

6. Translate the following sentences.

(1) 请问您一共几位？

(2) 请问是否还有空房？

(3) 请问您何时入住？

(4) 您要订双人间还是单人间？

(5) 能留下您的姓名和电话号码吗？

(6) 抱歉，我们现在没有空房间。

(7) 您能否改变预订日期呢？

(8) 团队预订可以打八折。

(9) 如果订五间房，房价可以享受八五折。

(10) 我们是一家五星级酒店。

Part Two Knowledge Extension

According to the part of Knowledge Extension, write the answers to the following questions on the sheet of paper by using your own words, not simply copying the sentences. When you have completed the test, ask your lecturer for the answers.

Hotel

_____

_____

Motel

_____

_____

Resort

_____

_____

Convention Center

_____

_____

Convention \ Tourism

_____

_____

Casino

_____

_____

Club

_____

_____

Informal Restaurant

_____

_____

Formal Restaurant (Fine Dining Room)

_____

_____

Cafe/Bistro
_____
_____

Pub
_____
_____

Fast Food Outlet
_____
_____

Section One 模块一
Front Office 前厅服务

Topic Two At the Airport 接机服务

Introduction

Meeting tourists at the airport is an essential first step during the whole reception process in tourism. It's much warmer for tourists being greeted at the airport with a smile, esp. in a foreign country. The whole process of meeting and greeting guests at the airport includes checking the guests' arrival time, arriving at the airport 30 minutes earlier in advance, finding the driver, checking the parking place, telling the driver about the itinerary, finding the guests, greeting them, introducing yourself, counting the guests' number, checking luggage, leading them to the coach, talking about such topics as weather, travel, sports, dress and cosmetics, and then taking them to the hotel.

Objectives

Competence Standard	Knowledge Standard
Ability to meet guests from the airport	Know about the working procedures of meeting guests at the airport
Ability to recognize and meet guests and tour groups	Learn the basic words, phrases and expressions of meeting guests at the airport
Ability to introduce oneself and others and make small talks to break the ice	Grasp the tips on meeting guests at the airport, check-in for flight, delay of check-in for flight, notice of flight cancellation and notice of diverted flight
Ability of listening, speaking and reading	Know about the function areas at the airport and address foreign guests properly

Working Procedures

- Get the expected arrival list.
- Prepare for pick-up service.
  Prepare the pick-up card.
  Make sure of the arrival time, airport and flight number.
- Meet the guests.
  Greet the guests.
  Carry the luggage for the guests.
  Lead the guests to the coach.
- Accompany the guests to take a coach.
  Have a small talk.
- Notify the hotel.

Dialogues

Dialogue 1

Situation Question: Do you know the limousine service? How can you get it?

【拓展音频】

Ask for Pick-up Service

R: Receptionist   B: Bob

R: Good morning. Hua Xia Hotel. How may I help you today?

B: Yes. I want to know if your hotel has pick-up service.

R: Yes, we offer airport limousine service to our guests. The airport representative will be at the airport to meet the guests.

B: OK, that is good. I want to reserve a pick-up service for one of my clients who will be staying in your hotel.

R: OK. May I have your name and number?

B: My name is Bob Xia, and my number is 99092215, and the guest's name is Michael Black.

R: Could you spell the name of the guest?

B: Yes. M-I-C-H-A-E-L, Michael. B-L-A-C-K, Black.

R: OK, may I know the arrival time and flight number?

B: Yes. He will arrive here tomorrow and the flight number is CN1287 from London Heathrow to Shanghai Pudong Airport.

R: Mr. Xia, we have Buick and Benz, which one would you like to choose for the service?

B: I choose Benz.

R: How would you like to pay?

B: Please put it on the room.

R: OK, sir. A pick-up service for Michael Black, and the flight number is CN1287. Is that right?

B: Yes, that is right.

R: OK, sir. We will arrange the pick-up service. Thank you for calling.

Notes:

(1) pick-up service 接机服务

(2) limousine 豪华轿车　limousine service 豪华礼宾车服务

(3) representative 代表　airport representative 机场代表

(4) client 客户；顾客

Dialogue 2

Situation Question: What should you talk about with a guest on the way to the hotel car?

Pick up the Guests with Reservation

A: Airport Representative　　G: Guest

A: Excuse me, are you Mr. Johnson from London to attend the small business meeting in Hua Xia Hotel?

G: Yes, I am.

A: Good morning, Mr. Johnson. I am the airport representative from Hua Xia Hotel. I am here to meet you. My name is David. Welcome to our city.

G: Thank you, David. Nice to meet you.

A: Nice to meet you, too, Mr. Johnson. Have you got your luggage?

G: Yes.

A: That's good. Would you like me to help you with your luggage?

G: No, thank you. I can manage it myself.

A: OK. Mr. Johnson, I'll show you the way to the coach. This way, please.

G: Great.

A: How about the trip?

G: Oh, it is good except that the flight was delayed for 2 hours.

A: I'm sorry to hear that. You know flights are usually delayed for weather reasons.

G: Yes, I understand.

A: Here we are. You can take the coach to hotel. Have a good rest there. Goodbye, Mr. Johnson.

G: Goodbye.

Notes:

(1) small business 中小企业

(2) luggage 行李　hand luggage 手提行李　carry-on luggage 随身携带的行李
(3) help sb. with sth. 帮助某人做某事
(4) manage 处理
(5) coach 旅客车厢　airport coach 机场大巴
(6) delay 延误

Dialogue 3

Situation Question: How would you deal with the request of limousine service from a walk-in guest?

Pick up Walk-in Guests

【拓展音频】

A: Airport Representative　　G: Guest

G: Excuse me, are you the airport representative of hotel?

A: Yes, I am the airport representative from Hua Xia Hotel. My name is David. Can I help you, sir?

G: Yes. What's the star rating of your hotel?

A: Hua Xia Hotel is a five-star hotel. It is located in the city center, 45-minute drive from the airport.

G: That's good. Is it near the City Conference Center? You know, I am going to attend a meeting there.

A: Yes. It's near the City Conference Center, only 5-minute drive from there, and you can walk there if you like.

G: Great. I have not made a reservation in your hotel. Can you help me?

A: Yes, it's my honor. I will call back the hotel to arrange it. May I have your name, sir?

G: My name is Larry King from King Software Co. London.

A: And what kind of room would you like to have?

G: I'd like a single room with bath.

A: OK, please wait for a minute.

...

A: OK. Mr. King. I have called the front desk, and there is a single room with bath for you. You can take our hotel coach there and go to the front desk and check in.

G: Thank you so much. You really help me a lot.

A: You are welcome. Now let me show you the way to the coach.

Notes:

(1) star rating（酒店的）星级　star hotel 星级酒店
(2) be located in /at 位于；坐落于
(3) drive 驾车旅行的路程

(4) conference 会议   conference center 会议中心

(5) show the way 带路   show sb. around 带某人参观

Dialogue 4

Situation Question: Do you know small talks? How would you do it with the guest in the car to the hotel?

On the Way to the Hotel

A: Airport Representative   G: Guest

A: Please get on the car, Mr. White. I will accompany you to the hotel.

G: OK, thank you.

A: You are welcome. Mr. White, what kind of drink would you like?

G: Please give me a bottle of mineral water.

A: Here you are. Would you like to have a look at the music menu and choose the music you like?

G: No, thanks.

A: Would you like to read the newspapers or magazines?

G: Yes, I would like to have an English newspaper.

A: OK. Mr. White, here it is.

G: By the way, how far is it to the hotel?

A: It's about 25 minutes' drive from here to the hotel. But during the rush hour, it will take 40 minutes to the hotel.

G: It is understandable.

...

A: Here we are at the hotel. Please follow me to check in, Mr. White.

G: OK. Thank you.

Notes:

(1) small talk 闲聊

　　small talk 常用话题

(2) accompany 陪伴

(3) mineral water 矿泉水   soda water 苏打水   purified water 纯净水

(4) rush hour 交通拥挤时间

Useful Sentences

- I want to know if your hotel has pick-up service. 我想知道你们酒店是否提供接机服务。
- We offer airport limousine service to our guests. 我们酒店有接机服务。
- The airport representative will be at the airport to meet the guests. 机场代表会去机场接客人。
- I want to reserve a pick-up service. 我想预订接机服务。
- Could you spell the name of the guest? 您能拼读一下客人的名字吗？
- May I know the arrival time and flight number? 可以告诉我您的到达时间和航班号吗？
- How would you like to pay? 您想怎么付款？
- Please put it on the room. 请记到房费上。
- I am the airport representative from Hua Xia Hotel. I am here to meet you. My name is David. Welcome to our city. 我是华夏酒店的机场代表，叫 David，来这儿接您，欢迎您。
- Have you got your luggage? 您取行李了吗？
- Would you like me to help you with your luggage? 需要我为您提行李吗？
- I can manage it myself. 我自己可以的。
- I'll show you the way to the coach. 我带您去酒店大巴。
- How about the trip? 行程顺利吗？
- It is good except that the plane was delayed for 2 hours. 除了飞机延误 2 小时，其他还好。
- What's the star rating of your hotel? 你们酒店是几星级？
- The Hotel is a five-star hotel. It is located in the city center, 45 minutes, drive from the airport. 我们是一家五星级酒店，位于市中心，离机场 45 分钟车程。
- It's my honor. / It's my pleasure.（为您服务）是我的荣幸。
- You can take our hotel coach there and go to the front desk to check in. 您可以乘坐酒店巴士前往，然后到前台办理入住。
- I will accompany you to the hotel. 我陪您前往酒店。
- What kind of drink would you like? 您要喝什么？
- Would you like to read the newspapers or magazines? 您要看报纸还是杂志？
- Would you like to have a look at the music menu and choose the music you like? 您要看一下我们的音乐单，并选出您喜欢的音乐吗？
- How far is it to the hotel? 这儿离酒店多远？

Knowledge Extension

- **Tips on Meeting Guests at the Airport**

When meeting guests are at the airport for the first time, the tips below are necessary to leave them a good impression:

Dress dark suits to show respect.

Prepare the notice board with the guests' names on it.

Give a brief self-introduction and some small talks to warm up the atmosphere when meeting guests for the first time.

Inquire the guests' journey by having some small talks with them.

Offer guests some help with luggage and give them some hints on leaving.

Focus on your attitude. It counts most in such occasion.

◆ Check-in for Flight

Ladies and Gentlemen, may I have your attention please: We are now ready for check-in for (supplementary) flight <u>CZ888</u> to <u>Hangzhou</u> at counter No. <u>15</u>. Thank you.

◆ Delay of Check-in for Flight

Ladies and gentlemen, may I have your attention please: Due to the poor weather condition at our airport (the poor weather condition over the air route/ the poor weather condition over the <u>Taoxian</u> airport/ aircraft reallocation/ the maintenance of the aircraft/ the aircraft maintenance at our airport/ the aircraft maintenance at the <u>Taoxian</u> airport/ air traffic congestion/ the close-down of <u>Taoxian</u> airport/ communication trouble), the (supplementary) flight <u>CZ888</u> to <u>Hangzhou</u> has been delayed. The check-in for this flight will be postponed (to 5:30). Please wait in the departure hall for further information. Thank you.

◆ Notice of Flight Cancellation

Ladies and Gentlemen, may I have your attention please: We regret to announce that (supplementary) flight <u>CZ888</u> from <u>Hangzhou</u> has been cancelled due to the poor weather condition at our airport/ the poor weather condition over the air route/ the poor weather condition at <u>Taoxian</u> airport/ aircraft reallocation/ the maintenance of the aircraft/ the aircraft maintenance at <u>Taoxian</u> airport/ air traffic congestion/ the close-down of <u>Taoxian</u> airport/ communication trouble. This flight has been rescheduled to tomorrow at <u>5:30</u>. Thank you.

◆ Notice of Diverted Flight

Passengers taking (supplementary) flight <u>ZH4737</u> from <u>Beijing</u> to <u>Shenyang</u>, attention please: Welcome to <u>Shenyang</u> airport. Due to the poor weather condition over the air route/ the maintenance of the aircraft/ air traffic congestion, your flight has been diverted to our airport for your security. Would you please wait in the waiting hall for further information. If you have any problems or questions, please contact the irregular flight service counter/ service counter/ information desk No. <u>15</u>. Thank you.

◆ Function Areas at the Airport

the conveyor belt   departure lounge   information desk

security check   first class   bus station

◆ **Address Foreign Guests Properly**

On formal occasions, you can address someone by his/her surname with prefix of "Mr." or "Ms.". Usually, a lady likes to be called "Ms." rather than "Miss" or "Mrs." because it can be used for both married and single women. It's a common way to ask people how they would like to be called and to tell what you would like them to call you. Don't feel shy. This can make introductions easier and get you a closer relationship with the guests.

Section Summary

- Meet tourists at the airport.
- Know about the process in tourism.
- Learn about the working procedures of meeting tourists at the airport.
- Learn about the tips on meeting guests at the airport.
- Know about the usual expressions for flight.
- Learn about the way of addressing foreign guests properly.

Practice

Part One   Dialogue

1. Fill in the blanks with correct sentences according to the context.

A: Airport Representative   G: Guest

A: Good morning. Are you Mr. Johnson from ABC Company? I am the airport representative of GH hotel. I am here to meet you. My name is Peter.

G: Yes, I am. Nice to meet you, Peter.

A: Nice to meet you, too, Mr. Johnson. Have you got all your luggage?

G: Yes.

A: That is good. _____. I will show you the way to the hotel coach.

G: OK. Thank you.

A: _____

G: It is good except there is a little bump during the flight.

A: Oh, I think it is because of the bad weather.

G: Yes. The weather is really bad recently.

A: _____

G: Yes, it is the first time for me to get here.

A: _____

G: I think the city is very big and modern. I have heard a lot about it before.

A: Yes, the population is very large now and there are lots of beautiful Imperial spots.

G: Can you recommend some to me?

A: Yes. We have some famous historical scenic spots, such as Imperial Palace.

G: I'm really interested in it. If I have free time, it will be my first choice.

A: _____. Please get on the coach.

G: OK.

A. Is this the first time for you to get here?

B. What do you think of the city?

C. Would you like me to help you with your luggage?

D. Here we are.

E. How about the trip?

2. Read the following telephone numbers and dictate them to your partner.

(1) CA982

(2) CZ2101

(3) MU5302

(4) CZ3602

(5) EU6615

(6) HU7613

3. Act in pairs to finish the following role-play activities.

(1) Student A: Act as a guest. Make a phone call to a hotel to reserve an airport pick-up service for your client, Mr. Smith. Leave your name, telephone number, and your flight number.

Student B: Act as the receptionist. Answer the phone call.

(2) Students A: Act as a guest, Mr. Smith. You are at the airport. The airport representative (student B) comes to meet you.

Student B: Act as the airport representative to meet student A.

(3) Student A: Act as a guest who has not reserved pick-up service. You will stay in GH hotel. You see the airport representative of GH hotel. Go to ask for pick-up service.

Student B: Act as the airport representative of GH hotel. Try to serve student A.

(4) Student A: Act as a guest who arrived at the airport but failed to find the airport representative. Call the hotel (GH Hotel) which you are going to stay in to ask for pick-up service.

Student B: Act as the receptionist. Answer the phone call of the guest (student A).

(5) Student A: Act as a guest from a foreign country. You are arriving at the airport and meeting with the airport representative.

Student B: Act as an airport representative to meet the guest and accompany him/her to the hotel. Have a small talk with the guest on the way to the hotel.

4. Discussion: Suppose you are the airport representative of a hotel and you encounter the following situations.

(1) What will you do if the guest you want to meet doesn't appear?

(2) What will you do if the guest is not satisfied with the car used to pick him/her up?

5. Translate the following sentences.

(1) 您好，我是来自 GH 酒店的机场代表。

(2) 请问您是来自香港 GP 公司的刘先生吗？

(3) 我们多久能到酒店？

(4) 我来帮您提行李好吗？

(5) 您的行李取完了吗？

(6) 旅途顺利吗？

(7) 您需要什么样的车接机？

(8) 费用记到房费上。

(9) 请问一共几位客人？

(10) 我想预订接机服务。

Part Two　Knowledge Extension

According to the part of Knowledge Extension, write the answers to the following questions on the sheet of paper by using your own words, not simply copying the sentences. When you have completed the test, ask your lecturer for the answers.

Tips on Meeting Guests at the Airport

_____

_____

Check-in for Flight

_____

_____

Delay of Check-in for Flight

_____

_____

Notice of Flight Cancellation

_____

_____

Notice of Diverted Flight

_____

_____

Function Areas at the Airport

_____

_____

Address Foreign Guests Properly

_____

_____

Topic Three Check-in 登记入住

Introduction

Check-in is the critical step in the process of hotel reception, and also the basic process of formal and legal relations built between the guest and the hotel. At hotels, guests are usually required to check in, register or sign in, which involves providing or confirming the guests' personal information and Signatures. According to the legal requirements of different countries, guests are required to fill in a registration card, provide such identification documents as a passport or driver's license, whose copies the hotel can keep. And only one guest per room is requested to sign in.

Objectives

Competence Standard	Knowledge Standard
Abilities to check in and confirm the information	Know about the working procedures of check-in
Abilities to check in with the advanced reservation or with the walk-in guest and receive group registration	Learn to fill in the check-in form, cope with the guests' check-in issues and identify their documents such as passports, visas and so on
Ability to introduce the check-in time in a hotel	Learn about the attributes of a professional waiter
Ability of listening, speaking and reading	Be familiar with the receptionist work. Know about the ways of payment used in a hotel and extending the stay

Working Procedures

- Greet the guest.
- Find out if the guest has a reservation.
- Check the details of the reservation.
- Check the related documents.
- Assist the guest to fill in the registration form.
- Ask the guest to pay a deposit.
- Offer a room card.
- Express wishes.

Dialogues

Dialogue 1

Situation Question: What documents should you check when you receive a guest with reservation?

Check in with Advanced Reservation

R: Receptionist   G: Guest

R: Good morning, Madam. What can I do for you?

G: Good morning. I reserved a double room last Wednesday.

R: May I have your name?

G: My name is Judy Bird.

R: Is it J-U-D-Y for Judy?

G: Yes. And B-I-R-D for Bird.

R: Please wait for a moment. Let me check it on the computer. Yes, you have reserved a double room. And you guaranteed your reservation by credit card. Is that right?

G: Yes, that is correct.

R: Ms. Bird, may I have a look at your passport?

G: Yes. Here you are.

R: Could you please sign your name here?

G: OK.

R: Ms. Bird, you are in Room 1605. Here is the key to the room and here is your passport. You may take the lift to the room. The lift is on your left side.

G: OK, thank you.

R: You are welcome. Have a good day, Ms. Bird.

Notes:

(1) passport 护照

(2) sign 标志　signature 签名

(3) key 钥匙

(4) lift 电梯　elevator 电梯　escalator 扶梯

(5) Have a good day! (表示祝愿) 过得愉快！

Dialogue 2

Situation Question: What should you do if a guest who has not made a reservation in your hotel wants to stay in your hotel?

【拓展音频】

Check in with Walk-in Guests (1)

R: Receptionist　　G: Guest

R: Good morning, ladies. What can I do for you?

G: We want to stay in the hotel. Do you have rooms available?

R: Have you made a reservation?

G: No.

R: How many people are there in your party?

G: Three.

R: What kind of room do you want?

G: We want a double room and a single room.

R: Please wait for a moment. I have to check the computer record. Thank you for waiting. We have the rooms you required but they are not on the same floor. They are on the 16th and 17th floor. Is it OK?

G: Yes. What is the room rate?

R: It's RMB700 *yuan* for a single room for one night, and RMB1,200 *yuan* for a double room for one night.

G: Is the breakfast included in the room rate?

R: Yes. Do you want to take them?

G: Yes. I'll take them.

R: May I have a look at your passport?

G: Yes, here you are.

R: Could you please fill in the registration form?

G: Yes. Here is the form.

R: Thank you. How would you like to pay the deposit, by card or cash?

G: By card. Here is my credit card.

R: OK. Here are your passport, credit card and the room keys. They are for Room 1602 and Room 1706.

G: Thank you very much.

R: You are welcome. I hope you will enjoy your stay here.

Notes:

(1) thank sb. for doing sth. 感谢某人做某事

(2) require 要求

(3) room rate 房费

(4) for one night 每个晚上，也可以说 per night

(5) registration form 登记表　registration 注册，登记

(6) deposit 押金，定金，保证金

(7) enjoy 喜欢　enjoy your stay 入住愉快

Dialogue 3

Situation Question: What will you do as a receptionist if you can't meet the needs of a walk-in guest?

Check in with a Walk-in Guest (2)

【拓展音频】

R: Receptionist　　G: Guest

R: Good afternoon, sir. Can I help you?

G: Yes, I want to stay in your hotel. Do you have a vacant room now?

R: Do you have reservation?

G: No.

R: What kind of room do you want?

G: I need a single room.

R: Could you please wait for a moment? I have to check with the computer. Oh, I am sorry, sir, we don't have single rooms now. Would you like to choose other type?

G: Can you recommend others to me?

R: We still have double rooms available.

G: What is the price of the double room?

R: It's RMB1500 *yuan* per night. Would you take it?

G: No, I still want to choose a single room. Can you contact other hotels for me?

R: I am sorry, sir. We don't have the room status of other hotels. So, I am afraid that I can not help you.

G: It's OK. Thank you all the same.

R: You are welcome. Look forward to serving you in the future. Goodbye.

G: Goodbye.

Notes:

(1) vacant room 空房

(2) contact 联系

(3) recommend 推荐，介绍　recommend sth. to sb. 向某人推荐某物

(4) room status 房态

(5) all the same 仍然

Dialogue 4

Situation Question: Do you know what documents should be prepared before checking in?

【拓展音频】

Receive Group Registration

R: Receptionist   G: Group leader

R: Good evening, sir. Can I help you?

G: Yes, I am the group leader, John Brown. We have booked 12 rooms in your hotel.

R: Just a minute, sir. Let me check the arrival list. Thank you for waiting. Yes, you have booked 12 double rooms for four nights. Is there any change in the group number?

G: No.

R: Could you please fill in the registration form?

G: Certainly. Here you are.

R: Thank you. Could you please show me your group visa? I need to photocopy it.

G: Here you are. These are our passports.

R: Thank you. Mr. Brown, here are the keys to the double rooms, and the rooms are on the 18th and 19th floors. Here are your passports and group visa.

G: OK. Thank you.

R: Is there anything else I can do for you?

G: Yes, does the room rate cover breakfast?

R: Yes, the room rate covers breakfast. The breakfast is buffet and served on the second floor. You just need to go to the second floor and tell the servant your room number.

G: OK, I see. Thank you very much.

R: You are welcome. Hope you have a pleasant stay in our hotel.

Notes:

(1) group registration 团队入住登记

(2) group leader 领队

(3) arrival list 到达者名单

(4) visa 签证　group visa 团队签证

(5) photocopy 复印，影印

(6) cover 包括

Useful Sentences

- I reserved a double room last Wednesday. 我上周三预订了一个双人间。
- May I have a look at your passport? 请出示您的护照。
- Could you please sign your name here? 请在此处签名。

- You are in Room 1605, and here is the key to the room. 您的房间在 1605，这是房卡。
- The lift is on your left side. 电梯在您的左侧。
- Do you have rooms available? 请问你们有空房吗？
- Do you have a vacant room now? 请问你们现在有空房吗？
- How many people are there in your party? 请问你们一行几个人？
- We have the rooms you required but they are not on the same floor. 您说的房型我们有，但不在同一楼层。
- What is the room rate? 房价多少？
- It is RMB700 *yuan* for a single room for one night, and RMB1,200 *yuan* for a double room for one night. 单人间一晚 700 元人民币，双人间一晚 1200 元人民币。
- What is the price of the double room? 双人间的房价是多少？
- Is the breakfast included in the room rate? 房费含早餐吗？
- Could you please fill in the registration form? 请您填写一下登记表。
- How would you like to pay the deposit? 您的押金怎么付？
- Can you recommend others to me? 能向我推荐一下其他的（房型）吗？
- We don't have the room status in other hotels. 我们没有其他酒店的房态。
- Thank you all the same.（无论如何）还是谢谢您。
- Look forward to serving you in the future. 期待以后为您服务。
- Let me check the arrival list. 我看一下到达旅客名单。
- Is there any change in the group number? 团队人数有变动吗？
- Could you please show me your group visa? 请出示您的团队签证。
- I need to photocopy it. 我需要复印一下。
- Is there anything else I can do for you? 还有其他能为您做的吗？
- The breakfast is buffet and served on the second floor. 早餐是自助餐，在二楼。
- Please wait for a moment. A bellman will show you to your room. 请稍等，服务员会带您到房间。
- Hope you have a pleasant stay in our hotel. 祝您在本酒店入住愉快。

Knowledge Extension

◆ Check-in Time

Check-in time changes and ranges from 12 p.m. until about 3 p.m. depending on the hotel's rules and regulations. Hotels usually define a check-in time expecting guests to check in after that. In general, if a guest wants to take up a room before that, some hotels will ask him/her to pay for an additional day. However, most hotels allow a grace time with 30—60 minutes on a guest's request without any extra charge if a guest wishes to occupy the room before the check-in time. Some hotels have a latest check-in time, and others have a deadline for checking in because the reception may come to an end for the night. In order to use hotel room occupancy effectively, a guest should try to come to the hotel at the hotel's check-in time and leave the hotel room at the hotel's check-out time.

◆ Attributes of a Professional Waiter

Punctuality—Always be on time for work. 'On time' means that you should be ready in uniform to start your duties at least 10 minutes before your shift begins.

Excellent personal presentation and hygiene—Clean and pressed uniform, appropriate hairstyle, polished shoes and a sense for cleanliness at work.

Efficiency—Being efficient means to perform one's work within a certain time and to a certain standard.

Courtesy—Always be polite and tactful.

Personality—Show a warm, friendly nature, good manners and plenty of common sense.

Honesty—Always being honest dealing with guests, staff and company property, which is a matter of course.

Good health/ability to work hard—Being a waiter, a great deal of efforts and energy is required at busy periods. Look after your health, exercise regularly, eat nutritious food and be moderate when drinking alcohol.

Sales/product knowledge—Knowledge of the products that you are selling is necessary to answer your customers' questions and help them in making decisions.

Industry trends, current affairs and general knowledge—In a competitive marketplace, you need to keep up with current food style and service trends by reading relevant magazines and attending courses and seminars.

Confidence—Customers and employers extremely value your confidence, so you should have profound knowledge and high-level skills to develop your confidence.

Guests—Customers always expect you to provide friendly and efficient attention though their expectations often vary.

Colleagues—You should be prepared to help your co-workers when they are busy.

Company—You should always be loyal to your employer and treat his/her affairs and property with respect.

◆ Receptionist Work

A receptionist should make sure that the guest's registration card is correctly filled out. The necessary items in a registration record are the guest's full name, address, nationality, passport or visa number, purpose of his/her visit and his/her signature. Besides, you should record the following information such as payment, arrival date, room type and rate.

◆ Registration Form

A registration form usually is in duplicate or triplicate, one kept by the front desk, one put on records by the public security department and the other used as the basis of opening a room by a floor attendant and the service for a guest. Three types of registration forms are used in China, namely "registration form of domestic guests", "registration form of overseas guests" and "registration form of group residence".

Registration Form of Domestic Guests

Name	In Chinese		Sex	Date of Birth	
	In Original Language			Nationality	
Place of Birth	Occupation		Passport No./Visa No.		
Permanent Address [ ]Home [ ]office					
Unit			Received by		
Arrival Date	From		Departure Date	To	Object of Stay
Room No.	Rate		Payment	Cash[ ]	Credit Card[ ]
Guest Signature			Transfer[ ]	Others[ ]	
Valuables: Please contact the cashier's desk for safe deposit services. Our hotel is not liable for any loss or damage.					Receptionist

Registration Form of Overseas Guest

Surname	Given Name		Photo
Chinese Name	Sex	Date of Birth Y M D	
Nationality or Area	Type of Certificate	Certificate No.	
Certificate Validity Y M D	Occupation	Object of Stay	
Type of Visa	Visa No.	Valid Time	Visa Issued at
Visa Expiry Date Y M D	Port of Entry	Date of Entry	
Date of Arrival Y M D	Date of Departure Y M D	Telephone Number	
Address in China			
Received by			
Type of Accommodation	[ ]Hotel [ ]Rented House [ ]Home Stay [ ]Dormitory [ ]Self-purchased House [ ]Others		
Name of Home Owner	ID No. of Home Owner		
	Home Owner's Telephone No.		
Contact in Emergency	Telephone No.		
Remarks	1. Fill in the form as complete as possible. 2. The form should be normatively filled according to the form instructions with neat handwriting.		

◆ Ways of Payment

The usual ways of payment are as follows:

Cash, Credit Card, Check, Written Permission and Guarantee

Note:

Some hotels don't accept personal checks.

Some hotels only accept the international credit cards, namely

Visa (VS)   American Express

Master Card (MC)   Dinners Club (DC)

Euro Card   Barclaycard (BC)

Federal Card   Great Wall Card

◆ Extending the Stay

If a guest wants to extend the stay, what can the hotel do for the guest?

Check to see whether there is a room available.

Require the guest to change the registration form with the dates.

If there is no room left, put the guest on the waiting list or help him/her find another hotel.

Section Summary

- Hotel check-in time can change and range from 12 p.m. until about 3 p.m..
- Eleven attributes of a professional waiter.
- A receptionist's work is to keep the guest's registration card correctly filled out.
- The way of filling in the registration form of domestic guests.
- The way of filling in the registration form of overseas guests.
- Usual ways of payment used in hotels.
- How to extend guests' stay in hotel.

Practice

Part One Dialogue

1. Fill in the blanks with correct sentences according to the context.

R: Receptionist   G: Guest

R: Good morning, madam. _____

G: I booked two single rooms last Thursday.

R: May I have your name?

G: Mary Miller.

R: Wait a moment, please. Yes, Ms. Miller, you have booked two single rooms. May I have a look at your passport?

G: Yes. _____

R: Thank you. How would you like to pay?

G: By credit card. Here it is.

R: OK. Could you please sign your name here?

G: Yes. Here it is.

R: OK. Ms. Miller, here are the keys to Room 1206 and Room 1207.

G: Oh, I forgot. Does the room rate cover breakfast?

R: Yes, it does. You may have breakfast on the second floor.

G: What time is the breakfast served?

R: _____.

G: OK. I see.

R: _____

G: Yes, I want to go to the city conference center. Could you tell me how I can get there?

R: You may go there by taxi or subway. We can help you to arrange a taxi if you like. Or you can take metro line 2. The station is 50 meters away from the hotel. You will see it on your left side when you step out of the hotel.

G: I get it. Thanks.

R: You are welcome. It is nice serving you. _____.

A. Here you are.

B. Have a good day.

C. From 7 to 9 o'clock in the morning.

D. Is there anything else I can do for you, Ms. Miller?

E. Can I help you?

2. Read the following room numbers and dictate them to your partner.

(1) 4203

(2) 1615

(3) 1923

(4) 1502

(5) 2308

(6) 4511

3. Act in pairs to finish the following role-play activities.

(1) Student A: Act as a guest. You have reserved a room in the hotel. Go to the front desk to check in.

Student B: Act as the receptionist.

(2) Student A: Act as a walk-in guest. Go to the front desk of LA Hotel to check in.

Student B: Act as the receptionist. Receive the walk-in registration.

(3) Student A: Act as a walk-in guest. You want to stay in the hotel for three days. You want a single room with the front view.

Student B: Act as the receptionist. The room the guest required is not available, and you recommend other rooms to him/her.

(4) Student A: Act as a walk-in guest having a child with you. You want a suite.

Student B: Act as the receptionist. The suite the guest required is not available. But a guest is just checking out. It will take 20 minutes to prepare the room. Ask if the guest would like to wait.

(5) Student A: Act as a group leader to check in.

Student B: Act as the receptionist. Receive the group registration.

4. Discussion: Suppose you are the receptionist of the hotel and you encounter the following situations.

(1) What will you do if the guest wants to change the room he/she has reserved?

(2) What will you do if the guest has arrived but you find the room reserved is not available because of overbooking?

5. Translate the following sentences.

(1) 早上好，先生。请问能为您做什么？

(2) 请问您有预订吗？

(3) 我上周二订了一个双人间。

(4) 请稍等，我查一下预订记录。

(5) 您怎么付押金，现金还是信用卡？

(6) 这是您的房卡。

(7) 房费包含早餐。

(8) 还有别的能为您做的吗？

(9) 我要一间可以看到海景的房间。

(10) 抱歉，先生。您要的房间目前没有。

Part Two Knowledge Extension

If you are a waiter in a hotel, can you introduce how the check-in time changes and ranges to the guest?

You know the attributes of a professional waiter are very important in a hotel. Can you tell us what they are?

You know a receptionist should make sure that the guest's registration card is correctly filled out. How can a receptionist do that?

_____

_____

You are a waiter in a hotel. When a domestic guest/overseas guest comes to check in at the hotel, what advice you can give him/her to fill in the registration form?

_____

_____

Please introduce the usual ways of payment used in a hotel to guests.

_____

_____

You are a waiter. If a guest in a hotel wants to extend his/her stay, please tell him/her the way of extending the stay.

_____

_____

Topic Four Bell Service 行李服务

Introduction

The bell service has the most frequent contact with the guests. The bellman greets the incoming guests at the gate, delivers luggage and escorts them to their rooms. The conversation on the way from the reception to the room is important on a guest's arrival. A deadly silence in the lift can be very embarrassing. After the guest is shown to the room, the bellman should describe the room, introduce all the hotel features and facilities. The bellman often does errands for guests upon check-in, such as hailing taxis. He hopes the guest will be free to ask any questions about the hotel services and does farewell to the guest at last.

Objectives

Competence Standard	Knowledge Standard
Ability to receive and escort the guests to the room	Know about the working procedures of the doorman and the bellman
Ability to answer guests' questions	Know about the duty of a bellman
Ability to get down luggage for guests	Have a good understanding of the three important rules when greeting a guest
Ability of listening, speaking and reading	Know something about greeting someone, making contact, the 10-foot and 5-foot rules and the ways to acknowledge people when you are busy

Section One 模块一
Front Office 前厅服务

Working Procedures

Working procedures of a doorman
- Greet the guest.
- Open the car door for the guest.
- Move the luggage from the car.
- Remind the guest if there are items left in the car.
- Express wishes.

Working procedures of a bellman
- Greet the guest.
- Count and confirm the luggage with the guest.
- Lead the guest to the front desk.
- Wait for the guest to check in.
- Deliver the luggage to the guest's room.
- Express wishes.

Dialogues

Dialogue 1

Situation Question: Do you think it is enough for a doorman only to know basic greeting English? Why or why not?

Receiving Guests

D: Doorman　　G1: the first guest　　G2: the second guest

D: Good morning, madam. Welcome to Hua Xia Hotel.

G1: Good morning.

D: Please wait for a moment. I will help you get the luggage from the trunk.

G1: Thank you.

D: You have one luggage and one suitcase. Is that right?

G1: Yes.

D: Please go straight to the front desk to check in. Have a good day.

G1: Thank you.

D: You are welcome.

Another guest is walking out of the hotel.

D: Good morning, sir.

G2: Good morning. Can you help me to get a taxi?

D: Yes. Could you tell me where you are going?

G2: Yes. I want to go to the White Swan Restaurant to meet a friend.

【拓展音频】

D: Is it a single trip or a round trip, sir?

G2: It is a single trip.

D: OK, I see. Please wait for a moment. The taxi will be here in 5 minutes.

G2: OK, thank you. By the way, do you happen to know how much I should pay for the taxi?

D: I think RMB40 *yuan* to RMB50 *yuan* will be enough.

G2: Thank you so much.

D: You are welcome. The taxi is coming. Please get on. Goodbye.

Notes:

(1) doorman 门童：是站在酒店入口处负责迎送客人的前厅服务人员

(2) luggage 行李箱　suitcase 手提箱　travelling bag 旅行包

(3) trunk 汽车车尾的行李箱

(4) single trip 单程　round trip 往返的行程

Dialogue 2

Situation Question: What should the bellman pay attention to when carrying luggage for guests?

【拓展音频】

Escort a Guest to the Room

B: Bellman　G: Guests

B: Good morning, ladies.

G: Good morning.

B: Are the three suitcases all your baggage?

G: Yes.

B: Are there any valuables or fragile items in the suitcases?

G: Yes, there is a bottle of wine which I plan to give one of my friends here.

B: So, could you carry it yourself, I am afraid of breaking it while carrying them.

G: OK, I will carry it myself.

B: Your rooms are on the 29th floor. Please follow me to take the lift.

G: OK.

(*in the lift*)

B: How was your trip here?

G: It was really tiring. You know, the flight took 14 hours.

B: That's a really long trip.

G: Yes. It is the first time for me to get here. But I find the city is very beautiful.

B: I hope you will like the city. There are many famous scenic spots in the city.

G: I hope I will have the chances to visit them.

B: OK. We are on the 29th floor. Shall I put the suitcases in one room or separately?

G: This one in 2901 and the other two in 2906.

B: OK. Here you are. Is there anything else I can do for you?

G: No, thank you.

B: You are welcome. Hope you will enjoy the stay with us. Goodbye.

G: Goodbye.

Notes:

(1) escort 陪同

(2) baggage 行李

(3) valuables 贵重物品　fragile items 易碎物品　breakable items 易碎品

(4) flight 航班

(5) scenic spots 旅游景点

(6) separately 分别地，各自

Dialogue 3

Situation Question: Do you think that the bellman should accept a tip? Why or why not?

Answer Guests' Questions

B: Bellman　　G: Guest

B: Here we are at the room, sir. Shall I put your luggage here?

G: Yes, thank you. Here is the tip.

B: Thank you, sir. Is there anything I can do for you?

G: Yes. I want to buy something online during staying at the hotel. Can I ask the seller to send it to the hotel?

B: Certainly, sir. You can find our hotel's address and postal code in the brochure which is in the drawer of night table. You also need to tell the seller your room number and name. When the item you buy is delivered here, we will send it to your room.

G: Very good. Another thing is that I may have a teleconference with my colleagues back home. Do you have the phone system?

B: Yes. There is an audio conference telephone in the room, but if you want to have a video conference, you can use the equipment in the business center.

G: OK, I see. Thank you so much.

B: I am glad to serve you.

Notes:

(1) tip 小费

(2) postal code 邮政编码

(3) brochure 小册子　pamphlet 小册子　leaflet 活页

(4) drawer 抽屉

(5) night table 床头柜

(6) colleague 同事

(7) teleconference 电话会议，远程会议

(8) audio conference 音频会议

(9) video conference 视频会议

Dialogue 4

Situation Question: Does the bellman finish his work when he has delivered the luggage to the front hall? Why or why not?

Getting Down Luggage for Guests

【拓展音频】

R: Receptionist   G: Guest   B: Bellman

R: Good morning. May I help you?

G: Yes, I want to check out. Could you ask the bellman to help me take my luggage down?

R: Certainly, madam. May I have your name and room number?

G: My name is Mary Bush, Room 1210 and 1216.

R: What time will you check out?

G: In an hour.

R: In an hour, that's 11 o'clock. I will send the bellman to your room in half an hour. Is it OK?

G: OK.

(*half an hour later*)

B: Good morning, madam. I'm here to take your luggage downstairs.

G: Good morning.

B: Have you packed your luggage, madam?

G: Yes. Here is my luggage, and you also need to go to Room 1216 to get luggage, too.

B: OK. Here is your claim tag, Ms. Bush. You'll get your luggage at the front hall.

G: OK, thank you very much.

B: You are welcome. I will go to Room 1216. See you downstairs.

G: See you.

Notes:

(1) claim tag 行李认领牌

(2) ask sb. to do sth. 让某人做某事

(3) check out 结账退房

(4) front hall 前厅

Useful Sentences

- I will help you get the luggage from the trunk. 我帮您把行李从汽车行李箱里拿出来。
- You have one piece of luggage and one suitcase. Is that right? 您有一个行李箱、一个手提箱，对吗？
- Please go straight to the front desk to check in. 请前往前台办理入住。
- Can you help me to get a taxi? 能帮我叫辆出租车吗？
- Could you tell me where you are going? 您要去哪儿？
- Is it a single trip or a round trip, sir? 先生，是单程还是往返？
- The taxi will be here within 5 minutes. 出租车5分钟内就会到。
- Do you happen to know how much I should pay for the taxi? 你知道车费大概是多少吗？
- Are there any valuables or fragile items in the suitcases? 您的手提箱里有易碎品或是贵重物品吗？
- I am afraid of breaking it while carrying them. 我担心会在搬运过程中打碎它。
- Please follow me to take the lift. 请跟我来去乘电梯。
- There are many famous scenic spots in the city. 我们城市有很多景点。
- Shall I put your luggage here? 可以把行李箱放在这儿吗？
- Here is the tip. 这是小费。
- You can find our hotel's address and postal code in the brochure. 小册子里有我们酒店的地址和邮政编码。
- I want to check out. Could you ask the bellman to help me take my luggage down? 我要退房。能否麻烦你叫行李员帮我搬下行李？
- What time will you check out? 您几点退房？
- I will send the bellman to your room in half an hour. 半小时后行李员会到您的房间。
- I am here to take your luggage downstairs. 我来取行李，帮您送下楼。
- Have you packed your luggage? 您的行李打包好了吗？
- Here is your claim tag. 这是行李提取牌。
- You'll get your luggage at the front hall. 您可以去前台领取行李。
- If there is anything I can do for you, please let me know. 如果有什么能为您做的，请通知我。
- Goodbye. Have a good trip. 再见，祝您旅途愉快。

Knowledge Extension

- **Duties of a Bellman**

Greet incoming guests and escort them to their rooms.

Provide guests with baggage handling and transport service upon arrival and checkout.

Deliver items such as flowers, and sundries, messages to guest rooms upon request.

Keep lobbies or entrance areas clean for guests. Assist in other front service areas including doorman services.

Additional duties such as delivering newspapers to guests' rooms and parking vehicles may be included.

Master the current knowledge of local area, attractions and events.

Carry out other duties assigned.

◆ Bellman Leaving Guests a Good First Impression

Bellmen are in charge of welcoming guests as they arrive at the hotel. They can leave guests a good first impression. They usually work in front of the hotel or near the front door. Since the bellman is the first hotel employee many guests contact, the warmth and courteous help he gives can have a great effect on the guests.

Bellmen do many things for guests, such as help guests enter and leave the hotel, help guests with luggage, store and handle baggage and aid guests getting in and out of autos by opening and closing doors. They also provide information about roads, local directions, and places of interest and so on.

Different cultures may welcome people in different ways. It is important to create a standard where you welcome everyone in the best possible fashion no matter where they are from, what they look like, or what gender they possess. There are three important rules when greeting guests:

Greet your guest warmly, sincerely and with a smile.

Check your attitude, and express your gratitude. This is very important because people can tell whether you are faking it.

Eye contact.

Drop what you are doing, look the customer in the eye, and greet them. Don't greet customers while doing something else, which is a very disrespectful behavior, unless you are helping another customer.

Acknowledge the guest immediately.

A simple nod of the head, eye contact, or a brief comment will let the person who is waiting know that you have seen them and will talk with them soon. Don't let a guest wait. Even a few seconds is impolite. Make the guest you are welcoming feel like they are important. It's your job to create an environment they can feel comfortable in! Welcome them into it! Welcome expressions are as follows:

Welcome (back)!

Welcome to our hotel!

Welcome! Please enjoy your stay/ lunch/ dinner/ day!

◆ Greeting Someone

Guests will feel welcomed when you acknowledge they are there. If guests feel at ease with you, they will feel free to ask for additional services, or purchase extras. Otherwise they may not do that.

Formal

Good morning! Good evening! Good afternoon!

Good to see you! Nice to see you again!

It's a pleasure to have you back with us!

Informal (Use with caution)

Morning! Evening! Afternoon!

Hello! Hello, there! Hello, everybody!

Hi! Hi, there!

◆ Making Contact

Sometimes you need to talk to some person, but you have no idea who they are. To confirm their identity, you can try the following phrases:

Excuse me, are you Mrs....?

Hello, you must be Mrs.....

You are Mr....., aren't you?

◆ The 10-foot, 5-foot Rule: The Zone of Hospitality

Whenever a guest comes to a staff member within 10 feet, the staff member should make a friendly eye contact and give them a warm smile to acknowledge them.

Whenever a guest comes to a staff member within 5 feet, the staff member should add a sincere greeting or gesture to the smile and eye contact.

These rules apply to all staff members, but there are a few things you should remember:

Don't greet guests from behind, which can surprise them.

Don't speak to each guest individually at times. Try to be open if they are in a large group, in a hurry or in conversation.

A nod of the head just means "good morning" or "nice day today!"

You should be natural when you greet guests.

◆ Ways to Acknowledge People When You Are Busy

Sometimes you have many things going on at once. The phone is ringing, several groups of guests are waiting for your service and you are alone. A great way to deal with this issue is to let the guest know that you see them, and you will help them as soon as possible by smiling and nodding. Let them know you will be right with them, and always thank the guests for their patience while they are waiting for your service.

Section Summary

- Know about the seven items of duties as a bellman.
- Learn the way of how a bellman leaves guests a good first impression.
- Know about the three important rules when greeting a guest.
- Learn to greet someone.
- Learn about making contact.

- Know about the rules of 10-foot or 5-foot, the zone of hospitality.
- Know about the ways to acknowledge people when you are busy.

Practice

Part One Dialogue

1. Choose the correct sentences to fill in the blanks according to the context.

D: Doorman   B: Bellman   G: Guest

D: Good morning, madam. _____

G: Good morning.

D: _____. Here is your luggage.

G: Thank you.

B: Let me help you with your luggage, madam.

G: Thank you.

B: This way please. _____

G: Good.

B: Madam, let me show you to your room. Let's take the lift.

G: OK, after you.

B: _____

G: Oh, it was a long trip. But the service on the flight was good.

B: Then you must be very tired.

G: Oh, yes.

B: Here we are at the room. _____

G: Yes, thank you.

B: You are welcome, madam. Have a good stay in the hotel. Goodbye.

G: Goodbye.

A. How was the trip?

B. Welcome to Hua Xia Hotel.

C. Shall I put the luggage here?

D. Let me help you get the luggage from the trunk.

E. Let's go to the front desk to check in.

2. Act in pairs to finish the following role-play activities.

(1) Student A: Act as a doorman. A taxi is coming, and you step up to greet the guest and offer help.

Student B: Act as the guest.

(2) Students A: Act as a bellman. Take the luggage for a new guest to the room and answer his/her questions.

Student B: Act as the guest. It is the first time for you to get to the city. Ask about scenic spots of the city.

(3) Student A: Act as a bellman. You escort the guest to his/her room and answer his/her questions.

Student B: Act as the guest. When you get to your room, you ask the bellman to help you to hire a taxi and give him tips.

(4) Student A: Act as a bellman. You escort the guest to his/her room and answer his/her questions.

Student B: Act as the guest. When you get to your room, you ask the bellman about Chinese festivals. And also you want to know if there is a Christmas party in the hotel.

(5) Student A: Act as a bellman. You are asked to go to pick up luggage for the guest to check out.

Student B: Act as the guest. The bellman comes to take your luggage downstairs to check out. Ask him to hire a taxi for you.

3. Discussion:

(1) Is it necessary for a doorman to take down the taxi plate number when the guest gets off? Why or why not?

(2) If you are a bellman, what will you do if a guest tells you that he/she lost one piece of luggage?

4. Translate the following sentences.

(1) 晚上好，先生，欢迎光临本酒店。
(2) 您一共有两件行李，对吗？
(3) 我来帮您拿行李吧。
(4) 这边请，女士。
(5) 我把您的行李放在这儿好吗？
(6) 请问您还有其他行李吗？
(7) 这是您的行李牌。
(8) 如有其他需要，请通知我。
(9) 祝您入住愉快。
(10) 请帮我叫一辆出租车。

Part Two Knowledge Extension

Suppose you are a bellman, please describe the seven items of duties as a bellman.

_____
_____
_____
_____
_____

Bellmen can leave guests a good first impression. Do you agree with it? If you agree, why do you think so? Where does a bellman work in a hotel?

_____
_____
_____
_____

Different cultures may welcome people in different ways and usually there are three important rules when greeting a guest. What are the three rules?

_____
_____
_____

As a bellman, when you are greeting someone, you usually use formal or informal ways of greeting people. What are they?

_____
_____

Can you say something about the 10-foot and 5-foot rules?

_____
_____
_____
_____
_____

When you are busy, what kind of ways do you usually use to acknowledge people?

_____
_____
_____
_____
_____

Topic Five   Currency Exchange
外币兑换

Introduction

Currency exchange is mainly for the convenience of overseas tourists. Exchange counters are not only in some major stores but also in the banks that are set up almost in every country. Overseas tourists are given exchange memos. Usually some of money will be lost in the exchanging process as fees are charged. The less you exchange, the more obvious it is.

Objectives

Competence Standard	Knowledge Standard
Ability to explain today's exchange rate to the guest	Know about the working procedures of foreign currency exchange
Ability to see the guest's passport, get the information as to the name, nationality and passport number	Learn to describe money exchange facilities. While changing money for a guest, what items should a cashier focus on?
Ability to fill in the exchange memo with the information such as passport number, total sum, room number or permanent address	Learn to describe foreign currency exchange service—TransForex
Ability to ask the guest to keep the memo well and exchange currency for the guest	Learn to identify whether the foreign currency is real or not and fill in the form of an exchange memo

Working Procedures

Working procedures of a cashier
- Greet the guest.
- Ask the guest to show his/her passport and room key.
- Inquire the guest's request of currency exchange.
  Amount.
  Type of currency.
  Denomination.
- Notify the guest of the exchange rate.
- Change the money for the guest.
- Ask the guest to fill in the exchange memo.
- Express wishes.

Dialogues

Dialogue 1

Situation Question: Is it necessary to look at a guest's passport and room key before exchanging money for the guest? Why?

Cash Exchange (1)

C: Cashier   G: Guest

C: Good morning, madam. Can I help you?

G: Good morning. I want to change some money.

C: What kind of currency do you have?

G: Euros.

C: May I look at your passport and room key?

G: Yes, here you are.

C: OK, Ms. White. How much money would you like to exchange?

G: 200 dollars. What's the exchange rate today?

C: It's 660.62 for cash purchases.

G: Is the exchange rate here the same as that in the bank?

C: Yes, it is the same.

G: Is there any extra charge?

C: No, there is not service charge for currency exchange.

G: OK, good. Then I will change it.

C: Ms. White, 200 dollars will be 1,321.14 *yuan*. What denomination do you want?

G: I want to have some 5-*yuan* notes and 10-*yuan* notes.

C: OK, Ms. White. Could you please fill in the exchange memo?

G: OK. Here you are.

C: Thank you. Here is the money. Please count it. And here is your receipt. Please keep it.

G: OK. I will. Thank you for your service.

C: You are welcome. Glad to serve you. Goodbye.

G: Goodbye.

Notes:

(1) exchange 交换 exchange rate 汇率

(2) cash 现金

(3) exchange for cash 兑换现金

(4) cashier 兑换员

(5) currency 货币

(6) service charge 服务费

(7) denomination 面额

(8) exchange memo 外汇兑换水单

(9) receipt 发票

Dialogue 2

Situation Question: Is it possible for a guest who consumes in the hotel but doesn't stay in the hotel to change currency? Why or why not?

Cash Exchange (2)

【拓展音频】

C: Cashier   G: Guest

C: Good evening, sir. How may I help you?

G: Good evening. I want to exchange for some RMB.

C: May I have a look at your room key and passport?

G: Sorry, I am not staying in the hotel.

C: I am sorry, sir. According to the hotel policy, we are not allowed to exchange currency for outside guests.

G: That's too bad. I used to live in your hotel for several times. The recent stay is half a year ago.

C: I am sorry, sir. I am afraid I can not help you.

G: You see, I come here to treat my friends but to find I am short of RMB. I am your established customer. I like your service and food in the restaurant, so I come back again. So could you do a favor and exchange it for me?

C: May I have your name and passport number?

G: My name is David King. This is passport.

C: How much would you like to change?

G: 100 dollars.

C: OK, sir. I will ask the supervisor. But I can't guarantee it. Please wait for a moment.

G: Thanks for your help.

Notes:

(1) hotel policy 酒店规定　policy 政策

(2) outside guest 店外客人

(3) established customer 老顾客

(4) be short of 缺少

(5) do a favor 帮忙

Dialogue 3

Situation Question: Do you know traveler's check? Do you think it is convenient for travelling abroad?

Exchange for Check

【拓展音频】

C: Cashier　　G: Guest

C: Good morning, sir. May I help you?

G: Good morning. I want to exchange for some RMB.

C: What do you want to exchange, notes or check?

G: Traveler's check.

C: Please sign your name on the check.

G: But I have signed it before.

C: Yes, but you have to sign it again. Please sign on the back.

G: OK. Here you are.

C: Thank you. May I have a look at your passport and room key?

G: Sure.

C: Thank you. Mr. Black, please fill in the exchange memo.

G: OK. Here you are.

C: The check is 100 pounds, and the exchange rate is 856.37. After deducting the discount interest, the total is 849.95 *yuan*. Please count it and make sure it is correct.

G: OK. Yes, it is correct.

C: And here is your receipt. Please keep it.

G: OK. I will. Thank you for your service.

C: You are welcome. Glad to serve you. Goodbye.

G: Goodbye.

Notes:

(1) check 支票　traveler's check 旅行支票是指境内商业银行代售的，由境外银行或专门金融机构印制，以发行机构作为最终付款人，以可自由兑换货币作为计价结算货币，有固定面额的票据。境内居民在购买时，须本人在支票上签名，兑换时，再次签名即可。

(2) deduct 扣除，减去

(3) discount interest 贴现利息

Dialogue 4

Situation Question: Do you think it is possible for the hotel to change RMB back to foreign currency? Why or why not?

Respond to Guest's Request

【拓展音频】

C: Cashier   G: Guest

C: Good morning, madam. May I help you?

G: Yes. Do you remember that I changed 500 dollars here yesterday?

C: Yes. I remember. I changed them for you. What happened?

G: The thing is the day before yesterday I caught sight of a bracelet in a shop. I wanted to buy it. So I changed money. But now I change my mind. Therefore, I don't need so much RMB. So I want to change it back. Could you help me?

C: Oh, madam. I can understand. But I am really sorry that I can't help you.

G: May I know why?

C: It is because of the policy. The hotel is not allowed to convert RMB to foreign currency in our country.

G: Then where should I go to change it?

C: You may get it changed at the airport or Bank of China and you will have to show the receipt of exchange memo.

G: OK, I see. Thank you for your help.

C: You are welcome. Goodbye.

G: Goodbye.

Notes:

(1) respond 回答

(2) catch sight of 看见

(3) bracelet 手链，手镯

(4) change one's mind 改变主意

(5) convert 转变

Useful Sentences

- I want to change some money. 我想兑换一些钱。
- I want to exchange for some RMB. 我想兑换一些人民币。
- What kind of currency do you have? 您想兑换哪种货币？

- May I look at your passport and room card? 能看一下您的护照和房卡吗？
- How much money would you like to exchange? 您想兑换多少钱？
- What's the exchange rate today? 今天的外汇牌价是多少？
- Is the exchange rate here the same as that in the bank? 这里的外汇牌价和银行的一样吗？
- Is there any extra charge? 你们收服务费吗？
- There is no service charge for currency exchange. 兑换货币不收服务费。
- Currency exchange serrice is free. 换汇免服务费。
- What denomination do you want? 您要什么面额的？
- I want to have some 5-*yuan* notes and 10-*yuan* notes. 我想要几张 5 元和 10 元的纸币。
- Could you please fill in the exchange memo? 请您填写兑换水单好吗？
- Here is the money. Please count it. 这是您的钱，请清点好。
- Here is your receipt. 这是您的收据。
- According to the hotel policy, we are not allowed to exchange currency for outside guests. 根据酒店规定，我们不可以为非住店客人兑换货币。
- I am afraid that I can not help you. 恐怕我帮不了您。
- I will ask the supervisor. But I can't guarantee it. 我请示一下主管，但是我不能保证一定行。
- What do you want to exchange, notes or check? 您要兑换钱币还是旅行支票？
- Please sign your name on the check. 请在支票上签名。
- Please count it and make sure it is correct. 请清点数目并确认无误。
- You may get it changed at the airport or Bank of China. 您可以去机场或者中国银行兑换。
- You are welcome. I am very happy that I can serve you. 不客气，很高兴为您服务。

Knowledge Extension

- **Money Exchange Facilities**

Money exchange facilities are available for both currency and travelers' cheques at major hotels, airports, and department stores. Please notice that exchange rates can change in line with international financial market conditions. The State Exchange Control Administration publishes the exchange rates every day. A cashier has to focus on the following items while changing money for a guest:

The cashier should attend the guests warmly, attempting to understand the needs of guests actively.

The cashier should recognize the foreign currency exactly, confirm whether it is true and decide whether it can be exchanged.

Fill in the foreign currency's type, exchange rate and amount clearly according to the demand.

The cashier should ask the guest to sign the list and fill in the room number.

Finally tell the guest to keep the exchange memo and currency exchange receipts, because he will need to show them while changing RMB back to his own currency at the end of his visit to China.

\multicolumn{5}{c}{Hotel Exchange Certificate and Exchange Memo}				
\multicolumn{5}{l}{Nationality_____ Passport No._____ Date_____}				
\multicolumn{5}{l}{Name & Signature _____ Address/ Hotel _____}				
Amount in foreign currency	Less discount	Net amount	Rate	Amount in R.M.B
Particulars				
\multicolumn{5}{l}{Please keep this for checking. Part of unused RMB can be turned back to foreign currency only for one time when the holder leaves China within six months.}				
\multicolumn{5}{c}{Voucher auditor Agent}				

◆ Foreign Currency Exchange Services

TransForex can change foreign currency cash, traveler's cheques, etc. into RMB or change RMB into foreign currencies at the exchange rates of TransForex on the transaction day. Foreign currencies accepted by TransForex include USD, EUR, GBP, JPY, HKD, CHF, SGD, SEK, DKK, NOK, CAD, AUD, MOP, etc. Non-major currencies accepted by TransForex include KRW, THB, PHP, RUB, MYR, etc.

◆ Exchange Memo

After the cashier identifies whether the foreign currency is real or not, he/she should fill in the exchange memo according to the exchanged amount of RMB, the foreign currency's amount and category based on the same day's exchange rate, date and the clerk's name and then let the guest sign, indicate the foreign currency's code, and write down the room number and certificate number.

Section Summary

- Know about money exchange facilities.
- Learn about foreign currency exchange service-TransForex.
- Know about the exchange memo.

Practice

Part One Dialogue

1. Choose the correct sentences to fill in the blanks according to the context.

C: Cashier   G: Guest

C: Good morning, madam._____

G: Good morning. I'd like to change some money.

C: _____

G: Pounds.

C: _____

G: 400 pounds._____

C: The exchange rate today is 829.70.

G: Do you charge service fee?

C: No, it's free of charge.

G: OK, please change it for me.

C: _____

G: Here you are.

C: Please fill in the exchange memo.

G: OK.

C: The total is 3318.8 *yuan*. Here is the money. Please count it. Here is your receipt.

G: OK, thank you. It is correct.

C: You are welcome, madam. Good-bye.

G: Good-bye.

A. What kind of currency do you have?

B. How may I help you?

C. May I have a look at your passport and room card?

D. How much would you like to change?

E. What's the exchange rate today?

2. Act in pairs to finish the following role-play activity.

(1) Student A: Act as an in-house guest. You go to the front desk to change 200 dollars.

Student B: Act as the cashier to exchange money for the guest.

(2) Student A: Act as an outside guest. You forget to bring your passport with you, but you want to change some pounds.

Student B: Act as the cashier. Decide whether to change the money for the guest or not.

(3) Student A: Act as an in-house guest. You go to the front desk to cash the traveler's check.

Student B: Act as the cashier to exchange money for the guest.

(4) Student A: Act as an in-house guest. You go to the front desk to change 200 dollars, but you find the amount is not correct.

Student B: Act as the cashier to exchange money for the guest, and respond to the guest's problem.

(5) Student A: Act as an outside guest. You used to stay in the hotel. This time you consume in the recreation center. You want the cashier to change 100 dollars for you.

Student B: Act as the cashier. Decide whether to change the money for the guest or not.

3. Discussion:

(1) What will you do if you find the guest exchanging counterfeit bank notes?

(2) What will you do if the guest wants you to change more than hotel limits?

4. Translate the following sentences.

(1) 请问您要兑换哪种货币？
(2) 今日的美元兑人民币的外汇牌价是多少？
(3) 外币兑换是免费的吗？
(4) 这项服务不收费。
(5) 请出示您的护照和房卡。
(6) 请填写一下兑换水单。
(7) 您要什么面额的钱？
(8) 我想兑换旅行支票。
(9) 请在背面签字。
(10) 不客气，很高兴为您服务。

Part Two Knowledge Extension

If you are a waiter in a hotel, can you summarize money exchange facilities and while changing money for a guest, what items does a cashier have to focus on?

_____
_____
_____

Perhaps you know foreign currency exchange services well. Can you tell us something about TransForex?

_____
_____
_____

Suppose you are a guest in a hotel, and you want to cash your traveler's check (GBP200). You require some information about the exchange rate between GBP and RMB, and

then you tell the cashier you need some small change. A cashier at the front desk is doing you a favor. Please make a dialogue to describe the above process.

_____
_____
_____
_____
_____

Topic Six Check-out 结账离开

Introduction

Check-out is one of the major jobs at the front desk in a hotel. Check-out time is different in different hotels, which is usually at 12:00 at noon or 1:00 p.m. If the guest checks out after the time, he/she will pay half or full of his/her room rates. Setting a clear check-out time is very important for the guest in a hotel. In general, many guests in hotels leave their hotels at about 8:00 a.m. or 9:00 a.m. and they may have to wait in a line of people for check-out if there are many tourists. Therefore, the guest had better notify the front desk to get his/her bill ready beforehand. Thus it will save his/her time when he /she checks out.

Objectives

Competence Standard	Knowledge Standard
Ability to check out the guest	Know about the working procedures of checking out
Ability to note the skill points of check-out	Learn to check out the guest
Ability to zero the account	Know about the way to zero the account
Ability of listening, speaking and reading	Have a good understanding of the skill points of check-out

Working Procedures

- Greet the guest.
- Confirm the guest's name and room number.
- Take back the room card.
- Inquire if the guest has signed a new bill within 2 hours.
- Print the bill.
- Ask the guest to confirm the consumption.
- Ask the guest about the method of payment.
- Settle the account for the guest.
- Express best wishes to the guest.

Dialogues

Dialogue 1

Situation Question: Do you know how to settle the account for guests who pay in cash? What should you pay attention to?

Pay the Bill in Cash

【拓展音频】

C: Cashier   G: Guest

C: Good morning, sir. Can I help you?

G: Good morning. I want to check out.

C: May I have your name and room number, please?

G: David King. Room 1403.

C: Have signed new bills within 2 hours?

G: No.

C: Please wait for a moment, Mr. King. I'll print the bill for you.... The total is RMB3,200 *yuan*. Please check it.

G: What is the figure, say, RMB200 *yuan*?

C: Let me see. Mr. King, you have asked for the room service last night, isn't right?

G: Yes.

C: The money is for room service and service fee.

G: OK, I see.

C: How would you like to pay the bill, sir?

G: I'd like to pay in cash.

C: Mr. King, you paid RMB1,000 *yuan* as deposit. Is it correct?

G: Yes.

C: So, you still need to pay RMB2,200 *yuan*.

G: Here you are.

C: Thank you. Here is your receipt.

G: Thanks.

C: You are welcome. Have a good trip. Good-bye.

G: Good-bye.

Notes:

(1) cashier 收银员

(2) total 总数，总额

(3) bill 账单   print the bill 打印账单

(4) figure 数字

(5) room service 客房送餐服务

(6) service fee 服务费

(7) pay the bill 付账

(8) deposit 押金

(9) receipt 发票

Dialogue 2

Situation Question: Do you know how to settle the account for guests who pay by credit card? What should you pay attention to?

Pay the Bill by Credit Card

【拓展音频】

C: Cashier   G: Guest

C: Good morning, sir. How may I help you?

G: Good morning. I want to pay the bill now.

C: May I have your name and room number?

G: Yes. My name is John Miller, and the room number is 1208.

C: Did you sign new bills half an hour ago?

G: Yes. Just now I asked for the room service.

C: I am afraid that your new bill has not reached here. Please wait for a moment, and I will check with the F&B Department.

G: OK.

(*After calling the F&B Department and get the new bill*)

C: Thank you for waiting. Here is the hotel bill, and the total is 3,500 *yuan*, including the room service fee. Please have a look at it.

G: How do you charge the service fee?

C: 15%.

G: OK. There is no problem with it.

C: How would you like to pay for it?

G: I'd like to pay by credit card. Here is the card.

C: OK, sir. Please sign your name here.

G: OK, here you are.

C: Here is the receipt. Is there anything I can do for you?

G: No, thank you.

C: You are welcome. Have a good trip. Good-bye.

Notes:

(1) credit card 信用卡

(2) F&B Department: food & beverage department 餐饮部

(3) receipt 收据

Dialogue 3

Situation Question: Do you know how to settle the account for guests who pay by traveler's check? What should you pay attention to?

【拓展音频】

Pay the Bill with Traveler's Check

C: Cashier　　G: Guest

C: Good morning, madam. May I help you?

G: Good morning. I want to check out.

C: May I have your name and room number?

G: My name is Sarah Turner and the room number is 1612.

C: Could I have your room card?

G: Here you are.

C: Have you used any hotel services after 10 o'clock today?

G: Yes. I used mini-bar. I drank a bottle of Coke in the room.

C: OK. I'll check with the Housekeeping Department. Please wait for a moment.

G: OK.

C: I am sorry to have kept you waiting. The total of your bill is 1,550 *yuan*. How would you like to pay it?

G: I'd like to pay with traveler's check. Here is the check. What's the exchange rate today?

C: The dollar-RMB exchange rate is 666.09. Your traveler's check is 200 dollars which is equivalent of 1,322.2 *yuan*. How would you like to pay the rest 227.8 *yuan*?

G: I'd like to pay it in cash. Here is the money.

C: Here is the change and here is your receipt. Please have a look at it.

G: OK. Thank you for your service.

C: You are welcome. Have a nice trip. Good-bye.

G: Good-bye.

Notes:

(1) mini-bar 迷你吧（指宾馆里放有酒类饮料的小冰箱）

(2) Coke 可口可乐

(3) equivalent *adj.* 等价的

(4) the rest of 其余的

Dialogue 4

Situation Question: If the guest says that there is some error on the bill, what will you do as a cashier?

Explain the Bills

C: Cashier   G: Guest

C: Good morning, madam. May I help you?

G: Yes. I want to check out.

C: May I have your name and room number?

G: Yes. My name is Judy Cotton and the room number is 1512.

C: Please wait for a moment. I will print the bill. Here is the bill, Ms. Cotton. Please check it.

G: I think there must be something wrong with the bill.

C: What's the problem, madam?

G: It says here 500 *yuan* for the room service, but I haven't used your hotel room service. And this 120 *yuan* for laundry service, I haven't used your laundry service, either.

C: I will check with the departments concerned. Could you please sit on the sofa and wait for a moment?

G: OK.

...

C: I'm sorry, madam. It is our fault. The staff mixed your room number with Room 1502. Both of the figures are for that room. Now we have corrected it. Sorry to have kept you waiting.

G: It's OK.

C: Madam, this is the new bill I've printed. The total is 1,200 *yuan*. Please check it.

G: OK, it's correct.

C: How would you like to pay for it?

G: In cash.

C: You have paid 1,000 *yuan* deposit. And you still need to pay 200 *yuan*.

G: Here you are.

C: Here is the receipt. Have a good trip. Good-bye.

G: Good-bye.

Notes:

(1) laundry service 洗衣服务

(2) concerned 有关的

(3) fault 过错

Useful Sentences

- I want to check out. 我想结账。
- I want to pay the bill now. 我想现在结账。
- May I have your name and room number, please? 请告诉我您的姓名和房间号？
- Have you signed new bills within 2 hours? 您两个小时内是否有新的消费？
- Have you used any hotel services after 10 o'clock today? 今天上午 10 点之后您还有其他消费吗？
- Please wait for a moment, Mr. King. I'll print the bill for you, Mr. King. 先生，请稍等，我为您打印账单。
- The total is RMB3,200 *yuan*. Please check it. 您一共消费 3200 元人民币，请核对一下。
- How would you like to pay the bill? 您想怎样付款？
- I'd like to pay in cash. 我想用现金支付。
- I'd like to pay by credit card. 我想用信用卡支付。
- I'd like to pay with traveler's check. 我想要旅行支票支付。
- You paid RMB1,000 *yuan* deposit. Is it correct? 您付了 1000 元押金，对吗？
- You still need to pay RMB2,200 *yuan*. 您还需要支付 2200 元。
- Please wait for a moment. I will check with the F&B Department. 请稍等，我和餐饮部确认一下。
- Here is the hotel bill, and the total is RMB3,500 *yuan*, including the room service fee. 这是账单，总额为 3500 元，含客房送餐服务费。
- I am sorry to have kept you waiting. 抱歉，让您久等了。
- How would you like to pay the rest RMB227.8 *yuan*? 还差 227.8 元，您怎么付款？
- I think there must be something wrong with the bill. 我觉得账单有误。
- What's the problem, madam? 有什么问题吗，女士？
- I will check with the departments concerned. 我和相关部门确认一下。
- Could you please sit on the sofa and wait for a moment? 请坐在沙发上稍等一会儿吗？
- I am sorry, madam. It is our fault. 抱歉，女士。这是我们的错。
- Here is your receipt. 这是您的收据。

Knowledge Extension

- **Skill Points of Checking Out**

The usual skill points used are checking out in cash, by credit card and with traveler's check. When checking out in cash, the cashier will ask the guest to give him/her the receipt of deposit; When checking out by credit card, the cashier will first make sure whether the credit card can be accepted or not in the hotel. And the guest must specially note the valid date and credit limit. When checking out with traveler's check, the cashier should examine whether the check is good or not and ask the guest to sign his/her name in the correct place. If the guest signs his/her name in the wrong place, the hotel can not cash the check.

◆ Post Introduction of Checking Out

When the guest in the hotel plans to depart, there should be some efficient check-out procedures. The front desk clerk usually checks out and settles the guest's bill, who is very important because his/her attitude toward the guest can directly affect the later discussion about the service and facilities of the hotel with his/her friends and business associates and whether they will come to the hotel or not. When the guest comes to the front office settling his/her bill and checking out, it is necessary for the front desk clerk to greet the guest warmly and handle check-out efficiently. The charges usually result from the guest's room and the use of telephone, laundry service, restaurant, and room service, and so on. After the guest signs his/her bill, the front desk clerk will keep and room key, release the notice of the guest's leaving and then record the information in the computer.

◆ Zeroing the Account

The term used by the front desk clerk refers to a guest's bill being settled. The guest has completely made his/her payment and now his/her account balance is zero. The hotel guest can have numerous payment options available, including the direct billing transfer method, which means the guest's account balance can be sent to the Accounting Office to be collected later. It is the Accounting Office that will be in charge of collecting payment.

Section Summary

- Know about the working procedures of checking out.
- Learn to check out the guest.
- Konw about the skill points of checking out.
- Know about zeroing the account.

Practice

Part One   Dialogue

1. Choose the correct sentences to fill in the blanks according to the context.

C: Cashier   G: Guest

C: Good morning, madam. May I help you?

G: Good morning. _____

C: May I have your name and room number?

G: Emily Brown in room 2016.

C: _____.

G: Here you are.

C: Please wait for a moment. _____ The total is RMB2,450 *yuan*. Please check it.

G: Could you tell me what this figure is, a cup?

C: Yes, Ms Brown. It is reported that you broke a cup in the room. _____

G: OK, how much should I pay for it?

C: RMB30 *yuan*.

G: OK, I see.

C: _____

G: In cash.

C: You have paid RMB1,000 *yuan* as deposit. So you still need to pay RMB1,450 *yuan*.

G: OK, here is the money.

C: OK, here is the change and receipt. Have a nice day. Good-bye.

G: Good-bye.

A. May I have your room card?

B. I want to check out.

C. You have to pay for it according to the hotel policy.

D. How would you like to pay the bill?

E. I will print the bill.

2. Act in pairs to finish the following role-play activities.

(1) Student A: Act as a guest. You go to the front desk to check out and pay in cash.

Student B: Act as the cashier. Settle the bill for the guest.

(2) Students A: Act as a guest. You go to the front desk to check out and pay with traveler's check.

Student B: Act as the cashier. Settle the bill for the guest.

(3) Student A: Act as a guest. You go to the front desk to check out and pay by credit card.

Student B: Act as the cashier. Settle the bill for the guest.

(4) Student A: Act as a guest. You go to the front desk to check out. You find the bill is overcharged than you expected. Ask the cashier to explain it to you.

Student B: Act as the cashier. Settle the bill for the guest and answer the guest's questions about the bill.

(5) Student A: Act as a guest. You go to the front desk to check out. You find the cashier forgot the 20% discount for long staying in the hotel for you stayed 20 days in the hotel.

Student B: Settle the bill for the guest and respond to the guest's question.

3. Read the following figures and then dictate to your partner.

(1) 3,450

(2) 4,569

(3) 3,470

(4) 25,000

(5) 46,700

(6) 2,350

(7) 330

(8) 150

4. Discussion:

(1) What should you pay attention to if the guest wanted to pay by credit card?

(2) What should you pay attention to if the guest wanted to pay in foreign currency?

5. Translate the following sentences.

(1) 我要结账退房。

(2) 请给我您的房卡。

(3) 请问您用什么方式付款?

(4) 你们接受信用卡付款吗?

(5) 抱歉，我们酒店不接受旅行支票付款。

(6) 您怎么支付余款?

(7) 这是找您的零钱和发票，请收好。

(8) 这是洗衣费用。

(9) 这是客房送餐和服务费。

(10) 抱歉，让您久等了。

Part Two Knowledge Extension

If you are a waiter, can you summarize the skill points of checking out?

_____

_____

Can you describe the post introduction of checking out in your own words?

_____

_____

Can you use your own words to explain zeroing the account?

_____

_____

Section Two

Housekeeping Service
客房服务

模块二

Introduction

Housekeeping service is very important in a hotel and it has the closest relationship with guests. If the work of housekeeping service is not done well, everything will be meaningless. If the work of that is done well, it will directly influence the operation, management and image of the hotel, including the atmosphere and economic benefits.

The housekeeping department is composed of the executive housekeeper and its staff, including housemaids, or housemen, floor clerks, porters, room attendants, and seamstresses. Relatively the job of a housemaid or houseman is more important.

Topic One   Room Cleaning Service
客房清扫

Introduction

A housekeeper in a hotel has a master key. He/She can enter an occupied room only in case there is an emergency circumstance. Before cleaning a room, the housekeeper's personal identification and the guest's permission are required. The housekeeper's job is to do a room cleaning and check the expenses of the expendables in the room consumed by the guest.

Objectives

Competence Standard	Knowledge Standard
Ability to clean rooms	Know about the working procedures of cleaning rooms
Ability to clean rooms with etiquette	Know about the etiquette of cleaning rooms
Ability to use tools and know about how to clean rooms	Learn about the tools used in cleaning rooms
Ability of listening, speaking and reading	Have a good understanding of the seven steps of cleaning rooms

Working Procedures

- Knock at the door and speak loudly "housekeeping".
- Open the door and (if the guest is in the room) greet the guest.
- Begin the cleaning process.
  Open the window.
  Turn off the air-conditioner.
  Clean the bedroom.
  Clean the bathroom.
  Close the windows.
  Switch on the air-conditioner.
  Remove all the linens and trash.
  Overview the whole room.
- Say goodbye to the guest.
- Fill in the room cleaning form.

Dialogues

Dialogue 1

Situation Question: Is it right to enter the room directly to do a room cleaning without knocking at the door? Why?

Regular Room Cleaning Service

【拓展音频】

R: Room attendant   G: Guest

(Room attendant knocks at the door)

R: Housekeeping, may I come in?

G: Come in, please.

R: Good morning, madam. May I clean your room now?

G: Yes, go ahead.

(*After a while*)

R: Madam, I've finished the room cleaning. Is there anything else I can do for you?

G: Yes. Do you know what is stuffed in the pillow? I think I am allergic to it. My face feels itchy after a night.

R: I am sorry to hear that. The pillow is down pillow which is stuffed with feather. But we also provide other kinds of pillows such as tea pillow, jasmine pillow and buckwheat pillow. You can choose the one you like.

G: Is there any extra charge?

R: No, there is not any extra charge for this service. Would you like me to change one for you?

G: Yes, I'd like a tea pillow.

R: OK, madam. I will get a tea pillow right now.

G: Thank you.

R: It is my pleasure.

Notes:

(1) room attendant 客房服务员

(2) housekeeping 家政　housekeeping service 客房服务

(3) room cleaning 房间清扫

(4) stuff 填塞

(5) pillow 枕头

(6) allergic 对……过敏的

(7) jasmine 茉莉

(8) buckwheat 荞麦

Dialogue 2

Situation Question: Do you know how to respond to the guest who wants to postpone the room cleaning service?

Postpone Room Cleaning

R: Room attendant　　G: Guest

R: Housekeeping, may I come in?

G: Yes, what's the matter?

R: Good morning, sir. I am here to clean your room. May I do it now?

G: Well, I am going to meet a friend, so I need to use the bathroom now. Could you come back later?

R: Yes, when would you like me to clean the room?

G: Let me see. Could you come back at 10:30? I think the room will be empty at that time.

R: OK, I will come to clean the room then. Is there anything else I can do for you?

G: Yes. I need a towel because the one in the room is wet.

R: OK, sir. I will bring a dry and clean towel for you right now.

G: Thanks.

R: You are welcome.

Notes:

(1) bathroom 浴室

(2) towel 毛巾

Dialogue 3

Situation Question: What will you do if a guest asks you to clean his or her room earlier?

【拓展音频】

Earlier Room Cleaning Request

R: Room Attendant   G: Guest

(The room attendant meets the guest in the corridor.)

R: Good morning, Mr. Clinton.

G: Good morning. Please wait a moment.

R: Yes, can I help you?

G: It's almost noon. But my room hasn't been cleaned yet.

R: I'm sorry, Mr. Clinton. I'm going to clean your room now.

G: I found that my room is always the last one to be cleaned. Why?

R: I need to clean check-out rooms first, and then the occupied rooms. You know, your room is the last one on this floor. And I clean rooms according to the sequence of the room number. So your room will be finished by noon.

G: OK, I see. But could you clean it earlier today? I have an important meeting to attend. Before that, I want to have a good nap.

R: No problem, sir. I will go to clean your room after finishing this one. Twenty minutes later, is it OK?

G: OK. That will be good.

R: Next time if you need an earlier cleaning, please do tell me. I will do as you request.

G: OK, thank you.

R: You are welcome.

Notes:

(1) request 请求

(2) corridor 走廊

(3) check-out room 已结账房

(4) occupied room 住客房，在住房

(5) nap 小睡

Dialogue 4

Situation Question: If a guest asks you to add an extra bed, what will you do?

【拓展音频】

Offer Help

R: Room Attendant   G: Guest

R: Housekeeping, may I come in?

Section Two 模块二
Housekeeping Service 客房服务

G: Come in, please.

R: Good morning, Mr. Li. I am here to clean your room now.

G: OK. Could you please clean the bathroom first? I just had a shower. And there is a mess now.

R: Certainly, sir.

(*After cleaning the room*)

R: Mr. Li, I have cleaned your room. Is there anything else I can do for you?

G: Yes. Does your hotel offer extra bed service?

R: Yes. We do offer extra beds to guests.

G: Good. How do you charge for it?

R: It depends. An extra bed for an adult is charged half of the room rate per night. It is free for an infant.

G: How about the charge for a child?

R: According to the hotel policy, the child under 12 is charged half the price, and a teenager is charged as an adult.

G: OK. That's reasonable. My son is coming to meet me this evening. Could you offer me an extra bed?

R: OK, sir. How old is your son?

G: My son is 14 years old.

R: When would you like to the extra bed?

G: This evening, say, before 8:00 o'clock p.m.

R: OK, Mr. Li. I will put the extra bed at the time and notify the front desk about it.

G: Thank you.

Notes:

(1) mess 混乱，脏

(2) extra bed service 加床服务

(3) adult 成年人

(4) teenager 青少年

(5) notify 通知，告知

Useful Sentences

- Housekeeping, may I come in? 客房服务，我可以进来吗？
- Come in, please. 请进。
- May I clean your room now? 我现在可以打扫房间吗？
- I have finished the room cleaning. Is there anything else I can do for you? 客房已经打扫完毕，请问还有什么能为您做的吗？
- Are there any extra charges? 有额外收费吗？
- What's the matter? 有什么事吗？

- I am here to clean your room. May I do it now? 我来打扫房间，可以开始吗？
- Could you come back later? 你能稍后再来吗？
- When would you like me to clean the room? 您想让我什么时间来打扫房间？
- Could you come back at 10:30? 你可以 10:30 过来吗？
- I will bring a dry and clean towel for you right now. 我现在就去给您拿干净的毛巾。
- Please wait a moment. 请稍等。
- But my room hasn't be cleaned yet. 但是我的房间还没打扫呢。
- I am going to clean your room now. 我马上给您打扫房间。
- I need to clean check-out rooms first, and then the occupied rooms. 我要先打扫已结账房，然后是住客房。
- So your room will be finished by noon. 您的房间中午前打扫完。
- But could you clean it earlier today? 今天可以早些打扫吗？
- I will go to clean your room after finishing this one. 我打扫过这个房间就去。
- Next time if you need an earlier cleaning, please do tell me. I will do as you request. 下次如果您需要提早打扫您的房间，请告诉我。我会按照您的要求做。
- Could you please clean the bathroom first? I just had a shower. And there is a mess now. 能否先打扫浴室？我刚刚洗了淋浴，里面比较乱。
- How do you charge for it? 怎么收费？
- It depends. 这要根据情况而定。
- An extra bed for an adult is charged half of the room rate per night. 成人加床，每晚按照房费的一半收费。
- Could you offer me an extra bed? 能否给我加一张床？
- When would you like the extra bed? 您想要什么时候加床？
- I will put the extra bed at that time and notify the front desk about it. 届时我会给您加床并通知前台。

Knowledge Extension

◆ Etiquette of Cleaning Rooms

Before doing the room cleaning, check the room status. When the sign 'Do Not Disturb' is on the door, don't knock at the door. Announce presence and knock lightly at the door with one of fingers, saying 'Housekeeping'. Don't use a key to do that. Wait for a response for a while. Knock again and repeat 'Housekeeping' if you don't hear an answer. You can open the door slightly and repeat 'Housekeeping' again if you still don't receive any answer after a second. You should leave quietly and close the door if you find the guest is in the bathroom or asleep in the room. Greet the guest with courtesy and ask him/her whether the room can be cleaned or not. You can open the door when the guest answers your knock. Otherwise excuse yourself, leave at once and close the door when you enter the room finding the guest is dressing. When the room is unoccupied, position your chart in front of the door. Keep the door open and begin cleaning. While you are doing the cleaning, the guest comes back. Ask the guest to take out his/her key to verify whether the key and room numbers match or not. Clearly report to the supervisor that the guest does not leave the room at noon, in the afternoon, or even in the evening before handing over to the next shift.

Don't touch and move the guest's valuables and his/her belongings. If necessary, handle them with care and put them back in place after cleaning up.

◆ Tools Used for Cleaning the Room

There are some tools used for cleaning rooms, such as trolley, mops, detergents, vacuums, rubber gloves, curtains and so on.

◆ Seven Steps of Cleaning Rooms

Step one: Pull Trash—Remove soiled linen, liners and reline all the waste containers.

Check and replace the needle box container according to the facility's specific guidelines. Clean all the waste receptacles.

Step Two: High Dust—High dust everything above shoulder level or out of reach by using an extension pole with duster head.

Step Three: Damp Wipe—Wipe everything in reach by using germicide for all surfaces except glass. And then use a dry cloth or paper towel to polish interior and low-level glass, including wall spotting, light switches, call buttons, telephones, wall moldings, dispensers, windowsills, and furniture. Begin with the door and work around the room in a circular pattern.

Step Four: Clean Bathroom—When cleaning the bathroom, it is usual to start at the door and end with the toilet by using a bowl mop inside the bowl and wiping the outside with a disinfectant damp wiper.

Step Five: Dust Mop Floor—Dust behind all the furniture and doors by moving them possibly.

Step Six: Damp Mop—Before you begin to mop the floor, remember to put a wet floor sign at the entrance by starting with the corner farthest from the door and work your way out.

Step Seven: Inspect the Room—Remember to report any repairs needed and correct any deficiencies.

Section Summary

- Know about the working procedures of cleaning rooms.
- Know about the etiquette of cleaning rooms.
- Learn about tools of cleaning rooms.
- Learn about the seven steps of cleaning rooms.

Practice

Part One Dialogue

1. Choose the correct sentence to fill in the blanks according to the context.

R: Room Attendant   G: Guest

R: _____

G: Come in, please.

R: Sir, I am here to clean your room. May I do it now?

G: Yes, go ahead.

R: I have cleaned your room. _____

G: Yes, I have some clothes to be washed. Can you help me?

R: _____

G: How can I do that?

R: You can call the housekeeping department for a valet to get your laundry. _____
The room attendant will take them to the Laundry Department.

G: OK, that will be good. _____

R: The number is in the brochure of the hotel which you can find in the drawer of the night stand.

G: OK, I see. Thank you very much.

R: You are welcome.

A. Is there anything else I can do?

B. You can use our laundry service.

C. Or you can put your laundry in the laundry bag and put it on the end of the bed.

D. How can I get the telephone number?

E. Housekeeping, may I come in?

2. Act in pairs to finish the following role-play activities.

(1) Student A: Act as a guest in the hotel room.

Student B: Act as the room attendant. Go to offer regular house cleaning service.

(2) Student A: Act as a guest in the hotel room. Ask the room attendant about laundry service.

Student B: Act as the room attendant. Go to the guest room to clean the room and answer his/her questions.

(3) Student A: Act as a guest in the hotel. You meet the room attendant in the corridor and ask for earlier cleaning for the rest days in the hotel.

Student B: Act as the room attendant. Meet a guest in the corridor during the working time. Greet the guest and correspond to his/her request.

(4) Student A: Act as a guest in the hotel room. Ask the room attendant to clean the room later and give reasons.

Student B: Act as the attendant to clean the room for the guest. Respond to his/her request.

(5) Student A: Act as a guest in the hotel room. Ask the room attendant to bring more cups for you.

Student B: Act as the room attendant to clean the room for the guest. Respond to his/her request.

3. Look at the following items in the hotel room and translate them into English.

(1) 浴缸　　　　　(2) 浴帽
(3) 洗发水　　　　(4) 床单
(5) 护发素　　　　(6) 毛毯
(7) 梳子　　　　　(8) 棉被
(9) 牙膏　　　　　(10) 床罩
(11) 牙刷　　　　 (12) 枕头
(13) 肥皂　　　　 (14) 床头柜
(15) 电吹风　　　 (16) 剃须刀
(17) 拖鞋　　　　 (18) 水杯

4. Discussion

(1) What should you do if you found the property left by the guest but he or she had checked out?

(2) What should you do if the phone in the room rang but the guest was not in the room?

5. Translate the following sentences.

(1) 我现在可以打扫房间吗？
(2) 还有什么能为您做的吗？
(3) 你能稍后再来吗？
(4) 您想让我什么时间来打扫房间？
(5) 我的房间还没打扫。
(6) 我马上给您打扫房间。
(7) 今天可以早点来打扫吗？
(8) 如果您需要提早打扫房间，请告诉我。
(9) 加床费是房费的一半。
(10) 房间打扫完了，请问还有什么能为您做的吗？

Part Two　Knowledge Extension

According to the part of Knowledge Extension, write the answers to the following questions on the sheet of paper by using your own words, not simply copying the sentences. When you have completed the test, ask your lecturer for the answers.

Etiquette of Cleaning Rooms

_____
_____
_____

Tools Used in Cleaning Rooms

_____

_____

_____

Seven Steps of Cleaning Rooms

_____

_____

_____

_____

_____

_____

_____

_____

_____

Topic Two   Laundry Service 洗衣服务

Introduction

Laundry service is one of the housekeeping service forms. Some hotels have this kind of service and charge extra. If a guest in a hotel requires this service, a laundryman comes to the guest's room to collect laundry. The guest fills in the laundry list, and chooses one of the laundry service types. After laundry, the guest's clothes will be delivered to the guest room.

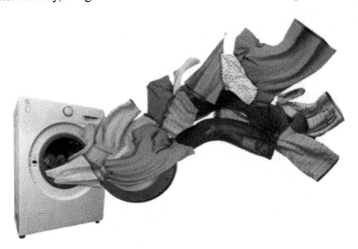

Objectives

Competence Standard	Knowledge Standard
Ability to know about the types of laundry service and laundry service guide	Know about the working procedures of laundry service
Ability to explain basic steps of laundry service	Learn to recognize the signs of laundry service
Ability to recognize washing signs	Know about the basic steps and process of laundry service
Ability of listening, speaking and reading	Know about the laundry service guide

Working Procedures

- Knock at the door.
- Greet the guest.
- Ask about the guest's needs for laundry.

- Confirm the service required by the guest.
- Explain the charge for laundry service.
- Fill in the laundry list.
- Ask the guest to sign.
- Place the laundry list together with the laundry in the bag.
- Thank the guest and say goodbye.

Dialogues

Dialogue 1

Situation Question: As a room attendant, what kind of information should he or she have about laundry service?

【拓展音频】

About Laundry Service

R: Room Attendant   G: Guest

R: Sir, your room has been cleaned. Is there anything else I can do for you?

G: Yes, I want to wash my suit. Can you help me?

R: Certainly. Our hotel offers laundry service to the guest.

G: That's good. How can I do that?

R: Please fill in the laundry list and then put your laundry together with the laundry list in the laundry bag. And I will take it to the Laundry Department for you.

G: How can I get the laundry list and the laundry bag?

R: They are in the wardrobe. Let me help you get it. Here you are.

G: Thank you. How do you charge for it?

R: There are details on the list. The charge is different according to the service itself.

G: OK, I see. How can I pay for laundry service?

R: Usually it is put on the room.

G: Suppose I need laundry service tomorrow, who should I give my laundry to?

R: You can put it on the end of bed. The room attendant will take it away. Or if you have any special request about laundry service, you could call the Housekeeping Department. The phone number is in the brochure of the hotel.

G: OK. Thank you so much.

R: You are welcome. So would you like me to take your laundry bag now?

G: Yes.

Notes:

(1) suit 套装

(2) laundry 洗衣店

(3) laundry service 洗衣服务

(4) laundry list 洗衣清单

(5) laundry bag 洗衣袋

(6) wardrobe 衣柜

(7) department 部门

Dialogue 2

Situation Question: Do you know the procedures of taking laundry? What are they?

Take Laundry

R: Receptionist   V: Valet   G: Guest

R: Good morning, Housekeeping Department. How may I help you?

G: Yes. I have some clothes to be washed. Could you send someone to get them?

R: Certainly, sir. May I have your name and room number?

G: My name is Jack Black in Room 1206.

R: Please wait in your room, Mr. Black. I will send a valet to your room now.

G: OK. Thank you.

(*After a while*)

V: Good morning, Mr. Black. I'm here to collect your laundry.

G: Good morning. Here are my laundry, one suit and one sweater.

V: Do you need a dry cleaning?

G: I think the sweater should be dry-cleaned. It will shrink if it is washed in water.

V: OK, I see. When would you like your laundry back?

G: How about tomorrow morning? Could you do that?

V: I am afraid you will not have the sweater tomorrow because it will take 2 days to dry and clean it. But you can have the suit around 10 o'clock tomorrow morning. Is it all right?

G: OK. By the way, there is a split on the coat, so could you stitch it for me?

G: Of course, sir.

V: Please have a look at the laundry list and sign on it.

G: OK. Here you are.

V: Thank you, Mr. Black. Good-bye.

Notes:

(1) valet 洗衣部服务员

(2) suit 套装

(3) sweater 毛衣

(4) dry cleaning 干洗

(5) shrink 缩水

(6) stitch 缝

Dialogue 3

Situation Question: If the guest wants to get laundry back in a short time, what kind of service will you recommend to him or her?

Express Laundry Service

【拓展音频】

V: Valet   G: Guest

V: Good afternoon, madam. I am here to collect your laundry.

G: Good afternoon. Here are the laundry, an overcoat and a skirt.

V: Do you need a dry cleaning service?

G: No, just a wet laundry.

V: OK. When would you like to have them back?

G: I need them this evening. Could I have them by 8:00 o'clock p.m. tonight?

V: Let me see. It's 3 o'clock. If you choose express service, then you can have it at that time.

G: I really need them. So I choose express service. How would you charge for express service?

V: We charge 50% more on normal service basis.

G: OK.

V: How would you like to pay for it?

G: I like to put it on the room.

V: OK, madam. Please fill in the laundry list and sign your name on it.

G: Here you are.

V: There is something in the pocket of the overcoat, madam.

G: Oh, yes, that's my credit card. Thank you so much. You have well helped me avoid a big trouble.

V: You are welcome. Glad to serve you. Have a nice day. Good-bye.

G: Good-bye.

Notes:

(1) express adj. 迅速的   express service 快洗服务，加急服务

(2) on the basis 在此基础上

(3) avoid 避免

Dialogue 4

Situation Question: Do you know how to deal with the damage of the laundry?

Damage

【拓展音频】

V: Valet   G: Guest

(The valet knocks at the door)

G: Who is that?

V: I am the valet to bring the laundry back. May I come in?

G: Come in, please.

V: Good morning, sir. Please check your laundry.

G: OK. The suit is well washed. But look at the sweater. Oh, it is out of shape. And it is dyed with other color.

V: I'm terribly sorry, sir. I will take it to the Laundry Department and the department will compensate you for the damage. May I know the price of the sweater?

G: I can't remember it.

V: Could you buy a new one here?

G: I am not sure.

V: If you could buy a new one, and give us the receipt of it, we will refund you the cost of the laundry and the sweater.

G: But I have no time to go shopping. You know I am here to attend an important meeting. I have a full schedule.

V: In that case, I recommend that you buy it back home and send us the receipt. Then we will send you a draft for the amount. What do you think of it?

G: OK. I think I have to do so.

V: Would you please fill in the form with your contact information?

G: OK.

V: I am sorry for the inconvenience caused to you. Thank you for your understanding.

Notes:

(1) out of shape 变形

(2) dye 染色

(3) compensate 赔偿

(4) damage 损毁

(5) receipt 收据

(6) refund 退款

(7) schedule 时间表

(8) in that case 假如那样的话

Useful Sentences

- Please fill in the laundry list and then put your laundry together with the laundry list in the laundry bag. 请填写洗衣单，然后连同要洗的衣物一起放到洗衣袋内。
- And I will take it to the Laundry Department for you. 我把待洗衣物送到洗衣部。
- How can I get the laundry list and the laundry bag? 怎么能拿到洗衣单和洗衣袋？
- They are in the wardrobe. 衣服在衣柜里。
- How do you charge for it? 怎么收费？
- The charge is different according to the service itself. 服务不同费用不同。

- Could you send someone to get them? 你能派人来取吗？
- I will send a valet to your room now. 我现在就让服务员去您房间。
- I am here to collect your laundry. 我是来收待洗衣物的。
- Do you need a dry cleaning or washing? 您需要干洗还是水洗？
- When would you like your laundry back? 您需要这些衣物什么时候送回来？
- It will take 2 days to dry and clean it. 干洗需要 2 天时间。
- Please have a look at the laundry list and sign on it. 请核对一下洗衣单并签字。
- How would you charge for express service? 快洗服务怎么收费？
- We charge 50% more on the normal service basis. 在普通洗基础上加收 50% 费用。
- I'd like to put it on the room rate. 我想把费用记到房费上。
- I am the valet to bring the laundry back. 我是服务员，来送还衣物。
- And it is dyed with other colors. 和其他衣物混色了。
- I'm terribly sorry for the inconvenience caused to you. 我对给您带来的不便深表歉意。

Knowledge Extension

- **Washing Signs of Laundry Service**

Dryclean		Do not dryclean	
Compatible with any drycleaning methods		Iron	
Iron on low heat		Iron on medium heat	
Iron on high heat		Do not iron	
Bleach		Do not bleach	
Dry		Tumble dry with no heat	
Tumble dry with low heat		Tumble dry with high heat	
Tumble dry with medium heat		Do not wash	
Handwash only		Wash with hot water	
Wash with warm water		Wash with cold water	
Line dry		Dry flat	
Hang dry		Dry	

- **Basic Steps of Laundry Service**

There are three basic steps of laundry service as follows:

A laundryman goes to the guest's room for his/her laundry.

A guest fills in the laundry list.

A laundryman delivers the laundry to the guest's room.

♦ Process of Laundry Service

The process of laundry service is a multi-step one, including collecting, sorting, washing, drying, finishing/folding and delivering. When collecting, the laundryman should not use dirty linen and terry as guestroom cleaning rags, place bloodstained linen or terry separately in a waste bag and put biohazard waste bags on every housekeeping cart; When sorting, the laundryman should sort laundry in terms of fabric types and degree of staining; when washing, the laundryman should monitor washing times, washing temperatures, chemicals and agitation length and strength, which is a complex process; when drying, the laundryman should vaporize or remove the moisture of fabrics by moving hot air and then cool them down; when finishing/folding, the laundryman should note the space for finishing laundry must be adequate; when storing, the laundryman should "rest" some fabrics for 24 hours for cleaned laundry and when delivering, the laundryman should lock the storage areas.

♦ Laundry Service Types

There are four types of laundry service, which are same-day service (A laundry attendant collects the laundry by 11:00 and returns them on the same day.), express service (A laundry attendant collects the laundry all day and returns them within four hours with 50% extra-charge.), next day service (A laundry attendant collects the laundry after 11:00 and delivers before 19:00 next day.) and express pressing service (A laundry attendant collects the laundry all day and returns them within one hour.)

♦ Laundry Service Guide

Please Contact for Laundry Service (8888)

Items	Unit price		Items	Unit price	
	Dry Cleaning	Pressing		Dry Cleaning	Pressing
Jackets	¥10	¥3	Cheongsam	¥29	¥9
T-Shirt	¥5	¥3	Jacket (long)	¥21	¥7
Upper Suit	¥11	¥6	Jean Jacket	¥10	¥4
Shirt	¥5	¥5	Jacket (normal)	¥20	¥8
Slacks	¥5	¥3	Down Jacket	¥26	¥7
Sweater	¥9	¥3	Overcoat (short)	¥16	¥6
Long Skirt	¥11	¥4	Scarf	¥9	¥5
Dress	¥13	¥4	Jacket (short)	¥15	¥7
Woolen Vest	¥9	¥2	Shawl	¥8	¥4
Miniskirt	¥5	¥5	Underwear	¥7	¥5
Pleated Skirt	¥12	¥3	Socks	¥6	¥3

续表

Items	Unit price		Items	Unit price	
	Dry Cleaning	Pressing		Dry Cleaning	Pressing
Open Sweater	¥10	¥3	Overcoat (normal)	¥17	¥7
Tie/Waist Coat	¥7	¥5	Overcoat (long)	¥22	¥9
Shorts	¥5	¥5	Chinese Costume	¥16	¥7
Chinese Costume (cotton)	¥12	¥6	Discuss the price on the spot		

Please Note:

Collect garments before 20:00 p.m. and return the next day 8:00 a.m.; Collect garments after 20:00 p.m. and return the next afternoon.

Express service is provided with the price of 200% normal price.

The laundry is not in charge of shrinkage, color fading, loosing thread and lost property in pockets.

The laundry compensates for loss and damage of garments within 10 times of the washing cost.

Section Summary

- Know about the washing signs of laundry service.
- Know about the basic steps of laundry service.
- Know about the process of laundry service.
- Know about laundry service types.
- Know about the laundry service guide.

Practice

Part One Dialogue

1. Choose the correct sentences to fill in the blanks according to the context.

V: Valet   G: Guest

V: Good morning, madam. _____

G: Good morning. Here is my laundry, one skirt and one coat.

V: How would you like your laundry to be washed?

G: _____The coat can be washed in a washing machine.

V: OK, madam. _____

G: I need them this afternoon. So, could you send them back before 1:00 p.m.?

V: We can. But according to the hotel policy, _____

G: Why? Is it different from tomorrow?

Housekeeping Service 客房服务

V: Yes. Now it's 11 o'clock. Laundry collected after 10:00 a.m. will be returned next day. If you want them back within 3 hours, you will have to pay twice charge of the service.

G: OK, I understand. But I really need them tonight. _____

V: OK, I will. Please have a look at the laundry list and sign your name on it.

G: OK. Here you are.

A. I'd like the skirt to be hand-washed in cold water.

B. When would you like to have it/them back?

C. So please get it/them back before 1:00 p.m. this afternoon.

D. I am here to collect your laundry.

E. You will have to pay extra money for the same service.

2. Act in pairs to finish the following role-play activities.

(1) Student A: Act as a guest. Call the Housekeeping Department for laundry service.

Student B: Act as the receptionist to answer the phone. Respond to the guest's request.

Students C: Act as the valet. Go to the guest room to collect the laundry. Respond to the guest's request.

(2) Students A: Act as a guest in the hotel room. You have laundry to be washed. Ask for express service.

Student B: Act as the valet. Go to the guest room to collect the laundry. Respond to the guest's request.

(3) Student A: Act as a guest in the room. You have laundry to be washed. Ask for normal service but leave something in the pocket.

Student B: Act as the valet. Go to the guest room to collect the laundry. Find the items in the pocket and return them to the guest.

(4) Student A: Act as a guest in the room. Go to open the door to get the laundry.

Student B: Act as the valet to send the laundry to the guest.

(5) Student A: Act as a guest in the room. Go to open the door to get the laundry, but find there is some damage to the laundry.

Student B: Act as the valet to send the laundry to the guest. Respond to the guest's request.

3. Look at the following words of laundry service and translate them into English.

(1) 洗衣单

(2) 洗衣袋

(3) 待洗衣物

(4) 普通洗衣服务

(5) 快洗服务

(6) 污渍

(7) 干洗

(8) 熨烫

(9) 丝绸

(10) 手洗

4. Discussion

(1) What will you do if the guest finds the laundry sent back is damaged?

(2) What will you do if you find some money in the pocket of the laundry to be washed?

5. Translate the following sentences.

(1) 请填写洗衣单并签字。

(2) 洗衣袋在衣柜里。

(3) 你能派人来取吗?

(4) 我来收待洗衣物的。

(5) 您需要干洗还是水洗?

(6) 请核对一下洗衣单并签字。

(7) 快洗服务怎么收费?

(8) 我想把费用记到房费上。

(9) 我的衣物和其他衣物混色了。

(10) 我对给您带来的不便深表歉意。

Part Two Knowledge Extension

According to the part of Knowledge Extension, write the answers to the following questions on the sheet of paper by using your own words, not simply copying the sentences. When you have completed the test, ask your lecturer for the answers.

Basic Steps of laundry Service

_____

_____

_____

Process of Laundry Service

_____

_____

_____

Laundry Service Types

_____

_____

_____

Topic Three   Turn-down Service
夜床服务

Introduction

In the hospitality industry, turn-down service is one of the hotel service forms, which refers to the practice of an attendant who enters a guest room to turn down the bed linen, clean and refresh the room, and preparing the bed for sleeping, usually during the period when the guest is not in the room.

Objectives

Competence Standard	Knowledge Standard
Ability to get some information of a turn-down attendant	Learn about the concept of turn-down service
Ability for turn-down attendants to know about the turn-down service duties	Know about the working procedures of turn-down service
Ability to know the detailed procedures of turn-down service	Know about the duties of turn-down attendants
Ability of listening, speaking and reading	Know about the detailed procedures of turn-down service

Working Procedures

- Knock at the door and speak loudly "housekeeping, turn-down service".
- Greet the guest if he/she is in the room.
- Begin the turn-down service (with the approval of the guest).
  Clean the room.
  Create the atmosphere of sleeping.
  Turn down the bed.
  Clean the bathroom.
- Leave the room (Express best wishes to the guest).

Dialogues

Dialogue 1

Situation Question: Do you know how to do the turn-down service? What should be paid attention to during the process?

Regular Turn-down Service

【拓展音频】

R: Room Attendant　　G: Guest

R: Good evening, turn-down service. May I come in?

G: Come in, please.

R: Good evening, sir. I'm here to do the turn-down service and may I start now?

G: Yes, please.

R: Sir, would you like me to draw the curtains for you?

G: No, thank you. I want to have a look at the beautiful night scenery.

R: That is true. Our hotel is the tallest building in the city. You can enjoy the beauty of the evening scenes.

(*After cleaning the room and finishing the turn-down service*)

R: Sir, is there anything I can do for you?

G: Could you bring me two more cups? I am expecting two friends. They are coming in a few minutes.

R: Certainly. I will bring the cups for you in a minute.

G: Thank you.

R: You are welcome.

Notes:

(1) turn-down service　夜床服务

(2) curtain　窗帘

(3) scenery 风景

(4) evening scene 夜景

Dialogue 2

Situation Question: If the guest asks you to postpone the turn-down service, what will you respond?

Postpone the Turn-down Service

R: Room Attendant   G: Guest

R: Housekeeping, may I come in?

G: Come in, please.

R: Good evening, madam. I am here to do the turn-down service. May I do it now?

G: Please wait a moment. Could you come back later? I need to meet some friends in the room in half an hour.

R: OK, madam. When would you like me to turn down your bed?

G: 8:00 o'clock p.m. Is it OK?

R: OK, I will come back at 8:00. Is there anything else I can do for you?

G: Yes, do you have the baby-sitting service?

R: Yes, we do have the service.

G: How can I get that? Tomorrow I will go to attend a very important meeting. I can not take my daughter with me. So I really need the service.

R: Don't worry, madam. You may call the Housekeeping Department to ask for the service. They will arrange it for you.

G: OK. Do you know how they charge for the service?

R: According to hours, I think. You may get the details from the Housekeeping Department. They have professionals in the field.

G: OK. Thank you for your help.

R: You are welcome.

Notes:

(1) baby-sitting service 托婴服务

(2) housekeeping department 客房部

(3) charge for 索价

(4) professional 专业人员

(5) field 领域

Dialogue 3

Situation Question: Do you think it is important for a hotel to provide personal service? Why or why not?

【拓展音频】

Personal Service (1)

R: Room Attendant　　G: Guest

R: Good evening, housekeeping, may I come in?

G: Come in, please.

R: I am here to do the turn-down service. May I do it now?

G: Sure, go ahead.

(After completing the turn-down service)

R: Sir, I have finished the turn-down service, and is there anything else I can do for you?

G: Yes. Do you have service for wedding anniversary? Tomorrow is our 10th wedding anniversary. I want to give my wife a surprise.

R: Congratulations.

G: Thank you.

R: We do have the service. You can get the service from the Housekeeping Department. Or you can contact the F&B Department to reserve a dinner for two. I think both of them are very good.

G: My wife will come here tomorrow evening at 10 o'clock. So it is too late to have dinner. But I think it may be a good idea to have the room decorated romantically. Could you do that?

R: Of course. Do you have any ideas about it?

G: I have prepared a gift. So I advise you to prepare flowers, music and wine. Is it OK?

R: No problem, sir. When would you like us to finish the arrangement?

G: How about 9 p.m.?

R: OK. We will do it.

Notes:

(1) personal service 个性化服务

(2) wedding 婚礼　anniversary 周年纪念日

(3) wedding anniversary 结婚纪念日

(4) surprise 惊喜

(5) F&B department 餐饮部

(6) reserve 预订

(7) decorate 装饰

(8) romantically 浪漫地

Dialogue 4

Situation Question: How many kinds of personal service do you know? What are they?

Personal Service (2)

R: Room attendant   G: Guest

R: Good evening, housekeeping, may I come in?

G: Come in, please.

R: Good evening, madam. I am here to do the turn-down service. May I begin now?

G: Yes, please.

(*After completing the turn-down service*)

R: Madam, I have finished the turn-down service. Is there anything else I can do for you?

G: Yes. Do you have personal service in your hotel?

R: Yes. We offer personal service according to guests' requests and custom, such as the service for wedding anniversary, birthday, and baby-sitting. Also we have the service for regular guests.

G: That's good. What does a regular guest mean?

R: It means that the guest stays in the hotel for a long time such as a month or a year. We will set up the guest archives and provide personal service to the guest.

G: OK, I see. Thank you.

R: You are welcome.

Notes:

(1) custom 习惯

(2) regular guest 常客

(3) guest archives 客史档案

Useful Sentences

- Good evening, turn-down service. May I come in? 晚上好，我来做夜床服务。我可以进来吗？
- I am here to do the turn-down service. May I start now? 我来做夜床服务，现在可以开始了吗？
- Would you like me to draw the curtains for you? 需要我为您拉上窗帘吗？
- Is there anything else I can do for you? 还有能为您效劳的吗？
- I will bring the cups for you in a minute. 稍后我把杯子送来。
- Please wait a moment. Could you come back later? 请稍等，你能晚点再来吗？
- When would you like me to turn down your bed? 您需要我什么时候做夜床服务？
- I will come back at 8:00. 我八点钟再来。

- Do you have baby-sitting service? 你们有托婴服务吗?
- You may call the Housekeeping Department to ask for the service. They will arrange it for you. 您可以给客房部打电话，他们会为您安排的。
- I have finished the turn-down service. Is there anything else I can do for you? 夜床服务已完成，请问还有什么能为您做的吗?
- When would you like us to finish the arrangement? 您需要什么时间为您准备好?
- Do you have personal service in your hotel? 你们酒店有个性化客房服务吗?
- We offer personal service according to guests' requests and customs. 我们会根据客人的要求和习惯提供个性化服务。

Knowledge Extension

◆ Turn-down Attendants

Turn-down attendants, who are very professional, good looking, observant and skilled, are in charge of providing the turn-down service. A turn-down attendant is naturally silent to avoid getting trouble to guests and usually arranges a guest room within five minutes.

◆ Duties of a Turn-down Attendant

In different establishments, turn-down attendants' duties can vary. For example, in some establishments, turn-down attendants turn down the bed sheets, put a chocolate or candy on a pillow with a card; in others, they place a morning breakfast card on the doorknob, fill an ice bucket, refill basket with fresh fruits, leave a fresh towel or a bottle of water for night.

◆ Detailed Procedures of the Turn-down Service

Get Ready

Collect room assignment sheets or giveaways given by a housekeeping supervisor. Check special notes or requirements for any guest.

Enter the Guest Room

Check the status of the room. Knock at the door first and then after getting the guest's permission for the turn-down service, enter the guest room. If the guest refuses, you can ask when you can do that or do something as the guest says. Remember to report about the refused service room to the supervisor. If you are allowed to enter the room or there is no guest in the room, you can follow the next step. Keep the door open and the cart in a proper position. And then switch on all the lights and keep them working fine. Look at the turn-down assignment sheet for special instruction.

Neaten and Fold One Corner of the Blanket

Remove the items from the bed and put them aside. Pull the bed cover lightly or fold the bed corner of the blanket back to form a right-angle triangle to make it easy for the guest to slide into the bed. Neaten all the edges properly and then fluff the pillows to make them look fresh.

Put Turn-down Amenities

Put the turn-down amenities and other necessary arrangements in a proper place, including mineral water. And put the foot mat on the floor along with slippers in front of the bed.

Clean the Room

Hang the guest's clothes in the hanger or keep them in the wardrobe. Collect all soiled utensils and replace them with new clean ones. Clean the whole room properly and arrange everything neatly.

Make the Guest's Bathroom Neat and Tidy

Clean the bathroom and keep it neat and tidy and then replenish the guest's supplies with new ones.

Create Pleasing Atmosphere

Try to create the pleasing atmosphere by closing curtains or blinds to give guests privacy at night, turning on bedside lights, spraying some air freshener as guests wish to make the room comfortable and appealing.

Double Check Everything

From beginning to end, scan the whole room and check whether anything has been missed or overlooked, especially handling some extra requirements needed by guests.

Exit the Room

Leave the room and lock the door properly to make the guest's belongings safe.

Take Note on the Assignment Sheet

Mark the worksheet as required.

Section Summary

- Know about turn-down attendants.
- know about the duties of turn-down attendants.
- Know about the detailed procedures of the turn-down service.

Practice

Part One Dialogue

1. Choose the correct sentences to fill in the blanks according to the context.

R: Room Attendant   G: Guest

R: Good evening, _____. May I come in?

G: Come in, please.

R: Good evening, sir. I am here to do the turn-down service. _____?

G: Wait a moment, please. I am expecting two friends. _____?

R: Certainly, sir. Is there anything I can do for you?

G: Yes, I need two coffee cups. Could you bring two cups for me?

R: Yes, _____. Anything else?

G: Could you clean the rest room first? I just had a shower.

R: OK. I will do it now.

(After cleaning the rest room, the room attendant goes to get cups)

R: Sir, here are the cups you wanted.

G: Good, thank you so much.

R: You are welcome. _____?

G: How about 9 o'clock?

R: OK, I will come back at 9:00.

A. So could you come back later

B. turn-down service

C. I will bring the cups in a minute

D. When would you like me to do the turn-down service

E. May I start now

2. Act in pairs to finish the following role-play activities.

(1) Student A: Act as a guest. You are in the room and respond to the room attendant.

Student B: Act as the room attendant. Come to do the regular turn-down service.

(2) Student A: Act as a guest. You are in the room, and ask the room attendant about scenic spots in the city.

Student B: Act as the room attendant. Offer the regular turn-down service and answer the guest's questions.

(3) Student A: Act as a guest. You are in the room, refuse the turn-down service and give reasons.

Student B: Act as the room attendant to offer the turn-down service to the guest.

(4) Student A: Act as a guest. You ask about the personal service in the hotel when the room attendant offers the turn-down service.

Student B: Act as the room attendant. Offer the regular turn-down service and answer the guest's questions.

(5) Student A: Act as a guest. Your wife/husband will come to meet you tomorrow evening in the hotel. Tomorrow is her/his birthday. Ask for personal service when the room attendant comes to offer the turn-down service.

Student B: Act as the room attendant. Offer the turn-down service and respond to the guest's request.

3. Read the following words and translate them into Chinese.

(1) pillow cases

(2) duvet cover

(3) bed sheets

(4) shower gel

(5) shampoo

(6) lotion

(7) shower cap

(8) toothbrush and toothpaste

(9) comb

(10) razor and shaving cream

4. Discussion:

(1) What will you do if you open the room to do the turn-down service, finding the guest is sleeping in the bed?

(2) What will you do if you find the guest has broken the mirror of the restroom?

5. Translate the following sentences.

(1) 我来做夜床服务，可以进来吗？

(2) 如果有任何需要，请随时联系我。

(3) 你们有托婴服务吗？

(4) 我想了解一下酒店的个性化服务。

(5) 我们酒店有专职照顾小孩的人员。

(6) 您需要我为您找医生吗？

(7) 我会马上把今天的报纸送过来。

(8) 女士，别担心，我马上派人过去处理。

(9) 您需要什么水果？

(10) 不客气，很高兴为您服务。

Part Two　Knowledge Extension

According to the part of Knowledge Extension, write the answers to the following questions on the sheet of paper by using your own words, not simply copying the sentences. When you have completed the test, ask your lecturer for the answers.

A turn-down attendant

_____

_____

_____

Duties of a turn-down attendant

_____

_____

_____

Describe the detailed procedures of the turn-down service.

Topic Four　Wake-up Call Service
叫醒服务

Introduction

Wake-up call service is a simplistic, straightforward and free service with the purpose of not letting you be late. In a word, it keeps calling every five minutes until you actually confirm that you're up. It's really more useful than a normal snoozing alarm. You can have the normal settings to let your call be repeated certain days of a week. You can actually choose the voice to make it a little more fun. Usually you can set the time you want to get a call for a limited time period.

Objectives

Competence Standard	Knowledge Standard
Ability to know about the detailed procedures of wake-up calls	Learn about the detailed working procedures of wake-up call service
Ability to grasp four features of wake-up call service	Have a good understanding of the four features of wake-up call service
Ability to know about the standards of wake-up call service requests and delivering a wake-up call	Know about the standards of wake-up call service requests
Ability of listening, speaking and reading	Know about the standards of delivering a wake-up call

Working Procedures

- Greet the guest.
- Ask the guest's name, room number and wake-up time.
- Confirm the details and keep a record.
- Express best wishes to the guest.
- Offer the wake-up call service on time.

Dialogues

Dialogue 1

Situation Question: Do you know how to offer wake-up call service to a guest?

【拓展音频】

Introduce Wake-up Service

R: Room Attendant   G: Guest

R: Sir, I have cleaned your room. Is there anything else I can do for you?

G: Yes. I want to take the morning plane to Beijing. But I am afraid that I will be late. So I want to use your morning wake-up service. Do you know something about it?

R: Yes. We have 3 types of wake-up service. They are wake-up call, knocking at the door and using our computer system. You can choose the one you like.

G: I think the wake-up call will be better. How can I get it?

R: You can call the front desk and tell them your room number, name, and the time you want to be woke up.

G: Generally, how many times will they call me?

R: We usually call the guest two times, in case the guest hasn't been woken up. After two times, if the guest didn't answer the phone, we will send a staff to knock at the door.

G: OK, I see. Thank you so much.

R: You are welcome. It's my pleasure to serve you.

Notes:

(1) wake-up call service 叫醒服务

(2) generally 通常

(3) in case 万一

Dialogue 2

Situation Question: Do you know computer wake-up call service? How would you do it?

Regular Wake-up Call Service

C: Clerk at Front Desk   G: Guest

C: Good afternoon, Front Desk. How may I help you?

G: Good afternoon. I want a morning wake-up call service for tomorrow.

C: May I have your name and room number?

G: Yes. My name is John Miller, and the room number is 1208.

C: Mr. Miller, what time would you like us to call you?

G: 5:30 a.m.

C: We have telephone wake-up call service, in-room computer wake-up call service and knocking at the door. Which one would you like?

G: How can I use the computer wake-up call?

C: I will type your room number and wake-up time in the computer. And when it's time to wake up, the computer will dial your room number automatically to wake you up.

G: OK, I see. I will use it. But how would you make sure that I am woken up?

C: The computer will print the file of the wake-up call and show the result of calling, such as "answered", "no answer", or "ring block". Then we will know whether or not the guest is woken up. If not, we will send a room attendant to knock at the door.

G: OK, Good. Thank you.

C: Then, Mr. Miller, you choose the computer wake-up call, and your room number is 1208 and the wake-up time is 5:30 a.m. tomorrow. Is it correct?

G: Yes, thank you.

C: You are welcome. Goodbye.

G: Goodbye.

Notes:

(1) dial 拨号
(2) automatically 自动地
(3) file 文件
(4) block 阻止

Dialogue 3

Situation Question: Do you know how to ask for group wake-up call service? What kind of information should be provided?

Wake-up Call for Group

【拓展音频】

C: Clerk   G: Guest

C: Good afternoon, Front Desk. May I help you?

G: Good afternoon. I want to have a wake-up call for my group.

C: Madam, are you the local guide for the group?

G: Yes. The group will go to watch sunrise. So we need a wake-up call service.

C: OK, Madam, could you come to the front desk to make registration for the group wake-up call service?

G: OK. I will come down soon.

(*After a while*)

C: Good afternoon, can I help you?

G: Yes, I want to book a group wake-up call service for my group. I called just now and I was asked to come down to register.

C: Yes, madam. We offer the group wake-up call service for guests. May I have your group number?

G: Yes, the group number is HT1203B from Happy Tour International Travel Agency.

C: May I have the room numbers to be called?

G: Room 2101 to 2118.

C: May I know the time the rooms should be called?

G: At 4:00 a.m. tomorrow morning.

C: OK. May I have your name and room number?

G: Yes. My name is Judy Wilson and my room number is 2105.

C: Please wait a moment. Let me check the rooming list. Thank you for waiting. Ms. Wilson, you have booked a group wake-up call service at 4:00 a.m. tomorrow morning for room 2101 to 2118. Is that correct?

G: Yes. That is correct.

C: Could you sign here?

G: Yes, here you are.

C: Thank you so much.

Notes:

(1) local guide 当地导游

(2) sunrise 日出

(3) registration 登记

(4) travel agency 旅行社

(5) rooming list 分房名单

Dialogue 4

Situation Question: What should you do if the guest complained to you about the wake-up call service?

Complain about Wake-up Call Service

C: Clerk of Front Office　　G: Guest

C: Good morning, madam. May I help you?

G: Yes. I want to make a complaint about your wake-up call service.

C: Could you have the seat there and talk about it?

G: Yes.

C: May I know what happened, madam?

G: OK. I called your front desk to reserve the wake-up call service last night. But this morning, you have not called me. And I missed my train to Xi'an, where I will have a very important meeting with my client.

C: I am very sorry about that. May I have your name and room number, please?

G: My name is Linda Brown in Room 1609.

C: OK, Ms. Brown. Could you please wait for a moment? I will check with the front desk and get back to you.

G: OK.

...

C: I am very sorry, madam. It is our fault. The computer system didn't work last night. Our staff didn't check it on time, so your room wasn't called this morning. We are very sorry about it. To express our sincere apology, we would like to refund your train ticket and help you book another one to Xi'an. What do you think of that?

G: But another train will be too late for me. Could you help me to book a flight ticket? Of course, I will pay for the flight ticket.

C: OK. I will contact our business center right away. Please wait a moment.

...

C: Ms. Brown, we have booked a flight for you. Then this is the money for the train ticket. And this is the VIP card. Next time you could use it in our hotel. We are sorry for the inconvenience.

G: OK, I am late for the train, but I am satisfied with your service. Thank you.

C: Thank you for your understanding. Have a good trip. Good-bye.

G: Good-bye.

Notes:

(1) complaint 投诉，抱怨

(2) client 客户

(3) get back to 回复

(4) contact 联系

(5) inconvenience 不便

Useful Sentences

- We have 3 types of wake-up service. They are wake-up call, knocking at the door and using our computer system. 我们提供三种叫早方式，电话、敲门和电脑系统叫早。
- How can I get it? 我该怎么得到这种服务？
- You can call the front desk and tell them your room number, name, and the time you want to be waked up. 你可以给前台打电话，然后说一下房号、姓名和叫早时间。
- Good afternoon, Front Desk. How may I help you? 下午好，酒店前台。我能为您做些什么？
- I want a morning wake-up call service for tomorrow. 我想预约明早的叫早服务。
- What time would you like us to call you? 您想让我们什么时间叫醒您？
- We will send a room attendant to knock at the door. 我们会派客房服务员去敲门。
- Madam, are you the local guide for the group? 女士，您是导游吗？
- The group will go to watch sunrise. So we need a wake-up call service. 游客明天早晨看日出，所以需要叫醒服务。
- Could you come to the front desk to make registration for the group wake-up call service? 您能到前台办理团队叫醒服务登记吗？
- May I have your group number? 可以告诉我您的团号吗？
- May I have the room numbers to be called? 可以告诉我叫醒房号吗？
- May I know what time the rooms should be called? 可以告诉我需要叫醒的时间吗？
- Please wait a moment. Let me check the rooming list. 请稍等，我核对下分房名单。
- You have booked a group wake-up call service at 4:00 a.m. tomorrow morning for room 2101 to 2118. 您预订了 2101 到 2118 房间的凌晨四点的叫醒服务。
- I want to make a complaint about your wake-up call service. 我想投诉你们的叫醒服务。
- Could you have a seat there and talk about it? 您请那边就座，然后谈好吗？
- May I know what happened, madam? 女士，能告诉我发生了什么事吗？
- I am very sorry about it. May I have your name and room number, please? 对此我很抱歉。能否告诉我一下您的名字和房间号？
- Could you please wait for a moment? I will check with the front desk and get back to you. 请稍等，我去前台核对一下再给您答复。
- I am sorry, madam. It is our fault. 抱歉女士，这是我们的过失。
- The computer system didn't work last night. Our staff didn't check it on time, so your room wasn't called this morning. 电脑系统昨天出故障了。我们的员工没有及时检查，导致今天早上没有叫醒您。
- To express our sincere apology, we would like to refund your train ticket and help you book another one to Xi'an. 为了表达我们的歉意，我们会退还给您火车票钱并为您重新订一张票。

- We are sorry for the inconvenience. 对于给您带来的不便，我们很抱歉。
- Thank you for your understanding. Have a good trip. 谢谢您的理解，祝您旅途愉快。

Knowledge Extension

- **Wake-up Call Service**

Wake-up call service is a daily service provided by room attendants in a hotel. In general, it is the room attendants on the night shift that make notes of the guests' requests and time for the wake-up call service. And then next morning the guests will receive a wake-up call by telephone or a hotel staff on schedule. In fact, the wake-up call service in different hotels may be different. In most hotels, the wake-up call service is done by operators. it is completed by computer.

- **Four Features of Wake-up Call Service Highly Configurable**

The configuration of the wake-up call service is high. For example, you can choose the way to be waked up. You can control the volume of the sounds and recordings independently. You can set how much time remains before you have to wake up and so on.

Simple Interface

The wake-up call service uses the clear digital display, which is very easy. On the alarm screen, there is a giant snooze button. With the extra drawer icon, you can notice whether the alarm is on or not.

Heavy Sleeper Options

With the nice custom snooze menu, it can let you skip the first class or meeting, and sleep for a couple of hours. But for the important times, you can turn on wake-up call's option to make sure you don't go back to sleep when you stop the alarm.

Audio Recordings

With audio recordings, wake-up call can not only use any installed system sound, but also make full use of the advanced audio capabilities of the Newton OS 2.1 to use as your own personal wake-up call.

- **Standards of Wake-up Call Service Request**

Answer the telephone within 3 rings or 10 seconds with proper greeting and the identified department. Otherwise, an appropriate apology should be offered. The background should be free of some noises or disturbances to make the conversation easy to hear. The hotel staff should confirm the caller's requests by repeating what he/she said to make sure of the correct understanding and before finishing the call, the hotel staff should offer some additional service, such as coffee in the morning or a second call.

♦ Standards of Delivering the Wake-up Call

Wake up calls should be private and should be made at the time designated by the guest. When making a wake-up call, the hotel attendant should first say hello to the guest and announce the current time.

♦ Detailed Procedures of Wake-up Call Service

Preparation

The sheet and ball pen for a wake-up call should be prepared well, which are easy for staff to keep a record at once.

Answer the Call

According to the standard procedures, the hotel staff should always be polite to the guest, answer the call within 3 rings and greet the guest politely, who is ready to offer the assistance to the caller.

Take the Request

If the guest asks for a wake-up call, the hotel attendant should fill in a wake-up call form, and write down the guest's name, room number, wake-up date and time, and whether a second wake-up call is required.

Repeat the Details

Once the hotel staff receives the information from the caller, he/she should repeat the details of the information to make them correct or carried out correctly.

Program the Wake-up Call in the Console

Recheck the guest's name and information. Program the wake-up call in the console immediately as the guest requests.

Update the Wake-up Call Sheet

Update the wake-up call sheet immediately if the guest changes some information or wishes to have a wake-up call for a few days to keep all the information correctly programmed.

Night Shift Checklist

The hotel staff should print the wake-up call report and check whether it is in accordance with the wake-up call sheet before closing the system. File the report for future reference.

Section Summary

- Know about the wake-up call service.
- Know about four features of the wake-up call service.
- Know about the standards of wake-up call service requests.
- Know about the standards of delivering a wake-up call.

- Learn the detailed procedures of a wake-up call.

Practice

Part One Dialogue

1. Choose the correct sentences to fill in the blanks according to the context.

C: Clerk at the Front Desk   G: Guest

C: Good afternoon, Front Desk. _____

G: Good afternoon. I'd like a wake-up call tomorrow morning.

C: _____

G: Emily Brown in Room 2016.

C: _____

G: At 7 a.m..

C: _____We have the wake-up phone call, knocking at the door and computer wake-up call. _____

G: Telephone call.

C: OK. Ms. Brown, a morning call at 7 a.m. tomorrow morning for Room 2016. Is it correct?

G: Yes.

C: Thank you for calling, goodbye.

G: Goodbye.

A. May I have your name and room number?

B. Which one would you prefer?

C. May I help you?

D. How would you like us to call you, madam?

E. When would you like us to call you?

2. Act in pairs to finish the following role-play activities.

(1) Student A: Act as a guest. You call the front desk to ask for a wake-up call.

Student B: Act as the clerk at the front desk. Answer the phone call from an in-house guest.

(2) Student A: Act as a guest. You call the front desk to change the time of the wake-up call.

Student B: Act as the clerk at the front desk. Answer the phone call from an in-house guest.

(3) Student A: Act as a local guide. You call the front desk to book a wake-up call for your group.

Student B: Act as the clerk at the front desk. Answer the phone call from an in-house guest.

(4) Student A: Act as a guest. You go to the front office to complain about the wake-up call service.

Student B: Act as the clerk working in the front office. Greet the guest and respond to the guest's request.

3. Read the following time and then dictate to your partner.

(1) 7:00 a.m.

(2) 7:30 a.m.

(3) 4:15 a.m.
(4) 4:30 a.m.
(5) 5:30 a.m.
(6) 6:00 a.m.
(7) 6:30 a.m.
(8) 5:00 a.m.

4. Discussion:

(1) What should you do if you got the complaint from the guest that the wake-up call service reserved didn't wake him/her up?

(2) What should you do if the guest in the room didn't answer the wake-up phone?

5. Translate the following sentences.

(1) 我想预约一下明天早晨的叫醒服务。

(2) 请告诉我您的叫醒时间。

(3) 我会派客房服务员去敲门。

(4) 我想预约团队叫醒服务。

(5) 您能到前台办理团队叫醒服务登记吗？

(6) 请告诉我您的团号？

(7) 请稍等，我核对一下分房名单。

(8) 我想投诉你们的叫醒服务。

(9) 对于引起的不便，我们很抱歉。

(10) 昨天我们的电脑出故障了。

Part Two Knowledge Extension

According to the part of Knowledge Extension, write the answers to the following questions on the sheet of paper by using your own words, not simply copying the sentences. When you have completed the test, ask your lecturer for the answers.

Wake-up Call Service

_____
_____
_____

Four Features of Wake-up Call Service

_____
_____
_____

Standards of Wake-up Call Service Request

_____

Standards of Delivering a Wake-up Call

Detailed Procedures of Wake-up Call

Section Three

F&B Department
餐饮部

模块三

Introduction

The food and beverage department, run by the food and beverage director, is responsible for supplying food and drink to the members of an organization and its guests. The staff in Food and Beverage Department should have multiple dining-related roles, including bartenders, baristas, servers, cooks, chefs, hostesses, dining room servers, food service attendants and dishwashers.

Section Three 模块三
F&B Department 餐饮部

Topic One Food and Beverage Reservation 餐饮预订

Introduction

When a guest reserves the food and beverage at a restaurant, he/she should pay attention to some special requirements at that restaurant, such as the room charge or minimum charge. There are four different ways of reserving a table: face-to-face reservation, telephone reservation, fax reservation and Internet reservation. No matter in which kind of way the guest makes a reservation, he/she should provide the following information: the name of the guest, his/her telephone number, the time of his arrival and the number of guests. Confirm the information at last.

Objectives

Competence Standard	Knowledge Standard
Ability to order food at a restaurant	Know about the working procedures of reserving a table in a restaurant
Ability to order food over the phone	Learn to order food over the phone or at a restaurant
Ability to make a table reservation and know something about a cover charge	Know something about a table reservation
Ability of listening, speaking and reading	Learn about a cover charge

Working Procedures

- Answer the phone call from guests (greeting the guests).
- Enquire the reservation.

  Time of dinning

  Number of people

  Food types

  Name and telephone number
- Confirm the reservation.
- Say goodbye to the guest.

Dialogues

Dialogue 1

Situation Question: Do you know how to answer a reservation phone call? What information will you get from the guest?

【拓展音频】

Accept a Reservation

R: Reservation Clerk   G: Guest

R: Good morning, White Swan Restaurant. How can I help you?

G: Yes, I want to reserve a table in your restaurant.

R: May I know when you would like to have it, sir?

G: Yes. It is for tomorrow evening at 7 o'clock.

R: OK, and how many people are there in your party?

G: Five, four adults and one child.

R: Would you like a table in the main hall or in the private room?

G: I prefer a private room.

R: May I have your name and telephone number?

G: My name is David Brown and I am staying in the hotel, Room 1216.

R: OK, Mr. Brown, a reservation for five at 7 o'clock tomorrow evening. Is that correct?

G: Yes.

R: Very well. Mr. Brown, thank you for calling. We are looking forward to serving you. Good-bye.

G: Good-bye.

Notes:

(1) White Swan Restaurant 白天鹅餐厅

(2) adult 成年人

(3) main hall 大厅

(4) private room 包间

(5) look forward to 期待

Dialogue 2

Situation Question: How would you handle the situation that there is no table for the time a guest requests?

Give Suggestions to Guests

R: Reservation Clerk   G: Guest

R: Reservation clerk, can I help you?

G: Yes, I want to book a table for two.

R: When would you like the table, sir?

G: This evening at 6 o'clock.

R: Sorry, all the tables have been reserved for that time tonight. Would you like to change to another time?

G: Yes, I want to celebrate a birthday for my girlfriend, so what is another time?

R: How about 7:30? We have tables available for that time.

G: OK, 7:30 then.

R: Do you have any special requests?

G: Yes. I would like the table by the window. In that case, we can enjoy the beautiful night sky of the city.

R: OK, I see. May I have your name and telephone number?

G: Larry Wong, my cell phone number is 136....

R: OK, Mr. Wong, you have reserved a table by the window for two at 7:30 this evening. Is that correct?

G: Yes, by the way, may I bring wine by myself?

R: According to the hotel policy, there is corkage for the wine brought in.

G: How do you charge for it?

R: 20% service charge based on the market price of the wine.

G: OK, I see. Thank you.

R: You are welcome.

G: Thank you very much. Good-bye.

R: Good-bye.

Notes:

(1) celebrate 庆祝

(2) available 可获得的

(3) in that case 假如那样的话

(4) corkage 开瓶费

Dialogue 3

Situation Question: Do you know how to handle the request of changing reservation?

Change a Reservation

R: Reservation Clerk   G: Guest

R: Good afternoon, Great Wall Restaurant, how may I help you?

G: Yes, I would like to change my reservation.

R: May I have your name, please?

G: My name is Peter Lee, and I reserved a private room for this evening.

R: Mr. Lee, please wait for a moment. I will check with the computer. Yes, you have booked private room at 7 o'clock this evening. How would you like to change it?

G: I would like to change it to tomorrow evening at the same time.

R: A moment, please. I am afraid all the private rooms have been reserved for tomorrow evening. But we still have tables in the main hall. Would you like to have a table there for that time?

G: Oh, that's too bad. I still prefer to have a private room. How about the day after tomorrow?

R: Let me check. Yes, we have a private room available for the day after tomorrow. Would you like to reserve it?

G: Yes.

R: OK, a private room under the name of Mr. Lee at 7:00 o'clock for the day after tomorrow, is that right?

G: Yes, thank you.

R: You are welcome.

Notes:

(1) check 核对

(2) prefer to 更喜欢

(3) under the name of 以……的名义

Dialogue 4

Situation Question: Do you know how to handle a banquet reservation?

Banquet Reservation

R: Reservation Clerk   G: Guest

R: Good morning, F&B Department. May I help you?

G: Yes, I want to arrange a party in your restaurant.

R: When would you like to hold the party?

G: Next Saturday, say, 28 th of July from 6:00 p.m. to 8:30 p.m.

R: How many people will there be in the party?

G: About 40.

R: Please wait for a moment. Yes, we have two banquet halls available for that time. One is on the 16th floor and the other is on the 2nd floor. Both of them are of the same size. Which one do you prefer?

G: I think the one on the second floor is better.

R: May I have your name and telephone number?

G: My name is Peter Lee and my number is ....

R: May I know what kind of party it is?

G: Yes. I want to have a party to celebrate my parents' 50th wedding anniversary.

R: I am so glad you choose our restaurant to celebrate your parents' golden wedding. I would like to congratulate them in the name of restaurant.

G: Thank you. How do you charge for it?

R: The minimum charge for a 40-person dinner party is 16,000 *yuan*, excluding beverages.

G: OK, I see.

R: Would you like us to have the banquet hall decorated?

G: No, thank you. I will arrange it myself.

R: How would you like to pay it?

G: By credit card.

R: OK, Mr. Lee reserved a banquet hall for July 28th. Is that correct?

G: Yes. That is correct.

R: Is there anything else I can do for you?

G: No, thanks.

R: Mr. Lee, thank you for calling. Good-bye.

Notes:

(1) F&B Department: Food and Beverage Department 餐饮部

(2) hold a party 举行聚会

(3) wedding anniversary 结婚纪念日

(4) golden wedding 金婚纪念（即结婚五十周年纪念）

(5) in the name of 以……的名义

(6) charge for 索价

(7) minimum 最低的

(8) excluding 不包括

Useful Sentences

- Good morning, F&B Department. May I help you? 早上好，这里是餐饮部，请问您需要什么帮助？
- I want to reserve a table in your restaurant. 我想在酒店订一张桌子。
- May I know when you would like to have it, sir? 您想什么时候用，先生？

- It is for tomorrow evening, at 7 o'clock. 明天晚上 7 点钟。
- How many people will be in your party? 你一行多少人?
- Would you like a table in the main hall or in the private room? 您想订大厅的桌子还是包间的桌子?
- I prefer the private room. 我想要包间。
- Mr. Brown, a reservation for five at 7 o'clock tomorrow evening. Is that correct? 布朗先生,您预订了明天晚上 7 点钟的五人桌,对吗?
- We are looking forward to serving you. 我们恭候您的光临。
- I want to book a table for two. 我想订一张两人桌。
- Sorry, all the tables have been reserved for that time tomorrow evening. 抱歉,明天晚上那个时间段的餐桌都订满了。
- Would you like to change to another time? 您愿意改成其他时间吗?
- We have tables available for that time. 那个时间段有空桌。
- Do you have any special requests? 您还有其他要求吗?
- I would like the table by the window. 我想要靠窗的桌子。
- I am afraid all the private rooms have been reserved for tomorrow evening. 恐怕明天晚上的所有包间都预订出去了。
- We have a private room available for the day after tomorrow. 后天有包间。
- Would you like to reserve it? 您要预订吗?
- When would you like to hold the party? 您想什么时候举行聚会?
- How many people will there be in the party? 聚会一共多少人?
- Both of them are of the same size. Which one do you prefer? 两个规模同样大,您要哪个?
- How do you charge for it? 怎么收费?
- The minimum charge for a 40-person dinner party is RMB16,000 *yuan*, excluding beverages. 40 人的晚宴最低收费 16 000 元,不含酒水。
- Would you like us to have the banquet hall decorated? 需要我们装饰宴会厅吗?

Knowledge Extension

- **Reserve a Table or Make a Reservation**

Some guest calls a restaurant to want to "make a reservation" at a restaurant. One of the hotel staff answers the phone and tells the guest the difference between "reserve a table" and "make a reservation". That is to say, if the guest wants to "make a reservation", he/she should reserve the entire restaurant, perhaps for a large party. If he/she wants the restaurant to hold a table for him/her for dinner, he/she should "reserve a table".

- **Order Food at a Restaurant**

Find a Seat

It's probably a better idea for clients to find a seat before getting their food to avoid all the seats being fully occupied after their food is collected. Otherwise, they will either eat standing up or walk around looking for a seat for quite some time. Some restaurants will ask you to find a seat or direct you to your seat.

Look at the Menu

A client should ask a member of staff for one menu, which should be on his/her table or perhaps it is not enough for everyone. On the menu there all the food sold with prices stated. Look at the menu and decide what to order.

Call the Waiter Over

Call the waiter over by attracting a passing waiter's attention or waiting until he/she comes to you. Tell him/her what you'd like to eat and make sure that he/she has put down the correct food after he/she arrives. Don't click your fingers to get his/her attention, because he/she will find it rude and offensive.

Wait for Your Food

Just be patient and your food should arrive within half an hour because the food you ordered might take some time to be cooked as soon as they get your order. If it hasn't arrived, tell some waiter. Perhaps they may have forgotten your order, or it might be a busy day.

◆ Order Food over the Phone

Decide Where You'd Like to Eat

Decide where you'd like to eat, which all depends on what you like. As long as the shop does deliveries, you can order almost whatever you like.

Find Their Phone Number

You can find their phone number by visiting their website, searching for their phone number online or reading one of their flyers to find their number.

Call Them Up

They might not answer immediately if they're busy. But just do your best to keep patient.

Place Your Order

Place your order and tell them what you'd like to eat. They will usually ask for your address and your name to deliver the food you ordered. Make sure that they confirm your order in order to deliver your food correctly.

Wait for Your Delivery

According to the place where you live and where you ordered from, the time that you wait for can vary. Usually though, you shouldn't be kept waiting for over half an hour. If you wait for over half an hour, call them up again to confirm whether your order has been delivered. They may have forgotten about it or not finished cooking it yet.

Pay the Delivery Person

Remember to tip the delivery person. If you don't like to do that, tell them to just keep the change.

◆ A Table Reservation

A table reservation is an arrangement which a client makes in advance to have a table available at a restaurant. Usually, it is not necessary to require a reservation, but some restaurants in the overcrowded cities often require a reservation. Some may have tables booked for weeks in advance. Especially at particularly exclusive venues, tables may be available at least one day before. The modern reservation system has evolved. People don't need to arrange catering at a restaurant. In recent times, many restaurants use a website to provide this service through online reservation system in place of the traditional pencil and notebook.

◆ The Way of Meeting the Food and Beverage Minimum

What a client chooses for food and beverage which go directly towards the food and beverage minimum. It all depends on what he/she chooses. In general, caterers will offer packages to make him/her easier to choose food and beverage, which are usually based on a per-person price. Per-person price multiplied by the total number of guests equals to the expenses that the client expects for the food and beverage prior to tax and service charge.

◆ A Cover Charge

A cover charge is an entrance fee which is sometimes charged at bars, nightclubs, or restaurants. According to the American Heritage Dictionary, it is defined as a "fixed amount added to the bill at a nightclub or restaurant for amusement or service". In some restaurants, a cover charge is included in the cost of food specifically ordered, but in some establishments, it is usually contained in the cost of bread, butter, olives and other accompaniments provided.

Section Summary

- Know about the working procedures of reserving a table at a restaurant.
- Know the differences between reserving a table and making a reservation.
- Order food over the phone at a restaurant.
- Learn about a table reservation.
- Know something about the way of meeting the food and beverage minimum or the cover charge.

Practice

Part One Dialogue

1. Choose the correct sentences to fill in the blanks according to the context.
R: Reservation Clerk   G: Guest

R: _____

G: Yes, I'd like to reserve a table for four at the Chinese restaurant.

R: _____

G: Tonight, at 6 o'clock.

R: _____

G: My name is Henry Lee and I am staying in the hotel, Room 1212.

R: _____

G: No.

R: Mr. Lee, _____, is that correct?

G: Yes.

A. When would you like to use the table?

B. F&B Department, can I help you?

C. Do you have any special request?

D. you have reserved a table of Chinese restaurant at 6 p.m. tonight

E. May I have your name and telephone number?

2. Act in pairs to finish the following role-play activities. Compensate necessary information.

(1) Student A: Act as a guest staying in the hotel room. Make a phone call to reserve a table for three.

Student B: Act as the reservation clerk. Answer the call and accept reservation.

(2) Student A: Act as an outside guest. Make a phone call to reserve a private room.

Student B: Act as the reservation clerk. Answer the call and accept the reservation.

(3) Student A: Act as an outside guest. Make a phone call to change the reservation.

Student B: Act as the reservation clerk. Answer the call and agree to change the reservation for the guest.

(4) Student A: Act as an outside guest. Make a phone call to reserve a table for five for tonight.

Student B: Act as the reservation clerk. Answer the call and tell the guest there are not tables available for the time. Ask if it is possible for the guest to change to another time.

(5) Student A: Act as an outside guest. Make a phone call to reserve a banquet hall for a wedding ceremony. Inquire about the price for the banquet.

Student B: Act as the reservation clerk. Answer the call and accept the reservation.

3. Look at the following items in hotel room and translate them into English.

(1) 餐台   (2) 包间

(3) 变更时间   (4) 押金

(5) 特别要求   (6) 营业

(7) 电话预订   (8) 网络预订

(9) 非吸烟区   (10) 开瓶费

(11) 服务费　　(12) 折扣
(13) 空桌　　　(14) 中餐厅
(15) 西餐厅　　(16) 预订

4. Discussion:

(1) What information should you get from the guest who wants to reserve a table in your restaurant?

(2) Please list the proper sequence of accepting the telephone reservation.

5. Translate the following sentences.

(1) 我想在酒店订一张桌子。

(2) 您想订大厅的桌子还是包间的桌子？

(3) 我们恭候您的光临。

(4) 我想要非吸烟区的桌子。

(5) 你们一共多少人用餐？

(6) 那个时间所有的包间都预订出去了。

(7) 你们怎么收费？

(8) 酒店对外带的酒水要收开瓶费。

(9) 宴会厅需要我们装饰吗？

(10) 您的预订我们只能保留到明晚8点。

Part Two　Knowledge Extension

According to the part of Knowledge Extension, write the answers to the following questions on the sheet of paper by using your own words, not simply copying the sentences. When you have completed the test, ask your lecturer for the answers.

Reserve a Table or Make a Reservation

_____
_____
_____

Order Food at a Restaurant

_____
_____
_____

Order Food over the Phone

_____
_____
_____

A Table Reservation

_____
_____
_____

The Way of Meeting the Food and Beverage Minimum

_____
_____
_____

A Cover Charge

_____
_____
_____

Topic Two F&B Service in Western Style 西餐席间服务

Introduction

As we know, F&B Department serves an important function in the guest service maintaining a hotel's valued reputation. In Western-style restaurants, the guests, their comfort, needs, and enjoyment, are the primary focus on the whole state. Respectful and personalized service is more important than anything else for creating a lasting impression on the guests. After greeting a guest, the Western food waiter should present the menu to him/her waiting to order dishes and beverage, and ask his/her taste and needs. When all the dishes are ready, the waiter should express good wishes for the guest to enjoy his/her happy time. By changing tableware, cleaning up the table, introducing new dishes and so on, the waiter tries his best to serve the guest at the Western table.

Objectives

Competence Standard	Knowledge Standard
Ability to receive food and beverage service in a Western style	Know about the working procedures of food and beverage service in a Western style
Ability to set the table, supply the food and beverage service, hostess service and present a menu technique	Know about the steps of setting the table, food and beverage service process, hostess service and the technique of presenting a menu
Ability to know about the waiter service process, taking order process, the methods of opening and serving a bottle of red wine, plate service procedures and end-of-service procedures	Know about the waiter service process, the methods of opening and serving a bottle of red wine, and the plate service procedures

Competence Standard	Knowledge Standard
Ability of listening, speaking and reading	Have a good understanding of the six ways of making reservations and seven types of hotel service.

Working Procedures

- Seat the guests.
  the guests with reservation
  the guests without reservation
- Take orders.
- Recommend specialties.
- Recommend dishes(starter, main course, dessert, etc).
- Serve dishes.

Dialogues

Dialogue 1

Situation Question: As a waiter or waitress, do you know how to seat the guests with reservation? How would you seat the guests without reservation?

Seating Guests

【拓展音频】

S: Server　　G: Guest

S: Good morning, sir.

G: Good morning.

S: Do you have a reservation?

G: No, I'm afraid we don't.

S: Sorry, sir. Now all the tables have been fully booked.

G: Oh, I'm sorry to hear that.

S: Do you mind waiting for a moment?

G: Of course not. How long should we wait for?

S: For about 20 minutes. I will tell you at once when there is a vacant table.

G: OK, I prefer to wait in my hotel room.

S: Would you like to leave your room number? When there is a vacant table, I will call you.

G: That's good. My room number is 1220.

S: And a table for two, yes?

G: Yes.

S: OK, sir. I will call you soon.

G: Thank you.

S: You are welcome.

Notes:

(1) reservation 预订

(2) be fully booked 订满

(3) mind 介意

(4) vacant 空闲的

(5) vacant table 空桌，空位

(6) prefer 更喜欢

Dialogue 2

Situation Question: Do you know the procedures of taking orders? How would you recommend dishes to guests?

【拓展音频】

Taking Orders (1)

S: Server   G1: Guest 1   G2: Guest 2

S: Good evening, Mr Johnson.

G1: Good evening.

S: Please be seated. How is everything going today?

G1: Good. The scenic spot you recommended yesterday was really good. My wife and I had a good time this morning. The scenery is amazing there.

G2: Yes. We really like the beauty of Imperial Gardens.

S: I am so glad you like it. What would you like to have today?

G1: We'd like to start with salad, say vegetable salad.

S: What salad dressing would you like?

G1: Thousand island dressing.

G2: French dressing.

S: OK. What would you like to have for the main courses?

G1: Australian T-bone steak. How about you, Lily?

G2: Me, too.

S: How would you like your steak cooked?

G1: Medium, please.

G2: Medium, please.

S: How about drinks?

G1: I would like to have mushroom cream soup.

G2: I want cream corn soup.

S: Would you like some dessert? Today's Italy Tiramisu is freshly made. You can have a try.

G2: Then give me one.

S: Yes, madam. So two vegetable salads, two T-bone steaks, one mushroom cream soup, one cream corn soup and one Italy Tiramisu. Please wait for a moment.

Notes:

(1) Thousand island dressing 千岛酱

(2) French dressing 法式酱

(3) main course 主菜

(4) Australian T-bone Steak 澳洲T骨牛排

(5) mushroom cream soup 奶油蘑菇浓汤

(6) cream corn soup 奶油玉米浓汤

(7) Italy Tiramisu 意式提拉米苏

Dialogue 3

Situation Question: Do you know how to ask guests about the desired doneness of steak and eggs?

Taking Orders (2)

S: Server   G1: Guest 1   G2: Guest 2

S: Good afternoon, sir. Do you have a reservation?

G1: Yes, I have reserved a table for two under the name of Johnson.

S: Oh, Mr. Johnson, we have been expecting to serve you. This way, please. Here we are. Please take your seats.

G1: That's good.

S: Here is the menu.

G1: Thank you.

(*After a while*)

S: May I take your order now?

G1: Yes, please. We would like to have Smoked Salmon to start with. As for steak, what is the specialty of the house?

S: Grilled Beef Rib-Eye Steak is the specialty. It is very tender.

G1: OK, I will choose the steak. How about you, Judy?

G2: Me, too.

S: So would you like your steak cooked, rare, medium or well-done?

G1: Medium, please.

G2: Mine, medium well-done.

S: How about vegetables? We have vegetables, peas and mushrooms. Which one would you like?

G1&G2: Vegetables.

S: Vegetables. Good. How about drinks?

G1: We would like to have a bottle of French red wine. Do you have any suggestions?

S: We have Beaujolais from Burgundy and Pauillac from Bordeaux. Which one would you like?

G1: Beaujolais, please.

S: So you would like to have Smoked Salmon, Grilled Beef Rib-Eye Steak with vegetables, one medium and medium well-done, and a bottle of Beaujolais.

G1: Yes.

S: Thank you for your order. Please wait for a moment.

Notes:

(1) menu 菜单

(2) order 订单，take your order 点餐

(3) Smoked Salmon 熏制鲑鱼

(4) steak 牛排

(5) specialty 招牌菜

(6) tender 嫩的

(7) rare 三分熟

(8) mushroom 蘑菇

(9) Grilled Beef Rib-Eye Steak 扒肉眼牛排

Dialogue 4

Situation Question: Do you know the serving order of Western food? What is it?

Serving Dishes

【拓展音频】

S: Server   G: Guest

S: May I serve the dish now?

G: Yes, please.

S: Here is the garden salad, steak and red wine. Please enjoy it.

G: Thank you.

(*After a while*)

G: Waiter.

S: Yes, madam, what can I do for you?

G: The steak is overdone and it is so tough. I don't think it is good to eat.

S: I am sorry, madam. I will take it back to the kitchen and ask the chef to prepare another one for you. Is that OK?

G: OK.

S: How would you like the steak cooked?

G: Medium.

S: OK, Please wait for a moment.

(*After a while*)

S: Madam, this is your steak. Here is the complimentary dessert for you. Thank you for your consideration.

Notes:

(1) dish 一道菜

(2) garden salad 田园沙拉

(3) overdone（肉）过老的

(4) tough 咬不动的

(5) kitchen 厨房

(6) chef 厨师

(7) prepare food 做菜

(8) complimentary 赠送的   complimentary meals 免费膳食

(9) dessert 餐后甜点

(10) consideration 体谅

Useful Sentences

- Do you have a reservation? 您有预订吗？
- All the tables have been fully booked. 所有桌子都预订出去了。
- Do you mind waiting for a moment? 您介意等一会儿吗？
- How long should we wait? 我们要等多久？
- I will tell you at once when there is a vacant table. 一有空位我就告诉您。
- Would you like to leave your room number? When there is a vacant table, I will call you. 您愿意把房号告诉我吗？有空位时我给您打电话。
- I have reserved a table for two under the name of Johnson. 我以约翰逊的名义订了一张双人桌。
- We have been expecting to serve you. 我们一直期待您的光临。
- Please take seats. 您请坐。
- May I take your order now? 现在要点菜吗？
- We would like to have smoked salmon to start with. 我想先点一道熏鲑鱼。
- What is the specialty of the house? 本店的招牌菜是什么？
- How would you like your steak cooked, rare, medium or well-done? 牛排您要怎么做，三分熟、五分熟还是全熟？
- Which one would you like? 您要哪一种（个）？
- How about French red wine? Many guests have said it tastes good. 要尝尝法国红酒吗？很多客人都说很好喝。

- I'd like to have French red wine. 我想喝法国红酒。
- Do you have any suggestion? 您有什么建议吗？
- May I serve the dish now? 现在可以上菜了吗？
- Please enjoy it. 请慢用。
- The steak is overdone and it is so tough. 牛排太老了，都咬不动。
- I will take it back to the kitchen and ask the chef to prepare another one for you. 我让厨房再给您做一份怎么样？
- Here is the complimentary dessert for you. 这是赠送您的甜点。
- Thank you for your consideration. 谢谢您的体谅。

Knowledge Extension

◆ The Style of Western Dining

There are two types of western dining: buffet and a la Carte. On the buffet table, there are a wide variety of foods, which are rich and can be divided into Chinese Buffet and Western Buffet. Guests can choose the food they like among many choices. Speaking of a la Carte, dishes are individually priced and guests may structure their meal in any way they choose.

◆ Steps of Setting the Table

The steps of setting the table are: table cloth, cutlery, napkins, flatware, glasses, condiments, flowers, lighting and music.

◆ Food and Beverage Service Process

The process of food and beverage service is reservation, greeting, seating, presenting the menu, food service, beverage service, informing the kitchen, taking orders, table service, tray changing, second order, cleaning the table, bidding farewell, cashier, presenting bill and coffee.

◆ Hostess Service

Hostess service includes greeting a guest, seating a guest and presenting a menu. When greeting the guest, the host should acknowledge the guest within five seconds with eye contact with the guest. The host should lead the guest to the table, rather than offering the guest a choice. During the show process, the host should walk one meter ahead of the guest and can't go too fast. It is fine to chat a little with the arriving guest but avoid a long conversation. If the guest brings his/her coats to the table, the host should repeat the offer to check the coats for them. The guest with children may need high chairs or booster seats. Disabled guests should be seated as quickly as possible and away from the busy aisles.

◆ The Technique of Presenting a Menu

When a menu is presented to guests, the host should carry the menu on the flat of the left arm, open the menu from the top with the right hand, present the menu to the guest's right and suggest the items which do not appear in the menu.

◆ Waiter Service Process

The waiter service process includes taking orders, informing the kitchen, beverage service and food service.

◆ The Way of Opening and Serving a Bottle of Red Wine

Hosts should know about the ways of opening and serving a bottle of red wine, which are as follows:

Cut the capsule by turning the blade of the waiter corkscrew.

Clean the lip of any residue.

Pull out the cork by the corkscrew.

Smell the cork to judge the wine quality.

After checking the cork, pour the one fifth red wine to taste.

Red wine is not usually chilled.

Red wine may be opened and placed in the center of the table.

Red wine should be poured to let air in.

During the process of pouring, never completely empty a bottle of an older vintage red wine.

◆ Plate Service Procedures

Food should be served to the right of the guest and the principle of serving ladies before gentlemen should be adopted. The plate service procedures include table service, which refers to clearing unwanted glasses, refilling the drink, clearing the dirty and crabbing bread, special requirement, second order and cleaning the table.

Section Summary

- Know about the working procedures of food and beverage service in a Western style.
- Learn about the style of Western dining.
- Learn about the steps of setting the table.
- Learn about food and beverage service process.
- Know about hostess service.
- Learn the technique of presenting a menu.
- Know about the waiter service process.
- Learn about the way of opening and serving a bottle of red wine.
- Know about the plate service procedures.

Practice

Part One Dialogue

1. Choose the correct sentences to fill in the blanks according to the context.

W: Waiter   G: Guest

W: Good afternoon. _____

G: Four. _____

W: RMB600 *yuan* altogether.

G: _____

W: RMB200 *yuan* for adults per person and RMB100 *yuan* for kids above 1.2 meters.

G: I see. _____

W: We do not charge for soft drinks. _____

G: Thank you.

W: You are welcome. Please enjoy your meal.

A. Two adults and two kids.

B. How do you charge for buffet?

C. How many people are there in your party?

D. But charge extra money for alcohol order.

E. Do I need to pay extra money for drinks?

2. Act in pairs to finish the following role-play activities.

(1) Student A: Act as a guest to go to a Western restaurant. You have booked a table for four.

Student B: Act as the waiter and seat the guest.

(2) Students A: Act as a guest in a Western restaurant. Order your food (appetizer, main course and dessert).

Student B: Act as a waiter in the Western restaurant. Take orders for the guest. Recommend wine for the guest.

(3) Student A: Act as a guest in a Western restaurant. You are allergic to seafood. Order your food.

Student B: Act as a waiter in the Western restaurant. Take orders for the guest.

(4) Student A: Act as a guest in a Western restaurant. The food you ordered is too tough. Ask the waiter for help.

Student B: Act as a waiter in the Western restaurant. Help the guest with the food.

(5) Student A: Act as a guest in a Western restaurant. Go to the manager to complain about the service of the hotel.

Student B: Act as the manager of the restaurant. Handle the complaints properly.

3. Look at the following words and translate them into English.

(1) 自助餐   (2) 沙拉

(3) 汤   (4) 蔬菜

(5) 甜点   (6) 主菜
(7) 海鲜   (8) 牛排
(9) 刀叉   (10) 汤匙
(11) 甜品勺   (12) 餐巾
(13) 沙拉酱   (14) 套餐
(15) 酒水单   (16) 招牌菜
(17) 厨师推荐   (18) 开胃菜
(19) 菜单   (20) 账单

4. Discussion:

(1) What should you do if you spilled the soup onto a guest's dress?

(2) What should you do if the guest's knife or fork dropped onto the ground?

5. Translate the following sentences.

(1) 请问您有预订吗?

(2) 靠窗的位子可以吗?

(3) 您是要含糖还是不含糖的食物?

(4) 您想要什么酒水?

(5) 对不起,自带的酒水需要收开瓶费。

(6) 您可以尝一下本店的招牌菜。

(7) 您想要什么沙拉酱?

(8) 牛排您要几分熟?

(9) 我们一直期待您的光临。

(10) 祝您用餐愉快。

Part Two   Knowledge Extension

According to the part of Knowledge Extension, write the answers to the following questions on the sheet of paper by using your own words, not simply copying the sentences. When you have completed the test, ask your lecturer for the answers.

The Style of Western Dining

_____

_____

_____

_____

Steps of Setting the Table

_____

_____

The Food and Beverage Service Process

Hostess Service

The Technique of Presenting a Menu

The Waiter Service Process

The Way of Opening and Serving a Bottle of Red Wine

The Plate Service Procedures

Topic Three F&B Service in Chinese Style 中餐席间服务

Introduction

In the restaurant industry, the food and beverage service in a Chinese style plays an important role in assuring the guest's pleasure and satisfaction in the course of their stay. Excellent Chinese-style service, which can bring the hotel guests pleasure and happiness, is mainly absorbed in traditional Chinese cuisine. Furthermore, Chinese service contains some features which are unique, traditional and complicated, including the chopsticks served with all food, except soup and dessert spoons, food presented and served attractively into platters, bowls, and other containers brought to the table for guests to choose and so on.

Objectives

Competence Standard	Knowledge Standard
Ability to receive the food and beverage service in a Chinese style	Know about the working procedures of the food and beverage service in a Chinese style
Ability to set the table	Acquire the knowledge about Chinese cuisine, and breakfast in Chinese hotels
Ability to deal with customer complaints	Know about the knowledge of the serving procedures of Chinese service, top ten meals for lunch that Chinese people eat
Ability of listening, speaking and reading	Acquire some knowledge about coping with customer complaints

Working Procedures

- Seat the guests.

    the guests with reservation

    the guests without reservation
- Take orders.
- Recommend specialties.
- Explain dishes (ingredients, cooking methods, etc).
- Serve dishes.

Dialogues

Dialogue 1

Situation Question: Do you know the differences between Chinese breakfast and American breakfast?

Serving Breakfast

W: Waiter   G1: Guest 1   G2: Guest 2

W: Good morning, sir. A table for two?

G1: Yes. My wife and I want to try the Chinese breakfast this morning. But we know nothing about it. So could you tell us something about it?

W: Certainly, it's my honor. The breakfast is buffet in the restaurant and there is a variety of food to choose from. We serve congee of different flavor, such as meat congee, vegetable congee, and mixed congee, etc. We usually serve milk and soybean milk instead of coffee or tea. We serve the steamed stuffed bun, dumpling and deep-fried dough sticks instead of bread. We also serve eggs like fried eggs and poached eggs.

G1: That's great. How about fresh juice? I mean vegetable juice and fruit juice. My wife prefers to have a cup of vegetables and fruit juice in the morning.

W: Yes, there is a stand offering vegetables and fruit juice in the restaurant.

G2: Terrific. Thank you.

W: You are welcome. This way, please. Is this table all right?

G2: Good. Thank you.

W: You are welcome. Enjoy your breakfast.

Notes:

(1) It's my honor. 这是我的荣幸。

(2) buffet 自助餐

(3) congee 粥   mixed congee 八宝粥

(4) soybean 黄豆，大豆   soybean milk 豆浆

(5) steamed stuffed bun 包子

(6) deep-fried dough sticks 油条

(7) poached egg 水煮鸡蛋

(8) vegetable and fruit juice 蔬果汁

Dialogue 2

Situation Question: Do you know the famous Chinese cuisine? Do you know how to explain Chinese dishes?

【拓展音频】

Taking Orders (1)

W: Waiter   G1: Guest 1   G2: Guest 2

W: Are you ready to order, sir?

G1: Yes. We like something light and fresh. What is your recommendation?

W: I recommend that you try our house specialty, Sauteed Shrimp with Green Tea.

G1: Is it made of shrimp?

W: Yes, it is made of shrimp together with green tea. You can have the tender and smooth shrimp meat together with the fragrance of green tea.

G2: Sounds great. I'd like to have a try. How about you, John?

G1: Me, too. Then let's have it. How about vegetables? We want some vegetables.

W: How about some Boiled Seasonal Vegetable ? It is cooked of seasonal and fresh vegetables. It is very delicious and nutritious.

G1: OK, we will have it.

W: Good. Would you like to have some soup?

G2: Yes. What kind of soup do you have?

W: We have chicken soup, mushroom soup, fish soup and some more.

G1: Mushroom soup, please. And we want some rice.

W: OK, You ordered Sauteed Shrimp with Green Tea, Boiled Seasonal Vegetables, Mushrooms soup and rice. Is it correct?

G1: Yes. Could you rush the order? You know, we are really hungry after a long trip.

W: Sure. I will tell the kitchen.

G1: Thanks.

W: You are welcome.

Notes:

(1) Sauteed Shrimp with Green Tea 西湖龙井虾仁

(2) Boiled Seasonal Vegetables 白灼时蔬

(3) light 清淡　light food 清淡饮食

(4) tender and smooth（口感）嫩滑

(5) fragrance 芳香

(6) nutritious 有营养的

(7) rush the order 快点上菜

Dialogue 3

Situation Question: Do you know how to help the kids and the senior with the food?

Taking Orders (2)

W: Waiter   G1: Guest 1   G2: Guest 2   G3: Guest 3—a kid of 5 years old

W: Are you ready to order, sir?

G1: Yes. We like to try some typical Chinese food. Could you recommend any for us?

W: There are eight cuisines in China. They have different flavors. The restaurant features Sichuan dishes and Su dishes.

G1: What is the difference?

W: Well, Sichuan dishes are featured with spicy and pungent flavors. The main ingredients are pepper and chilli pepper together with garlic and ginger which create the typical exciting tastes.

G2: I am afraid we can't try it because we are not spicy food lovers.

W: So you may try the Su dishes which is featured with fresh ingredients and cutting technique. The dishes are very exquisite and refined. The typical flavor is sweet.

G3: That's good. I like sweet food.

G1: OK. So we would like Su dishes. Could you recommend some in details?

W: Yes. How about some Sweet and Sour Pork Ribs and Wenxi Tofu? If you like vegetables, you may try Braised Bamboo Shoots.

G1: OK, we will have them. And we want to have some shrimp.

W: Then I recommend Fried Shelled Shrimp. It is soft and tasty.

G1: Good. Let's have it.

W: OK, So you ordered the Sweet and Sour Pork Ribs, Wenxi Tofu, Braised Bamboo Shoots and Fried Shelled Shrimp. Is it correct?

G1: Yes. And we would like some rice.

W: OK, Please wait a moment.

Notes:

(1) cuisine 菜系

(2) spicy 麻辣的

(3) pungent 辛辣的

(4) ingredient 配料

(5) exquisite 精致的

(6) refined 精炼的

Dialogue 4

Situation Question: What attitude should the server have when dealing with complaints?

Dealing with Complaints

【拓展音频】

W: Waitress   G: Guest   H: Head Waitress

W: Is everything to your satisfaction?

G: Satisfaction? No, see the fish. You told me that it was the specialty of the house. I ordered it, but it tastes so bad. It wasn't fresh at all.

W: I am sorry to hear that, sir. This is very unusual. Our seafood is bought from fishermen directly and all the fishes are live or refrigerated.

G: So, you mean I am not reasonable?

W: Sorry, sir. I don't mean that. I mean it was quite an accident. Shall I change another one for you?

G: No, I am not in a mood for fish now. I want to talk with your manager.

H: Good evening, sir. I am the head waitress. I am sorry about it. Do you wish to try something else? It would be on the house.

G: No, I don't want to try anything else. Give me the bill, please.

H: It is on the house. And here are some vouchers for you. Next time you can use them to pay when you dine in the restaurant. And I can assure you that the same thing will not happen.

G: OK. Thank you then.

H: You are welcome. We are looking forward to seeing you again.

Notes:

(1) head waitress 女领班

(2) the specialty of the house 招牌菜

(3) seafood 海鲜

(4) fisherman 渔夫

(5) refrigerated 冷冻的

(6) reasonable 通情达理的

(7) on the house 免费

(8) in a mood for 有心情……

(9) voucher 代金券

Useful Sentences

- So could you tell us something about it? 你能给我们介绍一下吗?
- We serve congee of different flavors, such as meat congee, vegetable congee, and mixed congee, etc. 餐厅有不同口味的粥, 如肉粥、蔬菜粥、五谷粥等。

- We usually serve milk and soybean milk instead of coffee or tea. 我们通常供应牛奶和豆浆，而不是茶或咖啡。
- We also serve eggs like fried eggs and poached eggs. 还有煎蛋和煮蛋。
- My wife prefers to have a cup of vegetable and fruit juice in the morning. 我妻子喜欢在早上喝一杯蔬果汁。
- This way, please. Is this table all right? 这边请，这个位子怎么样？
- Enjoy your breakfast. 祝您早餐愉快。
- What's your recommendation? 您推荐什么？
- I recommend that you try our house specialty. 我建议您尝尝餐厅的招牌菜。
- It is made of shrimp together with green tea.（这道菜）是由虾仁和蔬菜做的。
- It is cooked of seasonal and fresh vegetables.（这道菜）是由时令蔬菜做的，非常新鲜。
- It is very delicious and nutritious.（这道菜）既美味又有营养。
- Would you like to have some soup? 您要喝汤吗？
- We have chicken soup, mushroom soup, fish soup and some more. 餐厅有鸡汤、蘑菇汤、鱼汤等。
- So you ordered Sauteed Shrimp with Green Tea, Boiled Seasonal Vegetable, mushroom soup and rice. Is it correct? 您点的西湖龙井虾仁、白灼时蔬、蘑菇汤和米饭，对吗？
- Could you rush the order? 能快点上菜吗？
- They will go well with your dishes.（酒水）刚好和您点的菜搭配。
- Which one would you prefer? 您要哪一种？
- They are similar, but they have different flavors. 它们很像，但是味道不同。
- Is everything to your satisfaction? 一切还满意吗？
- I am sorry to hear that, sir. This is very unusual. 很抱歉，这很少发生。
- Our seafood is bought from fishermen directly and all the fish are live or refrigerated. 我们的海鲜都是直接从渔民那儿采购来的，而且所有的鱼都是鲜活的或者冷藏保存的。
- Shall I change another one for you? 我给您换道菜好吗？
- I am not in a mood for fish now. 我没心情吃鱼了。
- I want to talk with your manager. 我要找你们经理。
- It would be on the house. 免费的。
- And here are some vouchers for you, and next time you can use them to pay when you dine in the restaurant. 这里有一些赠券给您，您下次在餐厅用餐可以抵用的。

Knowledge Extension

◆ Chinese Cuisine

As a part of Chinese civilization, the art of cooking in China can trace back to several thousand years. Chinese cuisine, top world cuisine, can be found in the restaurants of any corner in the world, which attaches importance to the color, fragrance, taste, form and nutrition. It is estimated that there are about 5000 different local cooking styles in China. The most popular cuisine are those of Sichuan, Guangdong, Shandong and Jiangsu, which are subdivided into eight: Shandong, Hunan, Sichuan, Fujian, Guangdong, Jiangsu, Zhejiang and Anhui cuisine.

◆ Breakfast in Chinese Hotels

Except some five or four star hotels, most hotels in China only supply a Chinese-style breakfast. There is no Western food provided in the morning. The popular local breakfasts are as follows: soybean milk and deep-fried dough sticks, steamed buns stuffed with meat, soup, or nothing, tofu pudding, wheat noodles, rice noodles, steamed glutinous rice, rice porridge or congee, wontons and dumplings, pancakes with eggs, morning tea and dim sum. There are also some drinks like milk, orange juice, Coca-Cola and so on.

◆ Top Ten Meals for Lunch of Chinese People

In China, people can have many options for their lunch. There are ten top meals for Chinese people's lunch as follows: covered rice, oodles of noodles, steamed buns and dumplings, hot spicy soup, pancakes, Chinese burgers, canteen food, hand-held pancakes and hot pot.

◆ How to Deal with Customer Complaints

First, when someone is complaining about your business, breathe deeply and try your best to remain as calm as possible to help cope with the complaint successfully.

Second, when the customer picks up the phone from your call, remember to introduce yourself in a friendly way.

Third, after introducing yourself, address the problem and listen to him/her to take the complaint sincerely and seriously.

Forth, after listening to the customer's entire complaint, apologize and show a pity to him/her to let him/her know that you can understand him/her.

Fifth, when you understand the customer's complaint correctly, state it again and ask questions to help you understand the situation better.

Sixth, after thanking your customer for answering your questions, you should make sure that you will address the complaint and find the solution without delay.

Seventh, you should try to make a plan with the customer to follow up on his/her complaint.

◆ Follow up with Your Customer

First, before finding the solution to your customer's complaint, investigate the situation further on the basis of his/her description of the event.

Second, once having clarified the question, come up with a solution to the complaint.

Third, contact your customer with the solution you have for his/her complaint.

Forth, try to break the ice and offer your solution to him/her.

Fifth, thank your customer again for his/her concern and tell him/her that you are available if he/she needs your help again.

Sixth, try to learn more by taking addressing and following up on the complaint as a constructive way.

Section Summary

- Know about the procedures of food and beverage service in a Chinese style.
- Know about Chinese cuisine.
- Know about breakfast in Chinese hotels.
- Learn about the top ten meals for lunch of Chinese people.
- Learn to handle customer complaints.

Practice

Part One Dialogue

1. Choose the correct sentences to fill in the blanks according to the context.

W: Waiter   G1: Guest 1   G2: Guest 2

W: _____ Do you have reservation?

G: Yes, I've reserved a table for two under the name of Lee.

W: Yes. Sir. _____ Please be seated.

G1: The table is good.

G2: Yes, we can see the river and the tower.

W: _____

G1: Yes. We would like to have some vegetables and fish. What do you recommend?

W: Stirring Fried Broccoli is very good. I recommend you have a try. As for fish, how about Sweet and Sour Mandarin Fish? _____

G1: OK, We will have both of them, and Mushroom Soup.

W: _____

G2: Rice.

W: OK. Please wait for a moment.

A. It is the house specialty.

B. Good afternoon.

C. Are you ready to order?

D. What staple food would you like?

E. This way, please.

2. Act in pairs to finish the following role-play activities.

(1) Student A: Act as a guest to go to a Chinese restaurant. You have booked a table for two.

Student B: Act as the waiter and seat the guests.

(2) Student A: Act as a guest in a Chinese restaurant. Order your food (a cold dish, a hot dish, a soup and staple food).

Student B: Act as the waiter in the Chinese restaurant. Take orders for the guest. Recommend wine for the guest.

(3) Student A: Act as a guest in a Chinese restaurant. You are a vegetarian. Order your food.

Student B: Act as the waiter in the Chinese restaurant. Take orders for the guest.

(4) Student A: Act as a guest in a Chinese restaurant. The soup is so salty. All the dishes are very hot. Ask the waiter for help.

Student B: Act as the waiter in the Chinese restaurant. Help the guest with the food.

3. Translate the following words into English.

(1) 招牌菜

(2) 脆的

(3) 酸的

(4) 甜的

(5) 油腻的

(6) 清淡的

(7) 咸的

(8) 苦的

(9) 美味的

(10) 有营养的

4. Discussion:

(1) What is the general procedure of serving Chinese food?

(2) Do you know any famous Chinese dishes? What are they made of? Can you give the names of them in English?

5. Translate the following sentences.

(1) 我建议您尝尝餐厅招牌菜。

(2) 这道菜是由鸡肉和蘑菇做的。

(3) 它美味又有营养。

(4) 你能快点上菜吗?

(5) 我给您换道菜好吗?

(6) 我要找你们的经理。

(7) 这有一些优惠券送给您,您下次在餐厅用餐可以抵用。

(8) 炒西蓝花怎么样?

(9) 抱歉,给您上错汤了。

(10) 这是免费赠送给您的。

Part Two　Knowledge Extension

According to the part of Knowledge Extension, write the answers to the following questions on the sheet of paper by using your own words, not simply copying the sentences. When you have completed the test, ask your lecturer for the answers.

Chinese Cuisine

_____
_____
_____
_____
_____
_____

Breakfast in Chinese Hotels

_____
_____
_____
_____
_____
_____

Top Ten Meals for Lunch of Chinese People

_____
_____
_____

How to Deal with Customer Complaints

_____
_____
_____
_____

Topic Four Bar Service 酒吧服务

Introduction

Drinking is a natural form of socializing because tasty beverages can make people happier. Beverage service is one of the most profitable services, which can be provided for hotels, restaurants, coffee houses, tea shops and so on. Bars are the most common place for people to drink, where drinks are dispensed from a counter. According to different functions, bars are classified into main bars with exquisite decoration, sufficient bar counters and chairs, lounges with drinks and snacks, grand bars located in entertainment venues, banquet bars temporarily established, gentleman bars and service bars situated in restaurants.

Objectives

Competence Standard	Knowledge Standard
Ability to know about the steps of bar service	Know about the working procedures of bar service
Ability to learn about wine bar etiquette	Acquire the knowledge about the steps of bar service
Ability to grasp the key points and standards of bar service and the main types of wine glasses	Get the knowledge about bar service and the key points and standards of bar service
Ability of listening, speaking and reading	Have a good understanding of the main types of wine glasses

Working Procedures

- Greet the guest.
- Show the wine list to the guest.
- Take an order.
- Show it to the guest.
- Open the bottle.
- Serve the guest.

Dialogues

Dialogue 1

Situation Question: Do you know how to introduce Chinese wine to guests?

At the Restaurant

W: Waiter   G1: Guest 1   G2: Guest 2

W: Would you like to have some wine with your meal?

G1: Yes. What wine do you have?

W: Here is the wine list. There is a wide selection of wine for you to choose from. Please have a look at it.

G1: Thank you. I'd like to have a bottle of Chinese beer. Could you recommend one to me?

W: Certainly. I think Tsingtao and Yanjing beer are very good. They will go well with your dishes. Which one would you prefer?

G1: Tsingtao, please. How about you, Jane?

G2: I have no idea.

G1: Could you recommend some wine which is a little milder for my girlfriend?

W: We have the rice wine which is made of glutinous rice and tastes good. It is suitable for ladies.

G2: Is it like Japanese sake?

W: They are similar, but they have different flavor.

G2: OK, I will have a try.

W: So you ordered a bottle of Tsingtao and a bottle of rice wine. Is it correct?

G1: Yes.

W: Thank you. You will get it right away.

Notes:

(1) wine list 酒水单

(2) selection 选择   a wide selection of 种类齐全的

(3) go with 搭配

(4) mild 温和的

(5) glutinous rice 糯米

(6) sake 日本清酒

Dialogue 2

Situation Question: Do you know how to recommend drinks if a guest doesn't want to have alcoholic drinks?

At the Bar (1)

B: Bartender   G1: Guest 1   G2: Guest 2

B: Good evening, ladies. What can I make for you tonight?

G1: I would like to try some local beer. Can you recommend?

B: Sure. We have Tsingtao beer, Snow beer, Yanjing beer and Zhujiang beer. Which one do you like?

G1: I have heard about the first three, and I have tried all of them, but I have not heard about the last one. Is it a local beer?

B: Yes, it is a brand of beer made in Guangdong Province.

G1: Guangdong Province, I know it. OK, I would like to have a bottle of Zhujiang beer.

B: Good. How about you, my lady?

G2: I prefer to have some nonalcoholic drink. Do you have soft?

B: Certainly. We have fresh squeezed fruit juice and tea.

G2: I would like to have a cup of lemonade.

B: OK. Here is the beer. And here is the lemonade.

G1&G2: Thank you.

Notes:

(1) brand 品牌

(2) nonalcoholic 不含酒精的

(3) soft drink 软饮料

(4) fresh squeezed fruit juice 鲜榨果汁

(5) lemonade 柠檬水

Dialogue 3

Situation Question: Do you know something about alcohol and cocktail?

【拓展音频】

At the Bar (2)

B: Bartender   G1: Guest 1   G2: Guest 2

B: Good evening, madam and sir. Would you like to sit at a table or at the bar?

G2: I prefer to sit at a table. I don't like the bar stool.

G1: Me, too.

B: This way, please. Is this table all right?

G1&G2: Yes.

B: What would you like to drink?

G1: I prefer to have some whisky.

G2: Whisky is too strong. I don't think it is good for health.

G1: Just a cup. You know, I am so excited after watching the game.

G2: I know, but I still advise you not to have whisky.

G1: I will have it on the rocks, so it will not be too strong.

G2: OK, if you insist. A whisky on the rocks for him. I prefer to cocktail with little alcohol. Do you have any recommendation?

B: Yes. You may try our special cocktail. It is with a little alcohol and tastes good. It is popular with the ladies.

G2: OK, then I will try it.

B: Please wait a moment.

Notes:

(1) bar stool 酒吧的高脚凳

(2) whisky 威士忌酒

(3) on the rocks (酒等饮料) 加冰的

(4) strong wine 烈酒

(5) insist 坚持

(6) alcohol 酒精

(7) special cocktail 特制鸡尾酒

Dialogue 4

Situation Question: Do you know how to introduce Chinese wine?

At the bar (3)

B: Bartender   G1: Guest 1   G2: Guest 2   G3: Guest 3

【拓展音频】

B: Good evening. Here is the wine list. What would you like to drink?

G1: Let me see. I like to have a cup of Scotch.

B: How would you like your Scotch, straight or on the rocks?

G1: On the rocks.

B: How about you, madam?

G2: I would like to try some Chinese wine, but I prefer something milder. Can you recommend?

B: We have yellow wine and sticky rice wine. Both of them are less alcohol and suitable for ladies.

G2: What are the differences between them?

B: Yellow wine tastes like wine, but rice wine tastes sweet.

G2: I would like to have rice wine.

B: Good. How about you, sir?

G3: I want to have a cup of rum and coke.

B: May I repeat your order? A Scotch on the rocks, a rice wine and a rum and coke. Is that all right?

Notes:

(1) Scotch 威士忌，又称 Scotch Whisky

(2) straight 不加冰，直饮

(3) Rum and coke（鸡尾酒）朗姆加可乐

Useful Sentences

- Would you like to have some wine with your meal? 您用餐需要搭配什么酒水吗？
- What wine do you have? 你们都有什么酒？
- Here is the wine list. 这是酒水单。
- They will go well with your dishes. 这些酒都与您的菜肴搭配。
- Could you recommend some wine little milder? 你能推荐一些柔和点的葡萄酒吗？
- What can I make for you tonight? 今晚我需要为您调制什么酒？
- I would like to try some local beer. Can you recommend? 我想尝试当地的啤酒，你能推荐一下吗？
- I prefer to have some nonalcoholic drink. 我更想喝不含酒精的饮品。
- We have fresh squeezed fruit juice and tea. 我们有鲜榨果汁和茶。
- What would you like to drink? 您想要喝些什么？
- Whisky is so strong. I don't think it is good for health. 威士忌太烈了，我觉得对您的健康不利。
- It is with little alcohol and tastes good. It is popular with ladies. 它的酒精含量较低，口感好，很受女士欢迎。
- How would you like your Scotch, straight or on the rocks? 您要纯苏格兰威士忌还是加冰块的？
- Both of them are with less alcohol and suitable for ladies. 这两款酒的酒精含量都很低，非常适合女士饮用。
- May I repeat your order? 我能重复一下您的点单吗？
- So you ordered a bottle of Tsingtao and a bottle of rice wine. Is it correct? 您点了一瓶青岛啤酒和一瓶米酒，对吗？
- Thank you. Right away. 谢谢！马上（为您服务）。

Knowledge Extension

◆ Steps of Bar Service

First, take orders by asking, repeating and affirming and show wine to the guest. Next, open the bottle and at last pour wine for the guest.

◆ Wine Bar Etiquette

Assess the Environment

Give a quick scan of the area, learn to assess the bar by asking the server or bartender a simple question. Communicate with your server or bartender letting them know what you need. That is his/her big responsibility. Stick with what you know.

How to Choose

If you're not interested in or unfamiliar with the wines on the list, try to start a dialogue with your server to let him/her know your wine interests or immediately use the Vivino Wine List Scanner to know about rate and price details on all the wines. Never hesitate to ask for a sample of wines you are curious about. It's worthwhile for you to take your time to investigate your options. Don't be afraid to be indecisive. Many wine professionals take pride in helping someone find a wine they enjoy.

The Corkage Question

Bring your own wine and just check about the corkage policy in advance. Do not argue it and try to be polite. Pour your heart and soul into the wine list, and make sure of giving it a chance. Abandon your corkage fee and make an attempt to understand the concept of the wine program.

Wine Bar Socialization

Beware of wine snobs because truly experienced and committed wine people aren't so desperate to prove it. Don't be the wine snob because some wine professionals do have the tendency to be. If you are skillful at the wine, keep in mind to show your wine knowledge. A lot of wine joints will have a great sense of community. Keep it together.

Settling the Bill

In general, one person pays and everyone else settles up with that person while the server runs payment. This is the best way to pay the bill. Servers will love you for this. Try not to mix up payment too much. If you have a mix of cards and cash, offer the cash to the people with the card to consolidate. The included gratuity is usually 18%~22%. Keep an eye to make sure you don't double tip. Tips make up the majority of a restaurant employee's income, so if you were satisfied with the service, 20% should be the minimum. If the service was terrible, don't go back.

◆ Key Points of Bar Service

Serve the guest from his/her right side with the right hand. Remind the guest saying "Excuse me, sir/madam" when the employee in the bar is behind him/her to avoid accidents.

Name the drinks while presenting or adding them in the case of not disturbing the guest.

Be sure to ask the guest whether he/she'd like another cup before taking the empty one.

Listen carefully when guests speak and don't interrupt or urge guests, or show impatience because they drink too much, too little or too long.

Warmly receive all the guests. Don't make a fish of one and flesh of another. The guest who is drunk cannot have a slow attitude. When the drunken guest leaves the table, leave his/her original items as they are for verification.

- **Standards of Bar Service**

Ensure that all preparations are completed before opening, for example doing a good cleaning and checking whether bar chairs are properly furnished.

Receive orders at the bar, enter the computer according to the program, and then make and provide the service. Serve drinks for the guests. Establish a healthy relationship with them. Always consult with guests, and report to the supervisor.

Keep the equipment and utensils clean and ensure that the bar meets the requirements of high hygienic standards.

When receiving guests, be polite and smile.

Be familiar with drinks and wine snacks, so as to recommend them to guests. Seize the right time to sell drinks skillfully.

When the guest pays the bill, the waiter will take the bill according to the procedures.

- **Main Types of Wine Glasses**

There are twenty two types of wine glasses as follows: juice glass, shot glass, collins glass, old fashioned rock glass, high ball glass, champagne glass, water glass, cocktail glass, white wine glass, sherry glass, brandy snifter, champagne tulip, pilsner, liqueur glass, red wine glass, port wine glass, soda glass, Irish coffee glass, hurricane glass, whisky sour, sherbet and decanter.

Section Summary

- Know about the procedures of bar service.
- Learn about the steps of bar service.
- Know about the wine bar etiquette.
- Know about the key points of bar service.
- Know about the standards of bar service.
- Know the main types of wine glasses.

Section Three 模块三
F&B Department 餐饮部

Practice

Part One Dialogue

1. Choose the correct sentences to fill in the blanks according to the context.

W: Waiter   G1: Guest 1   G2: Guest 2

W: Good evening. _____

G1: We would like to try some Chinese alcohol. _____

W: We have white wine, beer, yellow wine and rice wine. Besides, we have grape wine made in China. _____

G1: We would like to try white wine first.

W: We have Maotai, Wuliangye, Luzhou and Fen wine.

G2: Let's have a bottle of Fen wine. I have heard there is a famous poem about the wine.

W: Yes. _____ So, a bottle of Fen wine. Anything else?

G1: _____

A. What kind of wine do you have?

B. Which kind do you prefer?

C. No, thank you.

D. In the poem, the place where the wine is made is mentioned.

E. What would you like to drink?

2. Act in pairs to finish the following role-play activities.

(1) Student A: Act as a guest. You are having dinner with friends in a Chinese restaurant. Ask the waiter to serve a traditional Chinese wine.

Student B: Act as the waiter in a Chinese restaurant. Go to serve the guest and respond to their request.

(2) Students A&B: Act as guests. You go to the bar to have a cup of wine. Talk with the bartender about the football game you just watched.

Student C: Act as the bartender. Serve the guests and make a small talk with them.

(3) Students A&B: Act as guests. You go to the bar to have a cup of wine. Ask the bartender to recommend a bottle of beer and a cup of cocktail.

Student C: Act as the bartender in the bar. Give recommendations to the guests.

(4) Students A &B: Act as guests. You are meeting in the bar. Ask the waiter to bring you some soft drinks.

Student C: Act as the waiter in the bar. Go to serve the guests and respond to their request.

3. Read the following words and translate them into Chinese.

(1) Rum

(2) Whisky

(3) Vodka

(4) Champagne

(5) Vermouth

(6) Liqueur

(7) Cocktail

(8) Gin

(9) Sherry

4. Discussion:

(1) Do you know the brands of Chinese famous wine? Do you know the history of them? Discuss with your partner.

(2) What should you do if you got drunk in the bar?

5. Translate the following sentences.

(1) 您想喝点什么呢?

(2) 这是酒水单。

(3) 您的威士忌要加冰还是直饮?

(4) 您想尝试一下中国酒吗?

(5) 请问您要再加一瓶酒吗?

(6) 这款酒很受女士欢迎。

(7) 我可以自带酒水吗?

(8) 现在打开酒瓶吗?

(9) 这款酒的酒精含量很低,适合女士饮用。

(10) 我能重复一下您的点单吗?

Part Two　Knowledge Extension

According to the part of Knowledge Extension, write the answers to the following questions on the sheet of paper by using your own words, not simply copying the sentences. When you have completed the test, ask your lecturer for the answers.

Steps of Bar Services

_____

_____

_____

_____

Wine Bar Etiquette

_____

_____

_____

_____

Key Points of Bar Service

Standards of Bar Service

Main Types of Wine Glasses

Topic Five Settling the Bill Service
结账服务

Introduction

At a restaurant, after a guest has a dinner, he/she will call for a bill. A waiter will go to the cashier and instruct him/her to figure the bill by the table number. After the cashier calculates the guest's whole sum, he/she will hand the bill to the waiter. The waiter goes through the bill, comes near to the table and then stands up straight to the guest's right side. At last, the waiter presents the bill to the guest and waits for the guest to examine his/her check.

Objectives

Competence Standard	Knowledge Standard
Ability to settle the bill by using a new method of uploading photos	Know about the working procedures of settling the bill by uploading photos
Ability to learn about the customs and standards of tipping	Know about the customs and standards of tipping
Ability to understand the definition of going Dutch and know about the methods of settling the bill in a restaurant	Know about the definition of going Dutch
Ability of listening, speaking and reading	Learn about the methods of settling the bill in the restaurant

Working Procedures

- Greet the guest.
- Bring the bill to the guest.
- Ask the guest for methods of settling the bill.
- Settle the bill for the guest.
- Thank the guest for consuming.
- Express best wishes to the guest.

Dialogues

Dialogue 1

Situation Question: Do you know the different ways of settling the bill?

Settling the Bill

【拓展音频】

S: Server   G: Guest

G: Waiter.

S: Yes, sir? How is everything?

G: Everything is good. I like them very much. May I have the bill?

S: Yes, sir. Would you like separate bills or one bill?

G: One bill for all is OK.

S: All right. Please wait a moment.

(*After a while, the waiter returns with the bill*)

S: Sir, this is the bill. The total is 1,820 *yuan* including 10% service charge. Please check it.

G: Yes, that's correct.

S: How would you like to pay it?

①

G: I'd like to put it on the room.

S: Could you please show me your room key?

G: Here you are. I am in Room 1220.

(*After checking the room key, and room number*)

S: Please sign your name here.

G: OK. Here you are.

S: Here is your receipt and your room key.

②

G: I'd like to pay in cash. Here is 1900 *yuan*.

S: OK. Please wait for a moment. I'll be back with the change.

(*After a while*)

S: Thank you for waiting. Here is your change and receipt.

G: Thank you.

③

G: I'd like to pay by credit card.

S: OK. May I have your credit card and passport?

(*After checking and confirming the related information*)

S: Would you please sign here?

G: Certainly.

S: Here is your copy and the receipt. Thank you.

G: Thank you.

Notes:

(1) bill 账单

(2) service charge 服务费

(3) put it on the room 记到房费上

(4) sign 签字

(5) cash 现金

(6) change 找回的零钱

(7) receipt 收据

Dialogue 2

Situation Question: What will you do if the guests have some questions about the bill?

Explaining the Bill

【拓展音频】

S: Server   G: Guest

S: Is everything all right?

G: Yes, the food is really good. We all enjoy the dishes very much.

S: I am glad to hear that. Would you like to have anything else?

G: Please give us two coffees and the bill.

S: Would you like to pay together or separately?

G: Together.

S: OK, Please wait for a minute.

(*After a while*)

S: Sir, here is your bill. The total is RMB1,480 *yuan*.

G: Is the service charge included? How much is it?

S: Yes, the service charge is included. It is 15% of the total.

G: I see. But what is this? 200 *yuan*?

S: This is for the wine, Fen Wine.

G: OK, I see.

S: How would you like to pay the bill?

G: In cash. Here is the money.

S: Please wait a moment will be back with the change.

(*After a while*)

S: Sir, here is your change and receipt.

Notes:

(1) service charge 服务费

(2) include 包括

(3) change 零钱

Dialogue 3

Situation Question: What's your opinion on tips? Would you accept tips if it was against the policy of your hotel?

Dealing with Mistakes

W: Waitress   G: Guest

W: How is everything, sir?

G: The food is good. Especially the specialty you recommended is really good. My wife and I enjoyed it very much.

W: I am glad that you like it. Would you care for anything else?

G: Yes. We would like two cups of green tea and the bill.

W: OK. Please wait a moment.

(*After a while*)

W: Sir, here is the bill. The total is RMB2,200 *yuan*. How would you like to pay for it?

G: Wait a minute. What's the figure? RMB1,000 *yuan* for Moutai. We have not ordered any wine.

W: Let me see. Oh, I am so sorry, sir. This is not your bill. I have brought the wrong bill to you. Please wait for a while, and I will go to get your bill.

G: OK.

W: This is your bill. The total is RMB1,560 *yuan* with a 15% service charge. Please have a look at it.

G: Yes, it is correct.

W: How would you like to pay for it?

G: In cash. Here is the money.

W: OK, Please wait for a moment. Sir, here is your change and receipt.

G: The change is for your tips.

W: Thank you, sir. But we are not allowed to accept tips in the hotel.

G: Thank you.

W: Thank you. We are looking forward to seeing you again.

Notes:

(1) care for 想要

(2) especially 特别地

(3) figure 价格

(4) order 点（菜，酒水等）

Useful Sentences

- The total is RMB1,820 *yuan* including 10% service charge. 您一共消费1820元，包括10%的服务费。
- How would you like to pay it? 您要怎么结账？
- I'd like to put it on the room. 我想记到房费上。
- I'd like to pay in cash. 我付现金。
- I'd like to pay by credit card. 我用信用卡支付。
- Please sign your name here. 请在这儿签名。
- Is everything all right? 您吃得还好吧？
- We all enjoy the dishes very much. 我们非常喜欢这些菜。
- Would you like to have anything else? 您还要点别的吗？
- Would you like to pay together or separately? 您是一起结账还是分开结账？
- Is the service charge included? How much is it? 里面含服务费吗？怎么收的？
- The service charge is included. It is 15% of the total. 包括服务费，是消费金额的15%。
- This is for the wine. 这是酒水的费用。
- Please wait a moment, and I will be back with the change and receipt. 请稍等，我去拿找零和发票。
- Would you care for anything else? 您还需要别的吗？
- We would like two cups of green tea and the bill. 请给我们两杯绿茶，并且把账单拿来。
- What's the figure? 这个数字是什么（的费用）？
- I am sorry. I have brought the wrong bill to you. 抱歉，我拿错账单了。
- Here is your change and receipt. 这是您的找零和发票。
- We are not allowed to accept tips in the hotel. 我们酒店是不收小费的。
- We are looking forward to seeing you again. 欢迎下次光临。

Knowledge Extension

- **Settle the Bill by Uploading Photos**

Now in London, there is a way of settling the bill for the meal that guests have by uploading photos of it to social networks. If a guest upload the photos of a two-course meal onto Twitter or Facebook, he/she won't have to pay for the meal. Some scientists claim taking a photo of their food before having it will make it taste better. The Picture House, a restaurant in London will be opened soon.

◆ People Tipped and Standards of Tipping

In the United States, tipping is very important, but it is not just a nice thing to do. In a sense, tipping is a way for people to say thanks to someone for his/her good service. However, now it is sad to say that people have to give tips even though the service is not good at all.

Remember to bring lots of change for tips. Here are the people tipped and the standards of tipping, which are as follows: taxi drivers ($2 to $3 each time, when they help to take the guest's bags), porters ($1 each bag, when they help the guest to take his/her heavy suitcase), hotel bellboys ($1 each bag, when they show the guest to his/her room), doormen ($1 each time, when they help the guest call a taxi except special service), hotel maids ($1 each night, when the guest stays for more than one night), waiters and waitresses (they can get 15%~20% tip of their pre-tax bill), tour guides (if you need to give a tip, the standards are: $1 for a half-day tour, $2 for a one-day tour, $5~$10 for a week-long tour).

◆ Go Dutch

Going Dutch is one of the ways of settling the bill, which means sharing the cost equally among each. That is used on the occasion where common consumption is paid together for a party and tourism, which comes from the British prejudice against the Dutch, because the ancient Dutch people were the ones who split the bill. British people thought they were ungentlemanly. There are several ways for that, such as splitting the bill, Dutch treatment, paying for ourselves and letting us go fifty-fifty.

◆ Methods of Settling the Bill in the Restaurant

There are some methods of settling the bill in the restaurant which are cash, personal check, Visa, traveler's check, credit card, and going Dutch and MasterCard.

Section Summary

- Know about settling the bill by uploading photos.
- Know about the working procedures of settling the bill.
- Know about the people that can be tipped and standards of tipping.
- Know about the definition of going Dutch.
- Learn to be familiar with the methods of settling the bill in the restaurant.

Practice

Part One   Dialogue

1. Choose the correct sentences to fill in the blanks according to the context.

W: Waiter   G: Guest

W: Would you care for anything else?

G: Yes, please give us two black coffees and the bill.

W: Would you like to pay the bill separately or together?

G: _____

W: _____

G: I'd like to put it on the room.

W: _____

G: Yes, here it is.

W: Sir, this is the bill. _____ Please check it.

G: Yes, that's correct.

W: _____

G: OK. Here you are.

W: Here are your room key and the receipt.

A. The total is RMB1,480 *yuan* including 15% service charge.

B. How would you like to pay?

C. May I have your room key?

D. Bill for all.

E. Please sign it.

2. Act in pairs to finish the following role-play activities.

(1) Student A: Act as a guest. You ask the waiter to bring the bill for you and give him/her the ways of settling the bill.

Student B: Act as the waiter. Settle the bill for the guest.

(2) Students A: Act as a guest. You find the waiter has brought you the wrong bill. Point it out and ask him/her to bring you the correct one and pay it.

Student B: Act as the waiter. Settle the bill for the guest.

(3) Student A: Act as a guest. You have some questions about the bill. Ask the waiter to explain to you.

Student B: Act as the waiter. Respond to the guest's request.

(4) Student A: Act as a guest. You find that you are overcharged. Ask the waiter to resettle the bill for you.

Student B: Act as the waiter. Respond to the guest's request.

3. Translate the following words into English.

(1) 结账

(2) 账单

(3) 折扣

(4) 赠券

(5) 服务费

(6) 现金

(7) 支票

(8) 信用卡

(9) 记账
(10) 收据

4. Discussion:

(1) What should you do if the guest has not enough money to pay the bill?

(2) What should you do if the bill is miscalculated?

5. Translate the following sentences.

(1) 您要再点别的吗?

(2) 您想怎么结账呢?

(3) 请问账单包括服务费吗?

(4) 这是甜点的费用。

(5) 打九五折。

(6) 您要合单还是分单?

(7) 请把账单给我,谢谢。

(8) 这是小费。

(9) 这是退还给您的钱。

(10) 欢迎下次光临。

Part Two   Knowledge Extension

According to the part of Knowledge Extension, write the answers to the following questions on the sheet of paper by using your own words, not simply copying the sentences. When you have completed the test, ask your lecturer for the answers.

Settle the Bill by Uploading Photos

_____
_____
_____
_____
_____
_____
_____

People Tipped and Standards of Tipping

_____
_____
_____

Go Dutch

Methods of Settling the Bill in the Restaurant

Section Four

Business Center
商务中心

模块四

Introduction

In a hotel, the business center refers to the room where there are many facilities and services such as a printer, a computer, a fax machine, photocopy machine, and a fax machine with high speed Internet access, which allows guests to work while they are staying at the hotel and offers a wide range of services for guests such as photocopy service, typing service, printing service, convention service and so on.

Topic One Photocopy and Fax Services
复印、传真服务

Introduction

Photocopy and fax service are part of facilities and services in a hotel. Here you can know something about photocopy, fax and the use of a copy machine. Photocopy refers to a copy of printed material made with a process in which an image is formed by the action of light usually on an electrically charged surface. Fax service refers to a device that sends and receives printed pages or images over telephone lines by digitizing the material with an internal optical scanner and transmitting the information as electronic signals.

Objectives

Competence Standard	Knowledge Standard
Ability to use a photocopy machine	Know about the working procedures of photocopy and fax services
Ability to use a fax machine	Learn to use a photocopy machine
	Learn to use a fax machine
Ability of listening, speaking and reading	

Section Four 模块四
Business Center 商务中心

Working Procedures

- Greet the guests.
- Enquire the request.
- Offer service as requested (photocopying or faxing).
- Return the originals and giving photocopies.
- Settle the bill.
- Say goodbye.

Dialogues

Dialogue 1

Situation Question: Do you know the working procedures of photocopying?

Photocopying (1)

【拓展音频】

C: Clerk   G: Guest

C: Good morning, sir. Can I help you?

G: Yes, I want to photocopy the document.

C: How many copies do you want?

G: In triplicate, I think.

C: Would you like them in the same size?

G: Yes.

C: OK. Please have a look at the sample. Is it all right?

G: Yes, it is good.

C: OK. Please wait a moment.

(*After a while*)

C: Sir, would you like me to staple them for you?

G: Yes, thank you.

C: Here you are.

G: How much should I pay?

C: 1 *yuan* per page. So the total is RMB45 *yuan*.

G: Here is the money.

C: Here is your change.

Notes:

(1) photocopy 复印

(2) document 文件

(3) triplicate 一式三份

(4) sample 样本

(5) staple 装订

Dialogue 2

Situation Question: Do you know how to use a photocopier?

Photocopying (2)

【拓展音频】

C: Clerk   G: Guest

C: Good morning, madam. Can I help you?

G: Yes, I want to make some copies of the document.

C: How many copies do you want?

G: One for each. And I want to enlarge it.

C: How big do you want it?

G: By 20%.

C: OK. Do you want me to make it a little darker?

G: Yes.

C: OK. Please have a look at the sample. Is it all right?

G: I think a litte darker will be better.

C: OK. Please wait a moment.

(*After a while*)

C: Madam, would you like it stapled?

G: No, thank you.

C: Here you are. RMB30 *yuan* altogether.

G: How much do you charge for photocopying?

C: 1 *yuan* per page. You have photocopied 20 pages in all.

G: Here is the money.

C: Thank you. Have a good day.

Notes:

(1) one for each 一式一份

(2) enlarge 扩大

(3) dark 深色的；light 浅色的

(4) altogether 一共；in all 一共

Dialogue 3

Situation Question: Do you know how to offer fax service to guests?

Sending Fax (1)

C: Clerk   G: Guest

C: Good afternoon, sir. Can I help you?

G: Yes, I would like to send a fax back home.

C: Where would you like to send the fax to?

G: London.

C: May I have the fax number?

G: Sure. It is 0044-20-12345678.

C: A moment, please.

G: OK.

C: OK, it went through. These are the transmission report and the original script.

G: Thank you.

C: How would you like to pay?

G: May I put it on the room?

C: Certainly. May I have your room key?

G: Here you are.

C: The total is 200 *yuan*. Please sign here.

G: OK.

C: Here is the receipt and your room key.

G: Thank you.

C: You are welcome.

Notes:

(1) fax 传真

(2) transmission report 发送报告

(3) original script 原件

Dialogue 4

Situation Question: What will you do if the original script of the fax is too thin?

Sending Fax (2)

C: Clerk   G: Guest

C: Good evening, madam. Can I help you?

G: Yes. I want to send a fax to Hong Kong.

C: Could I have your fax number?

G: Yes. It is 00852-12345678. By the way, how would you charge for it?

C: To Hong Kong, it is RMB15 *yuan* per minute.

G: Is there any service charge?

C: Yes, the service charge is 15% of the total.

G: I see.

C: Madam, your original script is too thin, so I think it is better to photocopy it first, and then faxing the copy of it would be better. Do you agree?

G: Sure. Good idea. You are so considerate.

C: OK. Do you think the copies are good enough?

G: Yes.

C: Sorry, madam. We have got an error report. Let me see what is wrong. There is no problem with the fax machine. So I think there might be some problem with the receiver. Do you have the other fax number?

G: OK. Please try this number: 00852-1234876.

C: Good. It went through.

G: Great. Thank you so much.

C: You are welcome. How would you like to pay?

G: In cash.

C: The total is RMB200 *yuan*.

G: Here is the money.

C: Here is your original and the copies.

G: Thank you.

C: You are welcome.

Notes:

(1) charge 收费

(2) considerate 周到的

(3) error report 错误报告

(4) receiver 接收机

Useful Sentences

- I want to photocopy the document. 我想复印这一份文件。
- I want to make some copies of the document. 我想复印这一份文件。
- How many copies do you want? 您需要复印几份?
- In triplicate, I think. 一式三份。
- One for each. And I want to enlarge it. 一式一份，我想扩印。
- Would you like them in the same size? 和原件一样大吗?
- Please have a look at the sample. Is it all right? 您看一下样本是否合适。
- Would you like me to staple them for you? 需要我为您装订一下吗?
- How much should I pay? 多少钱?
- Here is your change. 这是您的找零。
- How big do you want it? 您要扩印多大?
- I want to enlarge it by 20%. 扩印20%。
- Do you want me to make it a little darker? 需要我把颜色调暗一些吗?
- How much do you charge for photocopying? 复印怎么收费?

- You have photocopied 30 pages in all. 您一共复印了 30 页。
- I would like to send a fax back home. 我想往家里发一份传真。
- Where would you like to send the fax to? 您想往哪里发传真?
- May I have the fax number? 能告诉我您的传真号码吗?
- OK, it went through. This is the transmission report and the original script. 好的，传真发过去了。这是发送报告和原件。
- To Hong Kong, it is RMB15 *yuan* per minute. 传真到香港每分钟 15 元人民币。
- Is there any service charge? 收服务费吗?
- The service charge is 15% of the total. 服务费是总消费金额的 15%。
- Your original script is too thin 您的原件纸张太薄。
- We have got an error report. Let me see what is wrong. 传真没有发过去，我看看出了什么问题。

Knowledge Extension

◆ Photocopy

Photocopy can make a replica of something using a special machine that involves light reacting on a special surface. The main parts of a photocopy machine are cartage, ink, machine and drum. The main function of a photocopy machine/copy machine is to reproduce copies of documents. Other functions include enlargement and reduction.

◆ Fax

Fax machines can transmit any form of printed, typed or hand-written matter, drawings, diagrams and photographs from one location to another in this country or abroad by using the telephone within a few minutes. Replicas of documents can be sent any distance with complete accuracy because this equipment combines the speed of the telephone with the reproduction facility of the office copier. "Fax" actually is a short way of saying "facsimile telegraphy".

Nowadays fax can be done through the Internet with a fax machine and an e-mail address. Thus all kinds of written information is transmitted fast and easily. All the edited documents, written on paper or in the form of e-mail, can be faxed. There is no strict limitation on the writing of fax which is only a way of transmitting information, so all the documents should follow their own requirements. For example, the certificate of origin below follows its own style.

◆ The Use of a Copy Machine

Check the paper trays to ensure the appropriate size and amount of paper put in the machine.
Place one page of your document to be copied face down on the scanner.
If you are just copying one page, place it face down on the scanner.
On the control panel, select your settings such as the number of copies, one sided or double-sided copies you want.

Press the button of start to print the copies which come out in the output tray.

Grab your copies and take your original documents from the copy machine.

Section Summary

- Know about the working procedures of photocopy and fax services.
- Learn to use a photocopy machine.
- Learn to use a fax machine.

Practice

Part One Dialogue

1. Choose the correct sentences to fill in the blanks according to the context.

C: Clerk   G: Guest

C: Good afternoon, sir. Can I help you?

G: Yes, I'd like to make copies of the file.

C: _____

G: Four copies for each.

C: _____

G: Yes.

C: You see, your original is too dark. I am afraid the copies will not be very clear.

G: OK, make it lighter. _____

C: Here are your copies and original script. _____

G: In cash.

C: _____

G: Here is the money. Thank you.

C: You are welcome. Good-bye.

G: Good-bye.

A. Do you want the same size as the original?

B. Shall I make it a little lighter?

C. The total is RMB50 *yuan*.

D. How many copies would you like?

E. How would you like to pay?

2. Act in pairs to finish the following role-play activities. Compensate necessary information.

(1) Student A: Act as a guest staying in the hotel room. Go to the business center to make some copies of a document.

Student B: Act as the business center clerk. Offer photocopy service to the guest.

(2) Student A: Act as a guest staying in the hotel room. Go to the business center to ask some information of booking air tickets.

Student B: Act as the business center clerk. Respond to the request of the guest.

(3) Student A: Act as a guest staying in the hotel room. Go to the business center to send a fax to your company in London.

Student B: Act as the business center clerk. Offer fax service to the guest.

(4) Student A: Act as a guest staying in the hotel room. Go to the business center to receive a fax from New York.

Student B: Act as the business center clerk. Respond to the request of the guest.

(5) Student A: Act as a guest staying in the hotel room. Go to the business center to make some copies of a document. And then fax some pages to Hong Kong.

Student B: Act as the business center clerk. Respond to the request of the guest.

3. Look at the following items in a hotel room and translate them into English.

(1) 影印服务

(2) 传真

(3) 一式三份

(4) 一式四份

(5) 装订

(6) 双面复印

(7) 原件

(8) 国家代码

(9) 区域代码

(10) 接收传真

4. Discussion:

(1) What will you do if the fax machine doesn't work during the process of sending fax?

(2) What will you do if the photocopier is being repaired when a guest comes into the business center to have some documents photocopied?

5. Translate the following sentences into English.

(1) 您需要复印几份？黑白的还是彩色的？

(2) 需要我把颜色调深一些吗？

(3) 需要我把颜色调浅一些吗？

(4) 您是要双面复印还是单面复印？

(5) 请告诉我您的传真号码？

(6) 我先复印一份，然后把复印件传真过去，您看行吗？

(7) 请写下国家代码、区域代码和对方的电话号码。

(8) 抱歉，机器出故障了。

(9) 这是您的原件。

(10) 您的原件不是很清晰，我无法保证复印效果。

Part Two Knowledge Extension

According to the part of Knowledge Extension, write the answers to the following questions on the sheet of paper by using your own words, not simply copying the sentences. When you have completed the test, ask your lecturer for the answers.

Photocopy

___

Fax

___

The Use of a Copy Machine

___

Topic Two Typing and Printing Services
打字、打印服务

Introduction

Hotels provide typing and printing services. Typing refers to the process of inputting text by pressing keys on a typewriter, computer keyboard, cell phone, or calculator. And there are two kinds of typing: Chinese typing and English typing. Printing service is a process for reproducing text and images using a master form or template.

Objectives

Competence Standard	Knowledge Standard
Ability to know about typing and printing services	Know about the working procedures of typing and printing services
Ability to learn typing and touch typing	Learn the way of typing
Ability to learn how to print	Learn about touch typing
Ability of listening, speaking and reading	Know about how to print

Working Procedures

- Greet the guests.
- Enquire the request.
- Offer service as requested (typing and printing).

- Settle the bill.
- Say goodbye.

Dialogues

Dialogue 1

Situation Question: Do you know how to provide typing service for a guest? What information should you get from the guest?

Typing Service

【拓展音频】

C: Clerk　　G: Guest

C: Good morning, sir. What can I do for you?

G: Good morning. I want to have my manuscript typed. Do you have the service?

C: Yes, we have typing service.

G: How much do you charge for it?

C: RMB50 *yuan* per A4 page.

G: OK. This is the manuscript.

C: What fonts do you like?

G: Times New Roman font, size 12 and double spaced.

C: OK. I see.

G: When can I get it?

C: In an hour.

G: Could you call me when it is finished? I am staying in the hotel.

C: Certainly, sir. Which room are you staying in?

G: My room number is 1220 and my name is Henry Black.

C: OK. Mr. Black. I will call you when it is finished.

G: Thank you.

(*An hour later*)

C: May I speak to Mr. Black?

G: Speaking.

C: Mr. Black, could you come to the business center? Your manuscript is finished.

G: OK. I am coming down.

C: Mr. Black. This is your manuscript and this is the typed version. Could you check it?

G: Yes, very good. There is not any mistakes.

C: Would you like me to print it now?

G: Yes, please. And this is my USB drive. Please save it to the disk.

C: Sure.

C: All done. Mr. Black, how would you like to pay?

G: Shall I charge it to my room?

C: Certainly. Please sign your name on it.

G: Here you are. Thank you.

C: Thank you, Mr. Black. Have a good day. Good-bye.

C: Good-bye.

Notes:

(1) manuscript 原稿

(2) font 字体

(3) version 版本

(4) USB drive U 盘

Dialogue 2

Situation Question: Do you know how to provide printing service for a guest? What information should you get from the guest?

Printing Service (1)

C: Clerk   G: Guest

C: Good evening, Mr. Johnson. How may I help you this time?

G: Good evening. I want to print some photos. Do you have photo printing service?

C: Yes. Would you like them printed in black and white or color?

G: What is the difference? How much do you charge for them?

C: For black and white, RMB10 *yuan* per page, for color printing, RMB20 *yuan* per page.

G: I prefer color printing.

C: OK, please wait a moment. Here you are, sir. 5 pages in all.

G: Can you help me laminate them? I want to give them to my friends as gifts.

C: Sure. That is a good idea to keep photos.

G: How do you charge for the lamination service?

C: RMB10 *yuan* per page. OK, finished. Is there anything I can do for you, Mr. Johnson?

G: No, thank you. How much are they in all?

C: RMB150 *yuan*.

G: Here is the money.

C: Thank you. Good-bye.

G: Good-bye.

Notes:

(1) print in black and white 黑白打印

(2) laminate 塑封

(3) lamination service 过塑服务

Dialogue 3

Situation Question: What will you do if you are asked to print some documents in the company?

Printing Service (2)

【拓展音频】

C: Clerk　　G: Guest

C: Good afternoon, sir. Can I help you?

G: Yes, I have a form to be printed. Here is my USB drive. The name of the file is "form to be printed".

C: I see. How many pages?

G: 15 pages in all.

C: What type of paper do you need to print it?

G: A4.

C: Please wait a minute. I'm afraid I will have to check the USB drive with a virus scanner first.

G: OK. I understand.

C: Good. Now we can print it. Would you like it to be printed in black and white or in color?

G: I prefer black and white.

C: One for each?

G: Yes.

C: Here you are. RMB30 *yuan* in total. How would you like to pay?

G: In cash. Here is the money.

Notes:

(1) form 表格

(2) virus 病毒　　virus scanner 病毒扫描程序

Dialogue 4

Situation Question: Do you know something about printing a document from your inbox?

Printing Service (3)

【拓展音频】

C: Clerk　　G: Guest

C: Good afternoon, sir. What can I do for you?

G: I would like to print a document from my inbox. Could you help me?

C: Yes, it is my honor. What is your e-mail address?

G: Hotmail.

C: OK. Please log into your account, and download the document to the computer, say, desktop.

G: I see. You see, the file named "JKL" is the document to be printed.

C: OK. I will open it first, and please check if there is anything to be corrected.

G: Good. Just print it for me.

C: What type of paper do you need to print it?

G: A4.

C: Would you like it to be printed in black and white or in color?

G: Black and white.

C: One for each?

G: Yes.

C: Here you are. RMB50 *yuan* in total. How would you like to pay?

G: In cash. Here is the money.

Notes:

(1) inbox 收件箱

(2) log 登录

(3) account 账户

(4) download 下载

Useful Sentences

- I want to have my manuscript typed. Do you have the service? 我想把手稿打印出来，你们这儿能打印吗？
- How much do you charge for it? 怎么收费？
- RMB50 *yuan* per A4 page for typing. 打字每张 A4 纸 50 元。
- What fonts would you like? 您要什么字体？
- Times New Roman font, size 12 and double spaced. 新罗马字体 12 号，双倍行距。
- Could you call me when it is finished? I am staying in the hotel. 我住在酒店，打完可以给我打个电话吗？
- I will call you when it is finished. 打完后我给您打电话。
- This is your manuscript and this is the typed version (electronic version). 这是您的手稿和打印好的版本（电子版）。
- Would you like me to print it now? 需要我现在打印吗？
- And this is my USB drive. Please save it to the disk. 这是我的 U 盘，请存到里面。
- I want to print some photos. Do you have photo printing service? 我想打印一些照片，你们有照片打印服务吗？
- Would you like them printed in black and white or color? 您是要黑白打印还是彩色打印？
- For black and white, RMB10 *yuan* per page, for color printing, RMB20 *yuan* per page. 黑白打印每张 10 元，彩色打印每张 20 元。
- I prefer color printing. 我要彩色打印。

- Can you help me laminate them? 能帮我塑封一下吗？
- How do you charge for the lamination service? 过塑怎么收费？
- What type of paper do you need to print it? 您需要什么样的纸张打印？
- Please wait a minute. I am afraid I will have to check the USB drive with a virus scanner first. 请稍等，恐怕我得先查一下 U 盘病毒。
- I would like to print a document from my inbox. 我想打印收件箱里的文件。
- What is your e-mail address? 您的电子邮箱网址是什么？
- First, please log into your account. And download the document to the computer, say, desktop. 请先登录您的账号，然后将文件下载到电脑桌面上。
- The file named "JKL" is the document to be printed. 打印名为"JKL"的文件。

Knowledge Extension

◆ How to Learn Typing

Correctly sitting upright posture can speed up the learning process and also makes sure that minimum strain is put on the body.

Curl and place your eight fingers on the keyboard to keep them on the keys from left to right.

Obtain a main keyboard scheme to help your fingers press particular keys on the keyboard. It always keeps you starting from the home keys and then returns to them after typing.

Place your hands at the base of the keyboard and move them as much as is necessary.

Practice regularly and be patient with yourself. Your typing speed will increase slowly as you learn.

◆ Touch Typing

Touch typing is a kind of typing that does not need to use the sense of sight to find the keys because a touch typist will know their location on the keyboard by placing his/her eight fingers on the keyboard and having them reach for other keys. Both two-handed touch typing and one-handed touch typing are possible. Touch typing is one of the important skills which are of many benefits such as improving speed, increasing accuracy, saving time, reducing fatigue, improving health, increasing employment opportunity, focusing on one thing instead of two and editing.

◆ How to Print

Ensure to be on the same Internet. Turn on your printer and keep it connected.

Open start by clicking the Windows logo in the bottom-left corner of the screen.

Open file explorer by clicking the folder icon in the bottom-left of the Start window.

Click the folder containing the document to be printed on the left side of the file.

Explore the window. Usually the documents such as Word, Excel, PowerPoint documents, PDF files and photos can be printed.

Click the documents to be printed.

Click the Share tab in the upper-left corner of the window.

Find the button of print and click it.

Select your printer in the drop-down box.

Type in the number of copies of the documents to be printed in the "Copies" box.

Edit other print settings as you like concluding orientation, color, number of sides and so on.

Click Print and your document will start printing.

Section Summary

- Know about the working procedures of typing and printing services.
- Learn how to do typing.
- Know about touch typing.
- Learn how to print.

Practice

Part One Dialogue

1. Choose the correct sentences to fill in the blanks according to the context.

C: Clerk   G: Guest

C: Good morning, sir. What can I do for you?

G: I want to print an application form.

C: _____

G: 4 pages altogether.

C: _____

G: A4. How would you charge for it?

C: RMB10 *yuan* per page. _____

G: Black and white is OK.

C: OK, here you are. The total is RMB40 *yuan*. _____

G: Can I put it on the room? I am staying in the hotel.

C: Sure. _____

G: My name is Peter Wang and my room number is 1212.

C: OK, Mr. Wang. Please sign your name here.

A. What type of paper do you need?

B. Would you like black and white or color printing?

C. May I have your name and room number?

D. How many pages?

E. How would you like to pay?

2. Act in pairs to finish the following role-play activities.

(1) Student A: Act as a guest. Go to the business center to print a document. You want to pay by credit card.

Student B: Act as the business center clerk. Offer printing service to the guest.

(2) Student A: Act as a guest staying in the hotel room. Go to the business center to type a file. You want the bill put on the room.

Student B: Act as the business center clerk. Respond to the request of the guest.

(3) Student A: Act as a guest staying in the hotel room. Go to the business center to print some photos and then ask the clerk to help you to post the photos to a friend in Shenyang.

Student B: Act as the business center clerk. Respond to the request of the guest.

(4) Student A: Act as a guest staying in the hotel room. Go to the business center to print a file from your e-mail inbox.

Student B: Act as the business center clerk. Respond to the request of the guest.

3. Look at the following words and translate them into English.

(1) 打字

(2) 打印

(3) 塑封

(4) 校对

(5) 字体

(6) 字号

(7) 打印机

(8) U 盘

(9) 病毒检查

(10) 行距

(11) 草稿

(12) 电子版

(13) 手稿

(14) 定稿

(15) 下载

(16) 收件箱

(17) 电脑桌面

(18) 保存

(19) 黑白

(20) 彩色打印

4. Discussion:

(1) What will you do if you find virus in the guest's USB drive?

(2) What will you do if you find that there is some illegal information in the guest's document to be printed?

5. Translate the following sentences.

(1) 请问您需要什么字体，多大字号？

(2) 您需要打印多少页？

(3) 我什么时候来取？

(4) 请您来校对一下初稿。

(5) 帮我调成双倍行距，好吗？
(6) 请帮我保存到 U 盘里。
(7) 英语打字每页 10 元，打印每页 2 元。
(8) 我想打印电子邮箱里的文件。
(9) 您是要黑白打印还是彩色打印？
(10) 您要用什么样的纸打印？

Part Two   Knowledge Extension

According to the part of Knowledge Extension, write the answers to the following questions on the sheet of paper by using your own words, not simply copying the sentences. When you have completed the test, ask your lecturer for the answers.

How to Learn Typing

_____
_____
_____

Touch Typing

_____
_____
_____
_____
_____
_____
_____

How to Print

_____
_____
_____
_____
_____

Topic Three Convention Service
会议服务

Introduction

The business center service in a hotel provides many facilities and services such as a printer, computer, fax machine, photocopy machine, photocopy service, typing service, printing service and convention service and so on. Now you have a chance to learn something about meeting agenda, convention restaurant, meeting minutes and convention service, a kind of comprehensive system service with professional staff, professional departments, professional skills, professional marketing, and professional equipment.

Objectives

Competence Standard	Knowledge Standard
Ability to learn about convention service	Know about the working procedures of convention service
Ability to learn about meeting agenda	Learn about meeting preparation and meeting agenda
Ability to know something about convention reservation and meeting minutes	Acquire some knowledge about convention reservation
Ability of listening, speaking and reading	Learn about meeting minutes

Working Procedures

- Greet the guests.
- Enquire the request.
- Offer service as requested (convention service).
- Fill in the forms.
- Settle the bill.
- Say goodbye.

Dialogues

Dialogue 1

Situation Question: Do you know how to recommend translation or interpretation service to a guest?

Interpreting Service

C: Clerk   G: Guest

C: Good morning, sir. What can I do for you?

G: Good morning. I wonder if you offer interpretation service.

C: Yes, we do offer translation and interpretation service. What language interpretation would you like?

G: Chinese and English. We will have a conference this evening, but our interpreter is ill in the hospital. So we need a temporary interpreter.

C: OK, I see. When do you need the service?

G: At 6:00 p.m. in the meeting room of the hotel. How would you charge for it?

C: It is RMB2,000 *yuan* per day per person for a medium conference, and RMB4,000 *yuan* per day per person for a large conference.

G: Our meeting is a medium meeting.

C: Yes. Do you need to talk with the interpreter before the meeting?

G: Yes, I think we'd better meet before the meeting.

C: I will contact the interpreter now.

G: Thank you.

C: Sir, the interpreter will be here in 30 minutes. Would you please sit and wait for here?

G: OK.

Notes:

(1) interpretation 口译

(2) interpreter 口译译员

(3) temporary 暂时的

(4) contact 联系

Dialogue 2

Situation Question: Do you know how to respond if a guest calls to rent a conference room?

【拓展音频】

Renting Facilities (1)

C: Clerk   G: Guest

(*The telephone bell rings*)

C: Good morning, Business Center, how may I help you?

G: Good morning. I want to rent a conference room in your hotel.

C: What kind of room are you interested in?

G: We will have a department meeting, and there will be 30 members altogether.

C: What kind of facilities do you need?

G: We need a computer, video projector and internet connection.

C: OK, we have the meeting rooms you required. We have a small conference room for less than 30 people, a medium conference room for less than 60 people, and a large conference room for less than 100 people.

G: Are other rooms equipped with computers and Internet?

C: Yes.

G: How do you charge it?

C: They are different according to the size, equipment and duration.

G: What's about a small conference room for half a day?

C: It varies from RMB2,000 to RMB4,000 *yuan*.

G: I see. Which department should I contact if I come to see the meeting room?

C: You can come to the front desk and the receptionist will tell you what to do. Or you can also call the business center. The clerk here will show you around.

G: OK, I see. Thank you.

C: You are welcome.

Notes:

(1) department meeting 部门会议

(2) facility 设备

(3) video projector 投影仪

(4) internet connection 网络连接

(5) duration 持续时间，时长

Dialogue 3

Situation Question: Do you know how to respond when a guest comes to rent a laptop computer?

Renting Facilities (2)

C: Clerk   G: Guest

C: Good morning, sir. How may I help you?

G: I want to rent a laptop computer. Do you have the service?

C: Yes. When would you like to use it?

G: This afternoon.

C: For how long?

G: Two days.

C: Where would you like to use it?

G: I am staying in the hotel. So I just use it in the hotel room. How do you charge for it?

C: It's RMB300 *yuan* for a day. Would you like to rent it?

G: Yes.

C: Please wait a minute. Here is the laptop. Please check it.

G: OK, it is good. I will take it.

C: You have to pay RMB2,000 *yuan* as deposit. You will have the money back when you return the computer.

G: That's reasonable. Here is the money.

C: And how would you like to pay the rent?

G: I'd like to put it on the room. Oh, my room number is 1405. My name is Jack Brown.

C: May I have a look at your room key?

G: Here you are.

C: Good, Mr. Brown. Please sign your name here. OK, here is your receipt and here is the laptop. Please keep the receipt and show it when you return the computer.

G: OK, I will. Thank you.

C: You are welcome.

Notes:

(1) laptop computer 笔记本电脑

(2) rent 租金

(3) deposit 押金

Dialogue 4

Situation Question: What should you do if a guest calls from the conference for maintenance?

Request for Maintenance

C: Clerk　　G: Guest

(*The bell rings*)

C: Business Center, can I help you?

G: I am calling from the conference room. There is something wrong with the computer.

C: What is wrong?

G: I think there is something wrong with the internet connection.

C: Is there internet connection?

G: Yes, there is. But the speed is too slow. I can not download the file, I mean, my speech text. Could you send someone to check it? I am so worried about it.

C: I see. Which conference room are you in?

G: 105.

C: Don't worry, madam. I'll send a technician there right away.

G: OK, thank you.

Notes:

(1) maintenance 维修

(2) download 下载

(3) speech 演讲

(4) technician 技术人员

Useful Sentences

- Good morning, Business Center, how may I help you? 早上好，这里是商务中心，请问您需要什么帮助？
- I wonder if you offer interpretation service. 我想知道你们有没有口译服务。
- We do offer translation and interpretation service. What language interpretation would you like? 我们提供翻译服务，您需要哪个语种的口译？
- We need a temporary interpreter. 我们需要一位临时口译。
- It is RMB2,000 *yuan* per day per person for a medium conference, and RMB4,000 *yuan* per day per person for a large conference. 中型会议每位口译2 000元每天，大型会议4 000元每天。
- I will contact the interpreter now. 我现在就联系翻译官。
- I want to rent a conference room in your hotel. 我想在酒店租一个会议室。
- We will have a department meeting, and there will be 30 members altogether. 我们要开一个部门会议，共30人参会。

- What kind of facilities do you need? 您都需要什么设施？
- We need a computer, video projector and internet connection. 我们需要电脑、投影仪和网络连接。
- We have the meeting rooms you required. 我们有您要求的会议室。
- We have a small conference room for less than 30 people, a medium conference room for less than 60 people, and a large conference room for less than 100 people. 小型会议室可以容纳30人以下，中型会议室可以容纳60人以下，大型会议室可以容纳100人以下。
- Are all the rooms equipped with computer and the internet? 所有会议室都配有电脑和网络吗？
- They are different according to the size, equipment and duration. 区别和会议室大小，设备和使用时长有关。
- I want to rent a laptop computer. 我想租台笔记本电脑。
- Here is the laptop computer. Please check it. 这是笔记本电脑，请查看下。
- You have to pay RMB2,000 *yuan* as deposit. You will have the money back when you return the laptop computer. 您需要支付2 000元押金，押金在返还电脑时归还。
- And how would you like to pay the rent? 您怎么支付租金？
- Here is your receipt and here is the laptop computer. Please keep the receipt and show it when you return the laptop computer. 这是您的收据和笔记本电脑。请留好收据，归还笔记本电脑时请出示。
- Could you send someone to check it? I am so worried about it. 你能派人来看看吗？我很着急。
- Don't worry, madam, I'll send a technician there right away. 别担心，女士，我马上派技术人员过去。

Knowledge Extension

◆ Convention Service

Successfully preparing a meeting can test the working ability of a convention hotel and meeting planner. Convention service occurs before, during, and after the meeting. Convention service manager should keep communicating with the meeting planner, other individuals and departments. Three or six months before the meeting, guest room reservation information for meeting group should be recorded in the reservation system, including postal reply cards, rooming lists, a city housing bureau, toll-free numbers, meeting plans, meeting available facilities, and traffic matters, coordinating the staff's activities at the meeting, making a feasible budget or arranging related work in accordance with the established budget, determining the timing of all kinds of jobs, contacting with the parties concerned, and contacting with the conference speakers and distinguished guests and so on.

Service before the conference, the hotel convention service personal should be introduced to meeting planners at a meeting. The convention service manager should take charge of the set-up of meeting rooms and function rooms, which include exhibit halls, ballroom for banquets and conference rooms for meetings. Meetings perhaps call for breakfasts, luncheons, and dinners with entertainment or dancing. The refreshment breaks and cocktail receptions with beverage service and types of food are also provided.

Service during the conference means, if there are more guests than expected, the hotel convention service personal should prepare more cups than expected. They should be ready for desserts, tea, coffee and soft drinks during the refreshment break. They should raise or lower the air conditioning as guests like, or help a guest to make a multi-media presentation. Security in modern hotel is a big problem, which has four critical periods: move-in, open show hours, close show hours and move-out. They should make good preparations for other services, such as printing and duplication, decorations, reest packages, entertainment, telephone, convention hospitality suites, fashion shows, shopping trips, sight-seeing and city tours, etc.

Service after the conference includes paying bills, returning equipment, and evaluating the success or failure of the meeting.

◆ Meeting Agenda

A meeting agenda refers to the arrangements of different contents at the meeting, usually including the name of the meeting, meeting organizer, date, time, place, attendees, purpose, goals, introduction time, breakdown of objectives with description, time allocation, Q&A time, action item forms with description, date to complete and place for notes and so on. Here is an example.

Greeting U.S.A. Delegation
Agenda

1. Arriving
2. Visiting the Industrial Park
3. Meeting Room
4. Reports of Distinguished Guests
5. Tour for Qian Mountain
6. Lunch Dinner
7. Departure

8:00 a.m. Arrive
9:00 a.m. Visit the Industrial Park
10:00 a.m. Tour for Qian Mountain
12:00 Lunch
13:00 p.m. Departure

◆ Convention Reservation

Convention reservation includes ways of booking, which contains booking the conference on the phone, or on the spot, and the reception department, which contains the front office and the sales department. Some special attentions should be paid to conference scale or attendees, meeting types or the functions of meeting rooms, special requirements for conference facilities, special requirements for conference service, conference time, the requirements for housing, dining, rooms and restaurants and contact information of the other party.

- **Meeting Minutes**

Meeting minutes are an official record of things during the meeting, which must be accurate enough. It should include actions during the meeting and steps to be taken made before the meeting, the name of the organization, the type of the meeting, the purpose of the meeting and the time when the meeting begins and ends. Usually it uses past tense and contains thanks of the meeting presider and the decision of next meeting. After the meeting, the secretary should type it out as soon as possible. The following is an example.

December 10th, 2008

Human Resources Department
Meeting Minutes: Dec. 10th, 2008

Department Members:
Present/Attendees: Jack Smith, Rick Warner, Alex Lee, John Elmer Wolfe and Mary Smith.
Absent: Stella Willine
Minutes: The minutes of the November 2nd, 2008 special.
Proceedings/Action Items:
Jack Smith's Report: Analysing the present situation and predicting the future of the department.
John Elmer Wolfe's Report: Announcing the goals of development of the department.
Other Businesses:
Mary Smith's Speech: Reading some requirements of the department.
Meeting adjourned at 5:00 p.m..
Minutes submitted by Secretary, Mary Smith.

Section Summary

- Know about the working procedures of convention service.
- Learn about preparing a meeting.
- Know about meeting agenda.
- Learn about convention reservation.
- Know more about meeting minutes.

Practice

Part One Dialogue

1. Choose the correct sentences to fill in the blanks according to the context.

C: Clerk   G: Guest

C: Good morning, sir. Can I help you?

G: Yes. I'd like to book an air ticket to Beijing.

C: _____

G: Tomorrow morning about 10 o'clock.

C: There are 4 flights to Beijing tomorrow morning, exactly at 10 am. They are China Eastern Airline, JUNEYAO Airline and China Southern Airline. _____

G: I prefer Eastern Airline.

C: OK. _____

G: Business class.

C: _____

G: Here you are.

C: RMB1,080 *yuan*. _____

G: In cash. Here is the money.

C: Here is the change. Your flight is MU3852 at 10 tomorrow morning at Hongqiao International Airport. You can go to the airport check-in counter to get the boarding pass by showing your passport.

G: Thank you.

A. How would you like to pay?

B. When would you like to leave?

C. Which one do you prefer?

D. Economy class or business class?

E. May I have a look at your passport?

2. Act in pairs to finish the following role-play activities.

(1) Student A: Act as a guest. Go to the business center to rent a conference room.

Student B: Act as the business center clerk. Respond to the request of the guest.

(2) Student A: Act as a guest staying in the hotel room. Go to the business center to rent a digital camera.

Student B: Act as the business center clerk. Respond to the request of the guest.

(3) Student A: Act as a guest staying in the hotel room. Go to the business center to ask for an interpreter to accompany your family to have a tour in the city.

Student B: Act as the business center clerk. Respond to the request of the guest.

(4) Student A: Act as a guest in the conference room. Call the business center for help because the video projector suddenly broke down.

Student B: Act as the business center clerk. Respond to the request of the guest.

(5) Student A: Act as a guest in the hotel. Call the business center to book train tickets to Beijing.

Student B: Act as the business center clerk. Respond to the request of the guest.

3. Translate the following words into English.

(1) 投影仪

(2) 笔记本电脑

(3) 数据线

(4) 口译译员

(5) 桌牌

(6) 视听设备

(7) 可移动的

(8) 与会者

(9) 设备

(10) 商务中心

4. Discussion:

(1) What are the responsibilities of business center staff?

(2) Suppose you are a business center clerk, what will you do if the participants of the meeting exceed the seats of the conference room?

5. Translate the following sentences.

(1) 我想预订一个会议室召开部门会议。

(2) 我想租一台笔记本电脑。

(3) 请问会议室有网络吗?

(4) 电脑出故障了,你能派人来看看吗?

(5) 会议室有视听设备吗?

(6) 您需要支付 500 元押金。

(7) 请填写一下预订表。

(8) 您需要什么会议设施?

(9) 你们提供笔译服务吗?

(10) 我什么时候能拿到机票?

Part Two　Knowledge Extension

According to the part of Knowledge Extension, write the answers to the following questions on the sheet of paper by using your own words, not simply copying the sentences. When you have completed the test, ask your lecturer for the answers.

Convention Service

_____

_____

_____

_____

_____

_____

Meeting Agenda

Convention Reservation

Meeting Minutes

Section Five

Health and Recreation Center
康乐中心

模块五

Introduction

A health and recreation center plays a critical role in today's hotel industry. More and more hotels set up health and recreation centers, where many guests of all ages with different degrees of emotional and physical health go there. These health centers are equipped with superior items and facilities such as gymnasium, sauna and massage, swimming pool and tennis courts to do exercises for guests to relax themselves or enjoy nightlife. The recreation center organizes a variety of recreational and entertaining activities for guests focused on arts, sports and fitness, where there are all kinds of machinery, including treadmill and dumbbell. In a sports center or covered stadium are bowling, badminton, table tennis, snooker, tennis and golf. Health center attendants work there to welcome and serve guests. Recreation center can provide the guests with the places for dancing, drinking and dining to keep them relaxed.

Topic One Fitness Club Service
健身俱乐部服务

Introduction

A star hotel provides fitness club service for guests. The fitness clubs generally provide the guests in the hotel with free access to exercise equipment. Guests can do the following things, such as Pilates, aerobics, bodybuilding in fitness centers/studios/gyms, weight reducing, spas, sauna, Turkish baths, tanning salons, and similar things. In fitness clubs, there are some fitness attendants, who have an outgoing personality, knowledge of a fitness facility and physiology, love of fitness and the ability to serve the guests such as communicating well and teaching them well.

Objectives

Competence Standard	Knowledge Standard
Ability to acquire some knowledge about health club service	Know about the working procedures of health club service
Ability to know about health club	Know about health club
Ability to learn about facilities and services and personal training	Learn something about facilities and services in health clubs
Ability of listening, speaking and reading	Know about personal training in health club service

Working Procedures

- Greet the guests.
- Enquire the request of the guests.
- Respond to the request.
- Show facilities to the guests.
- Answer questions.
- Offer necessary help.

Dialogues

Dialogue 1

Situation Question: Do you know how to introduce the fitness machines to guests?

Introducing Facilities

C: Clerk   G: Guest

C: Good morning, sir, welcome to fitness center. How may I help you?

G: I want to know something about the facilities here. Could you tell me?

C: Certainly. The fitness club is well equipped with cutting-edge equipment like rowing machine, treadmill, and multifunctional fitness machine. They are very good aerobic exercise machines and strength training machines. Besides, guests can customize their workout plan here. We have special coaches to meet the exercise demands of the guests.

G: When do you open?

C: We open 24 hours a day.

G: That is good. Do you have ball games?

C: Yes, we have bowling room, snooker room and table tennis room. They are on the same floor.

G: How do you charge?

C: Generally, we don't charge for the guests staying in the hotel. For out-side guests, we charge differently according to apparatus and hours.

G: OK, I see. Thank you. I will come here tomorrow.

C: You are welcome. I am looking forward to serving you. Good-bye.

Notes:

(1) rowing machine 划船器

(2) treadmill 跑步机

(3) multifunctional fitness machine 多功能健身器材

(4) aerobic 有氧的

(5) customize 定做

(6) workout 体育锻炼

(7) coach 教练

(8) bowling 保龄球

(9) snooker 桌球

(10) apparatus 器械

Dialogue 2

Situation Question: Do you know how to offer help to the guests who meet some problems with the exercise machine?

Giving Help

C: Clerk   G: Guest

G: Excuse me, can you help me?

C: Yes, sir. What can I do for you?

G: I pressed the button, but the machine did not work.

C: Don't worry. Let me see. Sorry, sir. I think there is something wrong with the machine. Would you like to try something else? I will call for technician right away.

G: OK. But I don't know how to use this machine. Could you help me?

C: Oh, it is one of the latest running machines bought recently. It offers four modes for you to choose. They are summit trainer, elliptical trainer, exercise bike, and treadmill. Just press the button and select the mode suitable for you.

G: OK. I prefer to start from the moderate one.

C: Good. If there is anything else I can do for you, just call me. My name is David.

G: I will, thank you very much, David.

C: You are welcome. Enjoy your time.

Notes:

(1) button 按钮

(2) technician 技术人员

(3) latest 最新的

(4) mode 模式

(5) summit trainer 登山机

(6) elliptical trainer 空中漫步机

(7) moderate 适中的

Dialogue 3

Situation Question: Do you know how to respond to the guest's request to find a coach?

Getting a Coach

A: Attendant   G: Guest   C: Coach

A: Good afternoon, sir, welcome to the fitness center.

G: Good afternoon. Do you have coaches?

A: Yes. We have professional coaches for various sports. And they will assist the guests with planning and manage their sports. What sport are you interested in?

G: I am planning to play tennis. But I know little about it. So I hope to get professional instruction.

A: OK, I see. We have two tennis coaches here. One is male and the other is female. Both of them have very practical experience and good teaching methods.

G: I prefer the male coach. How do you charge for the service?

A: Are you staying in the hotel?

G: Yes. I am in Room 1609. My name is Black.

A: Good, Mr. Black. We don't charge the guests staying in the hotel for using the court. But the coach is RMB300 *yuan* per hour.

G: I see. Could you ask him to get here now. I want to arrange the time for playing tennis.

A: Sure. I will call him to get here at once.

(*After a while, the coach is here...*)

A: Mr. Black, this is the tennis coach, Mr. Wang.

G: Nice to meet you, Mr. Wang. I am Tom Black. Call me Tom, please.

C: Nice to meet you, Tom. Just call me John. And ....

Notes:

(1) coach 教练

(2) professional 专业的

(3) tennis 网球

(4) male 男性

(5) female 女性

(6) method 方法

Useful Sentences

- Good morning, sir. Welcome to the fitness center. How may I help you? 上午好，先生，欢迎光临健身中心。您有什么需要？
- I want to know something about the facilities here. 我想了解一下这里的设备。

- The fitness club is well equipped with cutting-edge equipment like rowing machine, treadmill, and multifunctional fitness machines. 我们健身中心配有最新的健身设施，像划船机、跑步机、多功能健身器等。
- They are very good aerobic exercise machines and strength training machines. 这些是很好的有氧运动器械和力量训练器械。
- Besides, guests can customize their workout plan here. 而且，在这儿客人可以定制锻炼方案。
- We have special coaches to meet the exercise demands of the guests. 我们有专门的教练满足客人需求。
- When do you open? 你们营业时间是什么时候？
- We open 24 hours a day. 我们全天24小时营业。
- We don't charge for the guests staying in the hotel. 住宿客人不收费。
- For out-side guests, we charge differently according to apparatus and hours. 非住宿客人，按照设施和使用时间收费。
- I pressed the button, but the machine did not work. 我按过按钮了，但是机器不启动。
- I will call for a technician right away. 我马上打电话叫技术人员过来。
- It is one of the latest running machines bought recently. 这是我们购置的最新款跑步机。
- I prefer to start from the moderate one. 我想从适中的运动模式开始。
- If there is anything else I can do for you, just call me. 如果有什么事情，请随时叫我。
- Do you have coaches? 你们有教练吗？
- We have professional coaches for various sports. 我们配有各项运动的专业教练。
- And they will assist the guests with planning and managing their sports. 教练会协助客人制定和管理锻炼。
- So I hope to get professional instruction. 我想得到专业指导。
- Both of them have very practical experience and good teaching methods. 他们两个都有非常丰富的实践经验和良好的教学方法。

Knowledge Extension

- ### Health Club

According to Wikipedia, a health club is a place that is equipped with exercise equipment with the purpose of physical exercise. The staff of a fitness club, which is also called fitness centre, health spa or simply a gym, can instruct and inspire the people in the club to start in the right way for exercising and improving physical fitness.

- ### Facilities and Services

Main Workout Area

In general, most health clubs have a main workout area, mainly including dumbbell, barbells and exercise machines. In order to maintain correct posture during their physical exercise, this area is often equipped with mirrors.

Cardio Area/Theatre

In a cardio area or theatre, there are many types of equipment related to cardiovascular training such as stationary exercise bikes, rowing machines, treadmills and elliptical trainers. Some audio-visual displays are placed on the walls or integrated into the equipment inside the areas so that the exercisers can be entertained and, at the same time, they can also keep exercising for a long time.

Group Exercise Classes

A majority of new health clubs set some exercise courses based on aerobics, which are provided by some qualified instructors, including boxing, cycling, spinning, high intensity training, Bikram yoga, Pilates, muscle training and swimming.

Sports Facilities

In health clubs, some sports facilities are provided and in some cases, if the exercisers use these facilities, they need to pay some additional fees such as boxing areas, swimming pools and squash courts. Some newer health clubs also offer such services as restaurants, health-shops, child-care facilities, snack bars, member lounges and cafes, where health clubs charge a fee.

◆ Personal Training

Most health clubs hire personal trainers for personal training. They can design a customized plan to meet the exercisers' personal needs including helping them achieve their goals. In normal conditions, hiring personal trainers needs to pay an additional hourly fee.

Section Summary

- Learn about the working procedures of health club service.
- Know about the health club.
- Acquire some knowledge about facilities and services.
- Know about personal training.

Practice

Part One Dialogue

1. Choose the correct sentences to fill in the blanks according to the context.

C: Clerk   G: Guest

C: Good morning, madam, can I help you?

G: Yes. _____

C: Yes. _____ Do you want to get one?

G: Yes. I am staying in the hotel and I will stay here for one month. I hope to practice yoga here every day. _____

C: Sure, I am glad to do that. _____

G: I prefer to have a personal coach. My working time is flexible so I can't attend the courses with others. By the way, how do you charge for that?

C: We don't charge the in-house guests for using the yoga room. The personal coach is RMB200 *yuan* per hour.

G: I see. Could you find one for me now? I want to talk with the coach about the timetable.

C: Certainly. Please wait a moment. _____

A. We have yoga rooms and professional coaches.

B. Do you want a personal coach or not?

C. Could you help me get a coach?

D. I will contact the coach at once.

E. Do you have a yoga room?

2. Act in pairs to finish the following role-play activities. Compensate necessary information.

(1) Student A: Act as a guest staying in the hotel room. Go to the fitness center to ask something about the facilities there.

Student B: Act as the clerk working in the fitness center. Respond to the request of the guest.

(2) Student A: Act as a guest in the fitness center. There is something wrong with the facility you are using. Ask the attendant for help.

Student B: Act as the clerk working in the fitness center. Respond to the request of the guest.

(3) Student A: Act as a guest staying in the hotel room. Go to the fitness center to find a table tennis coach.

Student B: Act as the clerk working in the fitness center. Respond to the request of the guest.

(4) Student A: Act as a guest staying in the hotel room. Go to the fitness center to get a VIP card.

Student B: Act as the clerk working in the fitness center. Respond to the request of the guest.

3. Look at the following items in a hotel room and translate them into English.

(1) 健身中心

(2) 教练

(3) 运动器械

(4) 跑步机

(5) 举重器械

(6) 进口器材

(7) 球馆

(8) 最新设施

(9) 有氧运动

(10) 专业指导

(11) 多功能设备

(12) 登山机

(13) 锻炼方案

(14) 贵宾卡

4. Discussion:

(1) What should you do as a fitness attendant if a drunken guest comes to the fitness center to do exercise?

(2) What information should you give to the guest who comes to the fitness center for the first time?

5. Translate the following sentences.

(1) 我们健身中心有最新的健身器械。

(2) 这些设备都是进口的。

(3) 你们什么时候营业?

(4) 我们上午 9 点到晚上 10 点营业。

(5) 我想找个瑜伽教练。

(6) 我们中心有专业的网球教练。

(7) 能介绍一下你们的健身器械吗?

(8) 我比较喜欢有氧运动。

(9) 请问您是中心的会员吗?

(10) 会员可以享受八折优惠。

Part Two Knowledge Extension

According to the part of Knowledge Extension, write the answers to the following questions on the sheet of paper by using your own words, not simply copying the sentences. When you have completed the test, ask your lecturer for the answers.

Health Club

_____
_____
_____
_____
_____
_____

Facilities and Services

_____
_____
_____

Personal Training

Topic Two Swimming Pool Service
游泳馆服务

Introduction

Some star hotels are equipped with swimming pool service. Swimming pools are fun for guests with family members because they can offer them a place to swim and relax. There are some professional trainers who teach them to learn swimming and some swimming pool service technicians in charge of doing general pool maintenance and serving major pool equipment such as pumps, motors, and filters. In the industry of swimming pool and spa, these technicians are also called "pool and spa service professionals".

Objectives

Competence Standard	Knowledge Standard
Ability to know something about swimming pool service	Know about the working procedures of swimming pool service
Ability to learn about the way of swimming	Know something about swimming pools
Ability to know about the general pool maintenance	Learn about the ways of swimming
Ability of listening, speaking and reading	Know about the general pool maintenance

Working Procedures

- Greet the guests.
- Enquire the request of the guests.
- Respond to the request.
- Show facilities to the guests (locker, shower and restroom).
- Answer questions.
- Offer necessary help.

Dialogues

Dialogue 1

Situation Question: As a clerk working in the swimming pool, do you know how to introduce the facilities to the guest?

【拓展音频】

Inquiring about the Facilities

S: Server   G: Guest

S: Good morning, sir. Welcome to the swimming pool.

G: Good morning. Could you tell me something about the swimming pool here?

S: Certainly, sir. Are you staying in the hotel?

G: Yes. It is the first time for me to stay in your hotel.

S: We don't charge for in-house guests. There are two kinds of swimming pool, one is for children, the other is for adults. The depth for adults is 2 meters, and for kids is less than half a meter. All the swimming pools are equipped with disinfection and circulation system and a heating system to keep clean and guarantee comfortable temperature for guests.

G: Good. How often do you change the water?

S: Because we have the disinfection and circulation system to keep the swimming pool clean, we change 20% of the pool water every day, which is higher than national standards.

G: How do you charge for non-in-house guests?

S: RMB350 *yuan* per person. But we have membership card, like monthly membership, quarterly membership and yearly membership.

G: OK, I see. Thank you for your service.

S: My pleasure.

Notes:

(1) in-house guest 住店客人

(2) adult 成年人

(3) depth 深度

(4) disinfection 消毒，杀菌

(5) circulation 循环

(6) guarantee 保证

(7) temperature 温度

(8) discount 折扣

Dialogue 2

Situation Question: Do you know how to show directions to the guest in the swimming center?

Showing the Way

S: Server   G1: Guest 1   G2: Guest 2

G1: Excuse me.

S: Good evening, sir. Can I help you?

G1: Yes. I forgot where my locker room is. Could you tell me?

S: Sure. The locker room is at both ends of the corridor. The locker room for gentlemen is on the left side, and for ladies is on the right side.

G1: Thanks.

S: You are welcome.

...

S: Good evening, madam, can I help you?

G2: Yes. I want to have a shower. Could you tell me where the shower room is?

S: Certainly. The shower room is next to the locker room. Please go straight and then turn right, you will find the locker room and shower room for ladies.

G2: Thank you for your help.

S: You are welcome.

Notes:

(1) locker room 更衣室

(2) corridor 走廊

(3) shower room 淋浴间

Dialogue 3

Situation Question: Do you know the names of swimming gears and how to give the price to the guests?

Service during Swimming

S: Server   G: Guest

S: Good afternoon, madam. Can I help you?

G: Do you have swimming suits for kids?

S: Yes. What size do you need?

G: I know nothing about the size. It is for an eight-year-old girl, my daughter.

S: We have two brands. Both of them are for eight to ten-year-old children. Please look at them.

G: How much are they?

S: This one is RMB400 *yuan*, and that one is RMB450 *yuan*.

G: Give me the pink one.

S: Is there anything else I can do for you?

G: Yes. A swimming cap and a pair of swimming goggles for her.

S: Here you are.

G: That's all. How much are they?

S: The swimming cap and swimming goggles are RMB200 and RMB600 *yuan* respectively. Add the pink swimming suit RMB400 *yuan*, so the total is RMB1,200 *yuan*.

G: OK. Here is the money. By the way, do you have swimming coach here?

S: Yes. We have professional swimming coaches.

G: Could you find one for my daughter?

S: Yes. Please wait for a moment. I will call for you.

G: Good. Thank you.

Notes:

(1) swimming suit 游泳衣

(2) swimming goggles 泳镜

(3) respectively 各自的

(4) professional coach 专业教练

Useful Sentences

- Could you tell me something of the swimming pool here? 你能跟我说说你们这儿的游泳池吗？
- We don't charge for in-house guests. 住宿客人不收费。
- There are two kinds of swimming pools, one is for children, the other is for adults. 这儿共有两种泳池，成人和儿童。
- The depth for adults is 2 meters, and for kids is less than half a meter. 成人泳池 2 米深，儿童泳池不到半米深。
- All the swimming pools are equipped with disinfection and a circulation system and a heating system to keep clean and guarantee comfortable temperature for guests. 泳池都配有消毒循环系统和供热系统，以保证水的清洁和舒适的水温。
- How often do you change the water? 你们多久换一次水？
- How do you charge for non-in-house guests? 非住宿客人游泳怎么收费？

- We have the membership card and it can offer discount for guests. 我们有会员卡可以为客人打折。
- Could you tell me where my locker room is? 能告诉我更衣室在哪儿吗？
- The locker room is at both ends of the corridor. 更衣室在走廊的尽头。
- The locker room for gentlemen is on the left side, and for ladies is on the right side. 男更衣室在左侧，女更衣室在右侧。
- Could you tell me where the shower room is？能告诉我淋浴间在哪儿吗？
- The shower room is next to the locker room. 淋浴间紧挨着更衣室。
- Please go straight and then turn right, you will find the locker room and shower room for ladies. 请直走然后右转，你会看到女更衣室和淋浴间。
- Thank you for your help. 谢谢你的帮助。
- Do you have swimming suits for kids? 你们有儿童泳装出售吗？
- What size do you need? 您需要多大号码的？
- It is for an eight-year-old girl, my daughter. 给我 8 岁的女儿穿的。
- Both of them are for eight to ten-years old children. Please look at them. 这两款都适合 8~10 岁儿童，请看一下。
- A swimming cap and a pair of swimming goggles for her. 给她一顶泳帽和一副泳镜。
- The swimming cap and swimming goggles are RMB200 *yuan* and RMB600 *yuan* respectively. 泳帽和泳镜分别是 200 元人民币和 600 元人民币。
- By the way, do you have swimming coach here? 顺便问一下，你们有游泳教练吗？
- Could you find a swimming coach for my daughter? 能帮我女儿找一位游泳教练吗？

Knowledge Extension

◆ Learning How to Swim

There are four steps in learning how to swim: getting comfortable in the water, beginning strokes and treading water, learning advanced techniques and being prepared for unlikely situations.

Getting Comfortable in the Water

Overcome your fear by not swimming alone, in moving water, in a depth you can not deal with, during the heavy weather or in too cold water. Get accustomed to floating by attempting to float on your back or your stomach as soon as you are prepared well. Remember not to be scared. Let you float on your back. In a shallow depth of water, take a deep breath and place your face under the water. Slowly breathe air until you are out of breath. Wear goggles under the water to make you see more clearly.

Beginning Strokes and Treading Water

When you can float on your back on the side of the pool, you should begin to learn kicking technique by attempting a flutter kick, a whip kick and an eggbeater kick. And then you should learn how to do a craw by trying a backstroke first and a front stroke. It is very important for you to learn treading water to help you catch your breath. Below water, you should attempt to use your arms to come up above the water from the bottom.

Learning Advanced Techniques

Once you feel more comfortable in the water, it's time for you to learn new advanced strokes by trying to learn the dolphin stroke, butterfly stroke, breaststroke, sidestroke, swimming laps and diving.

Being Prepared for Unlikely Situations

Be ready to deal with some situations that are impossible. For example, if you are swimming in the ocean, you might be caught in a rip current. You should learn how to get out of the trouble by not being scared and swimming directly to the shore or further into the ocean. Swimming in a stroke allows you to breathe or goes on swimming until you are out of the rip current when you can yell for help as loudly as you can. If you are caught in a river flowing too quickly or pushing you under the water, you should not panic, swim shoreline at a 90-degree angle or swim upstream. Point your feet in the direction that you are being carried to stop you from hitting your head on a rock or other obstruction.

♦ **General Pool Maintenance**

In general, the keys to swimming pool maintenance are cleaning the water of the pool and maintaining the chemical balance of water. Perform extra processing if the following situations occur, such as foul odor from the pool water, heavy rains and windstorms, more swimmers than usual, algae growth, extreme temperatures, murky and slimy water, or swimmers with burning and red eyes, including cleaning, balancing, chlorinating, shocking the pool or adding algaecide to the pool.

Section Summary

- Know about the working procedures of swimming pool service.
- Learn the ways of learning swimming.
- Know about the general pool maintenance.

Practice

Part One Dialogue

1. Choose the correct sentences to fill in the blanks according to the context.

S: Server   G: Guest

S: Good afternoon. Can I help you?

G: Yes. _____

S: We open from 9 a.m. to 10 p.m. every day, including weekends.

G: _____

S: It's about 26 degrees.

G: _____

S: The swimming pool for adults is 1.8 meters and 1meter for children.

G: How often do you change water?

S: _____

G: Good. _____

S: We have membership, and outside guests can buy them.

G: OK, I see. Thank you.

A. We usually change water every other day.

B. What's the depth?

C. What is the temperature now?

D. Do you have special offer for non-in-house guests?

E. What time does your swimming pool open?

2. Act in pairs to finish the following role-play activities.

(1) Student A: Act as a guest staying in the hotel. Go to the swimming pool to ask something about the facilities there.

Student B: Act as the clerk working in the swimming pool. Respond to the request of the guest.

(2) Student A: Act as a guest in the swimming pool. Ask directions for locker room and shower room.

Student B: Act as the clerk working in the swimming pool. Respond to the request of the guest.

(3) Student A: Act as a guest in the swimming pool. Go to the front desk to buy swimming tools and clothes.

Student B: Act as the clerk working in the swimming pool. Respond to the request of the guest.

(4) Student A: Act as a guest in the swimming pool. Go to the front desk to ask for a swimming coach for your kid.

Student B: Act as the clerk working in the swimming pool. Respond to the request of the guest.

3. Look at the following words and translate them into English.

(1) 游泳衣

(2) 泳镜

(3) 泳帽

(4) 游泳圈

(5) 拖鞋

(6) 浴巾

(7) 救生员

(8) 水温

(9) 更衣室

(10) 淋浴间

(11) 水深

(12) 卫生间

4. Discussion:

(1) What should you do when you greet guests in the swimming area?

(2) What should you do if a drunken guest comes to swim?

5. Translate the following sentences.

(1) 我们有室内外游泳池。

(2) 请出示您的房卡登记。

(3) 现在的水温是26℃左右。

(4) 泳池深多少?

(5) 我们有专职教练。

(6) 这是您的更衣室钥匙，请拿好。

(7) 请问淋浴间在哪儿?

(8) 我要买泳帽和泳镜。

(9) 住宿客人游泳不收费。

(10) 您可以办理会员卡，有月卡和年卡。

Part Two　Knowledge Extension

According to the part of Knowledge Extension, write the answers to the following questions on the sheet of paper by using your own words, not simply copying the sentences. When you have completed the test, ask your lecturer for the answers.

Learning How to Swim

General Pool Maintenance

Topic Three Night Club Service
夜总会服务

Introduction

Hotels usually provide night club service where guests in a hotel can relax and enjoy themselves. A night club, also called a nightclub or an entertainment venue, refers to an entertainment restaurant that works at night, the operating concept of which involves dancing with music, drinking alcohol and beverage and entertainment, which is a kind of licensed service with an entrance fee demanded under specific laws and regulations.

Objectives

Competence Standard	Knowledge Standard
Ability to know about night club service	Know about the working procedures of night club service
Ability to learn about entry criteria	Know something about entry criteria
Ability of listening, speaking and reading	Know something about night club

Working Procedures

- Greet the guests.
- Enquire the request of the guests.

- Respond to the request.
- Answer questions.
- Offer necessary help.

Dialogues

Dialogue 1

Situation Question: Do you know how to receive the guests who come to the KTV bar?

KTV Bar Service (1)

R: Receptionist   W: Waiter   G: Guest

R: Good evening, welcome to KTV bar. Can I help you?

G: Yes, we'd like a private room.

R: How many people is it for?

G: Six.

R: Are you an in-house guest or not?

G: I am staying in the hotel. Room 1612. Here is my room key.

R: According to the hotel regulation, we don't charge for the private room in KTV bar except drinks and beverages.

G: That's good.

R: All right, sir. Room 106 is a middle-sized room. It is big enough for 6 people. Please follow me. OK, here we are.

G: Thank you.

W: Good evening, gentlemen. I am your waiter, I am glad to be of your service. Here is the wine list. What would you like to have?

G: We'd like a dozen Heineken and some snacks, say, a bag of popcorn, a bag of chips and some dry fruit.

W: A dozen of Heineken and a bag of popcorn and chips respectively. Anything else?

G: No.

W: Please wait a moment. I will be back soon.

Notes:

(1) private room 包房

(2) regulation 规定

(3) wine list 酒水单

(4) Heineken 喜力（荷兰啤酒品牌）

(5) dozen 十二个

(6) popcorn 爆米花

(7) chips 薯条

Dialogue 2

Situation Question: Do you know how to recommend wine to guests in the KTV bar?

KTV Bar Service (2)

【拓展音频】

W: Waiter   G1: Guest 1   G2: Guest 2

W: Here is the beer you ordered. And here are the popcorn and chips. Please enjoy your time.

G1: Excuse me, waiter?

W: At your service, sir.

G1: Could you tell us how to order songs with this machine?

W: Sure. This song-order machine is of touch screen, so just use it like a smart phone. Choose the songs according to the category. All the songs under each category are arranged according to alphabetic order of their names.

G1: OK. I see. Thank you.

W: You are welcome.

...

G2: Excuse me, waiter.

W: Yes, sir. What can I do for you?

G2: I want to have some liquor, could you recommend any for me?

W: Sure. We have whisky, brandy and vodka imported from foreign countries. Which one would you like?

G2: I like a bottle of whisky.

W: With or without ice?

G2: With ice.

W: Please wait a moment. Here are the whisky and ice.

G2: Thank you.

Notes:

(1) song-order machine 点歌机

(2) touch screen 触屏

(3) smart phone 智能手机

(4) alphabetic order 字母顺序

Dialogue 3

Situation Question: Do you know how to help the guests settle the account?

KTV Service (3)

W: Waiter   G: Guest   C: Cashier

G: Excuse me, waiter?

W: Yes, sir. What can I do for you?

G: I want to pay the bill.

W: Please wait a moment, I will get the bill right away. Here is the bill, sir. The total is RMB2,000 *yuan*. Please have a look at it.

G: What's this, the 200 *yuan*?

W: This is the money for the cigarette. And this 300 *yuan* is for the snacks and the rest 1,500 *yuan* is for drinks.

G: OK. I see.

W: Please go to the cashier to pay the bill. The cashier is on the first floor, just beside the front desk.

(*After the guests leave the room, the waiter notices a cell phone left by one guest, and he hurries to the first floor.*)

W: Please wait a moment, sir. This is a cell phone left by one of your friend.

G: Thank you so much. I will give it to him.

W: You are welcome.

C: Good evening, the total is RMB2,000 *yuan*. How would you like to pay?

G: By credit card. Here you are.

C: Please sign your name here. This is your receipt and credit card.

Notes:

(1) cigarette 香烟

(2) cashier 收银员

Dialogue 4

Situation Question: Do you know how to recommend shows to guests?

Talk about Shows

R: Receptionist   G: Guest

R: Good evening, madam, can I help you?

G: Yes. I heard there would be some shows tonight. What kind of shows are they?

R: Tonight there will be Beijing Opera and song and dance opera.

G: I don't think that my kids will like them. Is there anything else?

R: If you would like to watch a show with your children, I recommend you to come tomorrow evening. At that time there will be a children's play—*Snow White*, which is particularly arranged for children. You know, Children's Day is coming.

G: But I don't think my children can understand the play in Chinese.

R: Don't worry. Actually it is a play in English, and a lot of Chinese parents come with their children to watch it. They want to practice English more.

G: That's good. What time is the play?

R: At 7:00 o'clock tomorrow evening. Would you like to reserve?

G: Yes, a table for three.

R: Are you staying in the hotel?

G: Yes. I am in room 802, and my name is Judy Bird.

R: OK, Mrs. Bird, a table for three for tomorrow's play. See you tomorrow.

G: See you.

Notes:

(1) show 表演

(2) Beijing Opera 京剧

(3) song and dance opera 歌舞剧

(4) Children's Day 儿童节

Useful Sentences

- Good evening, welcome to KTV bar. Can I help you? 晚上好，欢迎光临 KTV，需要为您做些什么吗？
- Yes, we'd like a private room. 是的，我们要间包房。
- How many people is it for? 一共多少人？
- Are you an in-house guest or not? 您是住宿客人吗？
- According to the hotel regulation, we don't charge for the private room in KTV bar except drinks and beverages for registered guests. 按照酒店规定，住宿客人 KTV 包房不收费，不含酒水。
- Room 106 is a middle-sized room. It is big enough for 6 people. Please follow me. 106 号包房中等大小，足够 6 个人。请随我来。
- I am your waiter, and I am glad to be of your service. 我是各位的服务员，很高兴为各位服务。
- Here is the wine list. What would you like to have? 这是酒水单，您想喝点什么？
- We'd like a dozen of Heineken and some snacks, say, a bag of popcorn, a bag of chips and some dry fruit. 我们要一打喜力啤酒和一些小吃，比如一包爆米花、一袋薯片和一些坚果。
- Could you tell us how to order songs with this machine? 你能告诉我们怎么用点歌机点歌吗？

- This song-order machine is of touch screen, so just use it like a smart phone. 点歌机是触屏的，就像智能手机的用法一样。
- Choose the songs according to the category. All the songs under each category are arranged according to the alphabetic order of their names. 根据类别选歌。每类下的歌曲是按照字母顺序排列的。
- I want to have some liquor. Could you recommend? 我想来点烈酒，您能推荐一下吗？
- We have whisky, brandy and vodka imported from foreign countries. Which one would you like? 我们有威士忌、白兰地和伏特加，全部从外国进口。您想要哪一种？
- Please wait a moment. I will get the bill right away. 请稍等，我马上去取。
- This is the money for the cigarette. And this 300 *yuan* is for the snacks and the rest 1,500 *yuan* is for drinks. 这是香烟的费用，这300元是小吃的费用，其余1 500元是酒水费用。
- Please go to the cashier to pay the bill. The cashier is on the first floor, just beside the front desk. 请去收银台结账。收银台在一楼前台旁边。
- What kind of shows are they? 他们在表演什么？
- Tonight there will be Beijing Opera as well as a song and dance opera. 今晚是京剧和歌舞剧表演。
- If you would like to watch a show with your children, I recommend you to come tomorrow evening. At that time there will be a children's play—*Snow White*. 如果您想和孩子观看演出，我建议您明晚来，届时会有儿童剧《白雪公主》。

Knowledge Extension

- ### Entry Criteria

Many nightclubs use bouncers to select the people who enter into a night club. Some expensive night clubs employ a group of bouncers to screen clients for entry to the main door. Some bouncers are sent to VIP areas, lounges and dance floors to check cliens' IDs. to see whether the prospective patrons are of legal drinking age and are not drunk. The bouncers in high-end and expensive nightclubs can screen patrons by using other criteria besides legal drinking age and not being drunk. The type of screening criteria varies in different nightclubs because dress standards vary in different nightclubs.

Cover Charge

Cover charge is a flat fee used for entering a nightclub. Early arrives can reduce the cover charge. Friends of the bouncers or the club owner can enjoy free entrance. At times, entrance fee and cloakroom expenses can be paid by cash. Only the drinks in the club can be paid by a pay card.

Guest List

Some clubs provide the chance for guests to sign up on their guest list, which can bring some benefits such as free entry, free drinks, discounted cover charge and the ability of skipping the line.

Dress Code

For the purpose of keeping a certain type of clients in the club, or preventing attendees from wearing trainers, sneakers or jeans, many nightclubs uniform a dress code. But there are also many exceptions.

◆ Exclusive Boutique Clubs

There are two features of this type clubs:

One is that there are less than 200 occupants and a very strict policy for entry, which requires an entrant must be on the club's guest list. Usually many celebrities favor this type of clubs. The other feature of exclusive nightclubs is that, besides being famous for a certain type of music, they are famous for some types of crowd, for example, fashion-forward, affluent or fashion models.

Section Summary

- Know about the working procedures of night club service.
- Know something about entry criteria.

Practice

Part One Dialogue

1. Choose the correct sentences to fill in the blanks according to the context.

W: Waiter   G: Guest

G: Excuse me, waiter?

W: Yes, madam. _____

G: Can I request a song here?

W: Sure. _____

G: Actually, I know nothing about Chinese songs. But today is one of my friends' big day. She has just won the first prize of a competition. So I want to request a song to congratulate her. But I prefer a Chinese song. _____

W: No problem. Do we need to mention her name?

G: Of course. _____

W: _____

G: At 8:30. She will be here then.

W: OK. I see.

A. Her name is Joyce Lee.
B. What can I do for you?
C. At what time do you need the song?
D. What song would you like?
E. Could you help me?

2. Act in pairs to finish the following role-play activities.

(1) Student A: Act as a guest in the night club. You and two friends go to KTV bar. Book a private room.

Student B: Act as the receptionist of the front desk of KTV bar and respond to the request of the guests.

(2) Student A: Act as a guest in the night club. You and two friends go to KTV bar. Order some drinks and ask the waiter to help you order songs.

Student B: Act as the waiter and respond to the request of the guests.

(3) Student A: Act as a guest in KTV bar. Ask the bill from the waiter and ask the waiter to explain the bill.

Student B: Act as the waiter and respond to the request of the guests.

(4) Student A: Act as a guest in the night club. You and two friends go to watch a show for tonight. But you are told the show is canceled.

Student B: Act as the receptionist at the front desk of the night club. Tell the guests the show is canceled and explain reasons.

3. Translate the following words into English.

(1) 歌舞剧

(2) 木偶剧

(3) 儿童剧

(4) 京剧

(5) 点歌机

(6) 烈性酒

(7) 鸡尾酒

(8) 演出

(9) 取消

(10) 音乐剧

4. Discussion:

(1) What are the working procedures of the waiter in the KTV bar?

(2) What should you do if guests complain to you about the song library in the KTV bar where you work as a waiter?

5. Translate the following sentences.

(1) 您能给我推荐一下今晚的表演吗？

(2) 表演什么时候开始？

(3) 多少钱一张票？

(4) 住宿客人点歌收费吗？

(5) 抱歉，点歌机坏了。

(6) 住宿客人只收饮料费，不收包房费。

(7) 请问明晚的演出还有位子吗？

(8) 谢谢您给我们提的意见。

(9) 很高兴为您服务。

(10) 请在收银台结账。

Part Two Knowledge Extension

According to the part of Knowledge Extension, write the answers to the following questions on the sheet of paper by using your own words, not simply copying the sentences. When you have completed the test, ask your lecturer for the answers.

Entry Criteria

___

Cover Charge

___

Guest List

___

Dress Code

___

Exclusive Boutique Clubs

___

Section Five 模块五
Health and Recreation Center 康乐中心

Topic Four Bath Service 洗浴服务

Introduction

The health and recreation center of a hotel is equipped with bath service. Guests in a hotel can take a bath or have a bath in a bath center, a bathroom or a bathtub for cleaning and refreshment, etc. The attendants usually provide guests with considerate service, such as exfoliating, scrubbing their back, shaving their legs and so on. People can go to a river, lake, water hole, pool or the sea for a bathing. Bathing refers to the washing of the body with a liquid, such as water and milk, etc. There are several types of baths. In public bathing situations, some people wear a swimsuit or underwear. Usually, people bathing is for personal hygiene. And bathing can also improve the social interactions when they are taking a bath, sauna, or massage.

Objectives

Competence Standard	Knowledge Standard
Ability to know something about bath service	Know about the working procedures of bath service
Ability to know about types of baths and clothing in bathing	Learn the types of baths and clothing of bathing
Ability to learn about benefits of sweating in a sauna or massage	Learn about the benefits of sweating in a sauna
Ability of listening, speaking and reading	Know something about massage

Working Procedures

- Greet the guests.
- Enquire the request of the guests.
- Respond to the request.
- Answer questions.
- Offer necessary help.

Dialogues

Dialogue 1

Situation Question: Do you know how to introduce the facilities of the bath center?

【拓展音频】

Introducing Facilities

R: Receptionist　　G: Guest

R: Good morning, welcome to the recreation center. How many people do you have?

G: Three in all.

R: What service would you like to choose today?

G: Could you introduce your facilities to us first, and then we will decide.

R: Certainly. We have shower, sauna, massage and spa services for our guests. They are on different floors.

G: We want to know something about sauna and massage service.

R: There are two kinds of sauna. One is dry sauna and the other is steam sauna. Both of them are good ways to relieve fatigue and improve one's health. But sauna is not suitable for the people with heart disease and high blood pressure. The change of temperature may cause the disease worse.

G: OK. I see. How about the massage service?

R: Massage is the popular way to relax which can reduce pain and fatigue. We have back massage, foot massage and full body massage. You can choose the one you like.

G: Thank you for your introduction.

R: You are welcome. Now, what would you like to choose?

Notes:

(1) recreation center 康乐中心
(2) sauna 桑拿浴
(3) massage 按摩
(4) spa 水疗
(5) relieve 缓解

(6) fatigue 疲劳

(7) heart disease 心脏病

(8) high blood pressure 高血压

Dialogue 2

Situation Question: Do you know how to introduce spa service to the guests as a receptionist of the recreation center?

Spa Service

R: Receptionist   G: Guest

R: Good afternoon, madam. Welcome to the recreation center. Can I help you?

G: Yes. I want to know something about your spa service. Could you tell me about it?

R: Sure. Spa service is one of the most popular services in the center. We have mineral spring spa, medical spa and natural essential oil spa etc. After enjoying spa service, you will get full relaxation and recovery of physical function.

G: Is it suitable for all the people?

R: Actually not. Some kinds of spa are not suitable for pregnant women and the people with heart disease.

G: Do I need to reserve it in advance?

R: Yes, you need to reserve it in advance. But it is very simple. Just call us 30 minutes earlier.

G: How do you charge for the service?

R: It depends on the service category. Here is the price list. Please have a look at it.

G: OK. I would like to try the natural essential oil spa.

R: This way, please. The attendant will show you the way.

Notes:

(1) mineral spring water 矿泉水

(2) natural essential oil 天然精油

(3) pregnant woman 孕妇

(4) category 类别

(5) price list 价目单

Dialogue 3

Situation Question: Do you know the procedure of receiving guests in the recreation center?

Reception Service

R: Receptionist   G1: Guest 1   G2: Guest 2

R: Good evening. Welcome to recreation center. Can I help you?

G1: I want to have a shower and sauna.

R: We have dry sauna and steam sauna. Which one would you like?

G1: Steam sauna.

R: Good. How would you like to pay?

G1: Put it on the room.

R: May I have your name and room number?

G1: My name is Bob Lee and I am in Room 1612.

R: Do you have a reservation?

G1: No.

R: Mr. Lee, please change your slippers.

G1: Here are my shoes.

R: Here is your tag. Please keep it and give it back to get your shoes. By the way, would you like to shine your shoes?

G1: No, thank you.

R: The shower room is on the first floor and massage room is on the second floor. This way please. Here we are, Mr. Lee. Here is the changing room. Please go ahead. The attendant will be your service there.

G1: Thank you.

R: You are welcome. Enjoy your time.

...

R: Good evening, can I help you?

G2: I'd like to pay the bill.

R: Could you show me your tag?

G2: Here you are.

R: Here are your shoes. The cashier is over here. Please pay the bill there.

G2: OK.

Notes:

(1) slipper 拖鞋

(2) shine shoes 擦鞋

(3) cashier 收银员

Useful Sentences

- Good morning, welcome to recreation center. How many people do you have? 早上好，欢迎光临康乐中心。请问你们一共几位？
- What service would you like to choose today? 您今天选择什么服务？
- Could you introduce your facility to us first? 能先介绍下你们的服务设施吗？
- We have shower, sauna, massage and spa service for our guests. They are on different floors. 我们有淋浴、桑拿浴、按摩和水疗，分别在不同的楼层。

Section Five 模块五

Health and Recreation Center 康乐中心

- We want to know something about sauna and massage service. 我想先了解一下桑拿和按摩。
- There are two kinds of sauna. One is dry sauna and the other is steam sauna. 桑拿浴有两种，干蒸汽浴和湿蒸汽浴。
- Both of them are good ways to relieve fatigue and improve one's health. 这两种都是缓解疲劳、改善健康的好方法。
- But sauna is not suitable for the people with heart disease and high blood pressure. The change of temperature may cause the disease worse. 但是桑拿浴不适合有心脏病和高血压的人，温度的变化会使病情加重。
- Massage is the popular way to relax which can reduce pain and fatigue. 按摩是很受欢迎的放松、减轻疼痛及疲劳的方式。
- We have back massage, foot massage and full body massage. 我们有背部按摩、足底按摩和全身按摩。
- Spa service is one of the most popular services in the center. 水疗服务是本中心最受欢迎的服务之一。
- We have mineral spring spa, medical spa and natural essential oil spa etc. 水疗有矿泉水、药物和天然精油等类型。
- After enjoying spa service, you will get full relax and full recovery of physical function. 水疗后，您会得到充分放松并且恢复体力。
- Some kinds of spa are not suitable for pregnant women and the people with heart disease. 有些水疗不适合孕妇和心脏病人。
- Do I need to reserve it in advance? 我需要事先预订吗？
- You need to reserve it in advance. But it is very simple. Just call us 30 minutes earlier. 你需要事先预订，但是很简单，只需提前30分钟给我们打电话就行。
- It depends on the service category. Here is the price list. Please have a look at it. 费用取决于服务类别。请看这份价目表。
- This way, please. The attendant will show you the way. 这边请，服务员会给您带路。
- We have dry sauna and steam sauna, which one would you like? 干蒸汽浴和湿蒸汽浴，您选哪一种？
- Here is your tag. Please keep it and give it back to get your shoes. 这是您的手牌，请拿好，凭手牌取鞋。
- By the way, would you like to shine your shoes? 顺便问一下，您需要擦鞋吗？
- The attendant will be your service there. 那儿会有服务员为您服务。

Knowledge Extension

- ## Types of Baths

In Western and many Eastern countries, specially in modern home, taking a bath or a shower in a bathtub is the most common form of bathing. In the bathroom, there is a tap, a bucket and a huge water pot. Heat the water in the pot, pour the water into a bucket and then on themselves in their home or use a private bath in a public bathhouse.

Sponge Bath

When a person is short of water or a standing bath is not fit for him, he usually uses a wet cloth or sponge material, or the person can wash by using the splashing water over his body.

◆ Clothing

Normally, people are completely naked when bathing so as to keep every part of their body clean no matter in private baths, in one's home or in a public bathhouse. In public bathing situations, some people wear an underwear or swimsuit based on the different social norm of the community. In a non-sex segregated area of a public swimming pool, people take a shower wearing their swimsuit. The customs can vary on the age of a person. In some communal bathing situations, people bathe without clothing no matter whether it is in a segregated situation or not and when swimming, some people do that without any clothing.

◆ Benefits of Sweating in a Sauna

In today's society, many people like to take a sauna after a day's hard work to have a good rest, so sauna is more and more popular, which has many benefits. Sweating in a sauna is one of the benefits of sauna, which can help detoxify your tissues. This kind of perspiration and detoxification can make you relaxed and lower your body's natural responses to pressure, which is beneficial to your heart and body organs and makes you feel lighter and more energetic.

◆ Massage

Generally speaking, massage is for the purpose of treating body pressure and pain by people professionally trained, with their hands, fingers, knees, elbows, forearm, feet or a device to work and act on the body with pressure. Massage can be done on different occasions such as in a massage chair, on a massage table, on a mat on the floor, on a bed or in a warm-water therapy pool.

Section Summary

- Know about the working procedures of bath service.
- Know about types of baths.
- Learn something about clothing in bathing.
- Acquire some knowledge about benefits of sweating in a sauna.
- Know about massage.

Practice

Part One Dialogue

1. Choose the correct sentences to fill in the blanks according to the context.

R: Receptionist   G: Guest

R: Good evening. Welcome to recreation center. Can I help you?

G: _____

R: We have back massage, foot massage and full body massage. _____

G: I hope massage can relieve fatigue and make me relaxed. I really feel tired recently and I need relaxation.

R: OK, in that case, _____ We have very good massage therapists. They will help you have a good relaxation.

G: Good. _____

R: Certainly. Please change your slippers.

G: Here are my shoes.

R: _____ And follow me.

A. Please keep your tag.

B. Please arrange a good massagist for me.

C. Which one would you like?

D. I suggest you choose full body massage.

E. I would like to have massage.

2. Act in pairs to finish the following role-play activities.

(1) Student A: Act as a guest staying in the hotel. Go to the recreation center to have a bath and massage.

Student B: Act as the receptionist in the recreation center. Respond to the request of the guest.

(2) Student A: Act as a guest in the recreation center. Ask something about spa service there.

Student B: Act as the receptionist in the recreation center. Respond to the request of the guest.

(3) Student A: Act as a guest in the recreation center. You want to have a sauna but your kid doesn't want to. Ask the receptionist for help.

Student B: Act as the receptionist in the recreation center. Respond to the request of the guest.

(4) Student A: Act as a guest in the recreation center. After sauna and spa, you go to the front desk to pay the bill.

Student B: Act as the receptionist in the recreation center. Respond to the request of the guest.

3. Read the following and translate them into Chinese or English.

(1) massage

(2) sauna

(3) spa

(4) heart disease

(5) high blood pressure

(6) 桑拿房

(7) 按摩浴缸

(8) 蒸汽

(9) 缓解疲劳

(10) 减轻疼痛

4. Discussion:

(1) How would you help the guests to pay the bill in the recreation center? Discuss with your partner.

(2) What should you remind the guests before having sauna?

5. Translate the following sentences.

(1) 我们有桑拿浴、按摩和水疗。

(2) 它们都有助于放松身体，减缓疲劳。

(3) 水疗有药物的和精油的，您选哪一种？

(4) 我们有非常好的按摩师。

(5) 心脏病和高血压患者不可以洗桑拿浴。

(6) 水疗的好处是什么？

(7) 您需要哪一种按摩？

(8) 您需要背部按摩还是全身按摩？

(9) 您需要擦鞋吗？

(10) 这是价目表，请过目。

Part Two Knowledge Extension

According to the part of Knowledge Extension, write the answers to the following questions on the sheet of paper by using your own words, not simply copying the sentences. When you have completed the test, ask your lecturer for the answers.

Types of Baths

_____
_____
_____
_____
_____
_____
_____
_____

Section Five 模块五
Health and Recreation Center 康乐中心

Clothing

_____
_____
_____
_____

Benefits of Sweating in a Sauna

_____
_____
_____
_____

Massage

_____
_____
_____
_____
_____

Section Six

Other Hotel Services
其他酒店服务

模块六

Introduction

In order to provide occupancy, hotels often offer many different services such as safe deposit box rental, television and in-room movies, fax service, copy service, room service, operator service and hotel shop service, etc.

Section Six 模块六
Other Hotel Services 其他酒店服务

Topic One Operator Service 话务服务

Introduction

Although the hotel operator may never be seen, he/she serves as an important part because they often contact guests. The operator must handle all the in-house, local, person-to-person, station, collect and long-distance phone calls. Many guests, especially business travelers, rely on the hotel operator for wake-up calls, and for important messages from outside callers. Operators must also be ready to deal with urgent matters at all times on behalf of the hotel or the guests.

Objectives

Competence Standard	Knowledge Standard
Ability to provide operator service	Know about the working procedures of operator service
Ability to learn about simple, efficient operator service and etiquette of transferring calls	Learn about simple, and efficient operator service
Ability to know about person-to-person, station, collect and long-distance calls	Learn about the proper etiquette of transferring calls
Ability of listening, speaking and reading	Know about person-to-person, station, collect and long-distance calls

Working Procedures

- Answer the phone.
- Greet the guests.
- Enquire the request of the guests.
- Respond to the request.
  Transfer phone calls.
  Offer wake-up call service.
  Take messages.
- Thank the guests for calling.

Dialogues

Dialogue 1

Situation Question: Do you know how to help the guests transfer their phone calls as an operator?

【拓展音频】

Transfer Phone Calls

O: Operator   C1: Caller 1   C2: Caller 2

O: Good morning, Great Wall Hotel, can I help you?

C1: Yes, could you put me through to Room 1609?

O: Could you tell me who you want to speak to?

C1: John Black. I am his colleague. I am calling from London.

O: OK, I will put you through at once. Sorry, sir. There is no reply from Room 16009. Would you like to leave a message?

C1: Yes. This is Henry Smith from London. Please tell John Black that I will come to meet him on Thursday. My plane is due to land at Hongqiao International Airport at 11:30 July 8th. I hope he could meet me there.

O: May I have your phone number?

C1: He has it.

O: OK, Mr. Smith, I will pass your message on to Mr. Black. Thank you for calling. Good bye.

...

O: Good morning, Great Wall Hotel, can I help you?

C2: Could you put me through to room 1218?

O: Yes, please hold on. Sorry, madam, the line is engaged. Could you call later?

C2: OK. I will call later. Thank you.

O: Thank you for calling. Good-bye.

Notes:

(1) put through 接通电话

(2) due 到期，到时

(3) engaged 使用中的，忙碌的

Dialogue 2

Situation Question: Do you know how to help the in-house guests to call from the hotel?

Incoming Calls

O: Operator   G: Guest

O: Thank you for calling the service center, how may I help you?

G: I want to call a friend in the hotel. Could you tell me how to do it?

O: Sure. Just dial the room number of your friend.

G: OK. I see. By the way, how can I call my friend in the city?

O: Please dial 9 first, and then dial the number you want.

G: Could you help get the telephone of City Theater? I need to book tickets.

O: Please wait a moment, madam. Madam, please take the number down. It is 12345678. And if you want to book tickets, you can do it online, or call the business center of the hotel. There is ticket booking service in the business center.

G: OK. Thank you. Could you give the phone number of business center?

O: Yes, it's 23412356.

G: Thank you very much.

O: You are welcome. Good-bye.

G: Good-bye.

Notes:

(1) dial 拨号

(2) theatre 剧院

Dialogue 3

Situation Question: Do you know how to help guests make long-distance calls?

Long-Distance Calls

O: Operator   G: Guest

O: Good evening, thank you for calling the service center. Can I help you?

G: Good evening. I want to call back my company in New York. Can you help me?

O: Is it a collect call or a pay call?

G: Pay call.

O: May I have your name and room number?

G: My name is David White in room 1003.

O: Could you tell me the number you want to call, including area code?

G: The number is 212-12345678.

O: May I have the name of the person you are calling?

G: Alan Cook.

O: Thank you. Please hang up now and we will contact him and call you back.

(*After a while*)

G: Hello?

O: Is that Mr. White speaking?

G: Yes.

O: Mr. White, Mr. Cook is on the line. Please go ahead.

G: Thanks.

Notes:

(1) collect call 对方付费电话

(2) pay call 自费电话

(3) area code 电话地区号

(4) hang up 挂断电话

(5) contact 联系，联络

Useful Sentences

- Good morning, Great Wall Hotel, can I help you? 上午好，长城酒店，我能帮您什么吗？
- Could you put me through to Room 1609? 能帮我接通 1609 号房间吗？
- Could you tell me who you want to speak to? 能告诉我您要和谁通话吗？
- John Black. I am his colleague. I am calling from London. 我找约翰·布莱克，我是他的同事，从伦敦打来电话。
- I will put you through at once. 立刻为您接通。
- Sorry, sir. There is no reply from Room 1609. Would you like to leave a message? 抱歉，先生。1609 号房间无人接听。您需要留言吗？
- Mr. Smith, I will pass your message on to Mr. Black. Thank you for calling. 史密斯先生，我会将留言传递给布莱克先生的。感谢您的来电。
- Sorry, madam, the line is engaged. Could you call later? 抱歉，女士，电话占线。您能否稍后再打过来？
- Thank you for calling service center. How may I help you? 谢谢致电服务中心，我能帮您什么吗？

- I want to call a friend in the hotel. Could you tell me how to do that? 我想给在酒店的一个朋友打电话，该怎么拨号？
- Sure. Just dial the room number of your friend. 当然。直接拨您朋友的房间号即可。
- Please dial 9 first, and then dial the number you want. 请先拨9，然后拨您要呼叫的号码。
- Madam, please take the number down, it's. ... 女士，请记录，电话号码是……
- Could you give the phone number of the business center? 能否给我商务中心的电话号码？
- I want to call back my company in New York. Can you help me? 我想给纽约公司打电话，你能帮我一下吗？
- Is it a collect call or a pay call? 是对方付费电话还是自费电话？
- Could you tell me the number you want to call, including area code? 请告诉我您要呼叫的电话号码，包括区号。
- May I have the name of the person you are calling? 请告诉我您要和谁通话？
- Please hang up now and we will contact him and call you back. 请先挂断电话，我们立即联系对方然后给您回电。
- Mr. White, Mr. Cook is on the line. Please go ahead. 怀特先生，库克先生在线，请讲话。

Knowledge Extension

◆ Operator Service Is Simple

The responsibility of hotel staff is to offer guests services quickly and efficiently. Operators provide a kind of simple, fast, excellent and efficient service, which will make the stay of guests in a hotel convenient and comfortable.

Ready-made and easy to use. You can get started with our operator services right away for free which you can use any infrastructures, equipment or support resource. Operators can cope with everything for guests in a hotel, so guests can enjoy easy access to national and international calling assistance at any time.

◆ Proper Etiquette of Transferring Calls

Proper etiquette of transferring calls is extremely important. In order to left callers have a pleasant experience and avoid mistakes made by the automated attendants, follow the steps below.

Listening to the callers in an active manner can help you determine the way that you help them best.

Using your active listening techniques, listen to the callers' needs and determine how you can best help them.

Offer the information of the persons transferred to, such as name, and telephone number to avoid their getting disconnected and need to call back in.

Update the caller information in your computer system to avoid repeating the same information they need to deal with the call.

Start the transfer and keep in touch with the caller on line until the call is answered.

Announce you need to transfer the caller to the new person and explain why you transfer the call. At the same time you offer them as much information as you can before entering into the computer system.

Say goodbye to the caller and thank them for calling and complete the transfer.

◆ **Person-to-person Calls**

A person-to-person calls refer to the call with the person whose name is designated by an operator. The telephone is not charged when the designated receiver is not in or is not yet connected. However, the efficiency of this kind of call is higher in unit time.

◆ **Station Calls (Station-to-station Calls)**

The charge of a station call is cheaper than that of a person-to-person call. The caller agrees to talk to anyone who is answering the phone. If the telephone is connected, the long-distance charges will begin.

◆ **Collect Calls (Reverse Charge Calls)**

Collect calls can be got through only after the operator asks for the advice of the other person if he/she is willing to pay for it. The charge is the same with the person calling.

◆ **Long-Distance Calls**

A long-distance call refers to a telephone call which is made to a place outside a defined local calling area in telecommunications, the charges of which are higher than that of local calls.

Section Summary

- Know about the working procedures of operator service.
- Know about fast, simple and efficient operator service.
- Learn about the proper etiquettes of transferring calls.
- Learn some information about person-to-person calls.
- Learn some information about station calls.
- Learn some information about collect calls.
- Learn some information about long-distance calls.

Practice

Part One Dialogue

1. Choose the correct sentences to fill in the blanks according to the context.

O: Operator   C: Caller

O: Good morning, Great Wall Hotel. Can I help you?

C: _____

O: Could you tell me the room number of Mr. Johnson?

C: _____

O: What's the full name of Mr. Johnson?

C: _____

O: _____

C: This is Mike Wong from New York.

O: OK, Mr. Wong, please wait a moment. Let me check. OK, sir, Mr. Johnson is in Room 1212. But the line is engaged. _____

C: In that case, I will call back later. Thank you anyway.

O: Thank you for calling. Goodbye.

C: Goodbye.

A. Henry Johnson, that is H-E-N-R-Y.

B. I am afraid I don't know.

C. Would you like to hold on or call back later?

D. May I know who's calling please?

E. Could you put me through to Mr. Johnson?

2. Act in pairs to finish the following role-play activities. Compensate necessary information if necessary.

(1) Student A: Act as a guest staying in the hotel room. You want to contact a friend in other cities of China. Ask the operator for help.

Student B: Act as the operator. Answer the phone and respond.

(2) Student A: Act as a guest staying in the hotel room. You feel dizzy this morning. You want the hotel doctor to come to see you. Ask the operator for help.

Student B: Act as the operator. Answer the phone and respond.

(3) Student A: Act as a caller. You want to contact a friend staying in the same hotel. Ask the operator for help.

Student B: Act as the operator. Answer the phone and respond.

(4) Student A: Act as a guest staying in the hotel room. You want to make a phone call to a friend in Hawaii. Ask the operator for help.

Student B: Act as the operator. Answer the phone and respond.

3. Look at the following items in a hotel room and translate them into Chinese.

(1) IDD

(2) person-to-person calls

(3) DDD

(4) long-distance calls

(5) house phone

(6) area code

(7) country code

(8) collect call

(9) operator

(10) emergency call

(11) telephone directory

(12) extension

(13) outside call

(14) taking message

(15) leaving message

(16) put through

4. Discussion:

(1) What should you do as an operator if a caller wants you to tell him a guest's room number?

(2) What qualities should a hotel operator have?

5. Translate the following sentences.

(1) 抱歉先生，您呼叫的电话占线。

(2) 您想留个口信吗？

(3) 请您再说一遍好吗？

(4) 如果愿意，请留下姓名和电话号码，我让他给您回电话。

(5) 我想打个电话，对方付费。

(6) 我想打个国际直拨电话。

(7) 请稍候，我这就为您接通 1206 号房间。

(8) 您要和谁通话？

(9) 请问您是哪位？

(10) 抱歉，声音不清楚，请您大点声说好吗？

Part Two Knowledge Extension

According to the part of Knowledge Extension, write the answers to the following questions on the sheet of paper by using your own words, not simply copying the sentences. When you have completed the test, ask your lecturer for the answers.

Operator Services Made Simple

Section Six 模块六
Other Hotel Services 其他酒店服务

Proper Etiquette for Transferring Calls

_____
_____
_____
_____

Person-to-person Calls

_____
_____
_____
_____

Station Calls (Station-to-station Calls)

_____
_____
_____
_____

Collect Calls (Reverse Charge Calls)

_____
_____
_____
_____

Long-Distance Calls

_____
_____
_____
_____
_____

Topic Two　Hotel Shopping Service
酒店购物服务

Introduction

Star hotels can provide guests with hotel shopping service, which is convenient for them to go shopping. When serving them, hotels should pay attention to the way of treating guests and give them some hints on prices of goods.

Objectives

Competence Standard	Knowledge Standard
Ability to provide hotel shopping service	Know about the working procedures of hotel shopping service
Ability to know about the way of treating guests while serving them	Know about the way of treating while serving them
Ability to know about prices of goods	Know about prices of goods
Ability of listening, speaking and reading	Know something related to hotel shopping service

Working Procedures

- Greet the guests.
- Enquire the request of the guests.
- Respond to the request.
- Answer questions.
- Introduce goods.
- Settle the bill.
- Offer other help.
- Say goodbye.

Dialogues

Dialogue 1

Situation Question: As a salesperson in the shopping center of a hotel, do you know how to introduce souvenirs to guests?

Introducing Souvenirs

S: Salesman   G: Guest

S: Good morning, madam. Welcome to the shopping center. Can I help you?

G: I want to buy some souvenirs for my friends. Do you have some advice?

S: Certainly. We have some traditional Chinese handicrafts, and they are very good souvenirs for friends and relatives. Please have a look at them.

G: They look like face masks of Beijing Opera.

S: Yes, they are Beijing Opera masks. There is a character introduction in Chinese and English on the back of the mask.

G: Good. They are different figures, right?

S: Yes. This set is the figures of *The Romance of the Three Kingdoms*, which is one of the Four Classical Novels in China.

G: Yes, I heard about it before. I know Guan Yu, the famous general.

S: Yes. A very faithful general.

G: I like them. How much are they?

S: The prices are different according to the size of the mask. The large one is RMB200 *yuan*, and the middle and small one are RMB150 *yuan* and RMB100 *yuan* respectively.

G: I want to have the middle size.

S: Do you want to have a set or just one piece?

G: A set.

S: There are 3 in total, so the total is RMB450 *yuan*. How would you like to pay?

G: Credit card.

Notes:

(1) souvenir 纪念品

(2) handicraft 手工艺品

(3) Beijing Opera mask 京剧脸谱

(4) figure 人物

(5) *The Romance of the Three Kingdoms* 《三国演义》

(6) general 将军

Dialogue 2

Situation Question: As a salesperson in the shopping center of a hotel, do you know how to introduce cosmetics to guests?

Introducing Cosmetics

S: Salesman   G1: Guest 1   G2: Guest 2

S: Good afternoon, ladies. Can I help you?

G1: We just look around.

S: Enjoy your time. If there is anything I can do for you, please tell me.

G1: OK.

G2: Excuse me.

S: What can I do for you?

G2: Is this facial cleanser?

S: Yes, it is a famous Chinese skin care brand. It is made of Chinese traditional herbs together with modern technology. The facial cleanser is very mild and suitable for dry skin.

G2: Is it suitable for oily skin?

S: No, I recommend the one over there for oily skin. It works very well for oily skin. It has good oil control effects and is kind to the skin.

G2: Sounds good. I would like to have a try. Give me one bottle.

S: Yes, madam. Anything else?

G1: I want to have a facial cleanser, too. But give me the one for dry skin.

S: OK. This way, please. Do you want to pay the bill together or?

G1: Together. I pay the bill.

Notes:

(1) facial cleanser 洗面奶

(2) Chinese traditional herb 中药

(3) dry skin 干性皮肤

(4) oily skin 油性皮肤

Dialogue 3

Situation Question: As a salesperson in the shopping center of a hotel, do you know how to introduce tea products to guests?

Introducing Tea

S: Salesgirl   G: Guest

S: Good afternoon, sir. Can I help you?

G: Yes, I'd like to buy some tea. I know China is a large tea producing country. And before I came, my friends recommended me to buy some tea.

S: You are right. China is famous for tea planting, producing and export. There are so many kinds of tea in China, and according to the processing methods, they can be classified into four major kinds, such as green tea, black tea, oolong tea, and scented tea.

G: Could you tell me how to choose tea?

S: First, you can choose tea according to seasons. Usually people prefer to have scented tea in spring, green tea in summer, oolong tea in autumn and black tea in winter. Each kind has its own effect for people's health. Second, you can choose tea according to flavors. But the water you use to make tea will affect the flavors of tea.

G: Oh, there is so much knowledge behind it.

S: Yes.

G: I want to buy green tea. Could you recommend any?

S: Yes. We have Dragon Well, Biluochun and Maofeng. All of them are famous brands of green tea.

G: Give me Dragon Well, please. How much is a box?

S: RMB1,680 *yuan*. How many boxes would you like?

G: Two.

S: How would you like to pay?

G: In cash.

S: The total is RMB3,360 *yuan*.

G: Here is the money.

S: Thank you. Here are the change and the receipt.

Notes:

(1) planting 种植

(2) processing 加工

(3) classify 分类

(4) oolong tea 乌龙茶

(5) scented tea 花茶

Useful Sentences

- Good morning, madam. Welcome to the shopping center. Can I help you? 上午好，女士。欢迎光临购物中心。我能帮您做什么吗？
- I want to buy some souvenirs for my friends. Do you have some advice? 我想给朋友买纪念品，您有什么建议吗？
- We have some traditional Chinese handicrafts, and they are very good souvenirs for friends and relatives. 我们这儿有中国传统的工艺品，都非常适合赠送亲友。
- This set is the figures of *The Romance of the Three Kingdoms*, which is one of the Four Classical Novels in China. 这一套是中国四大名著里《三国演义》中的人物。
- The prices are different according to the size of the mask. The large one is RMB200 *yuan*, and the middle and small ones are RMB150 *yuan* and RMB100 *yuan* respectively. 价格根据脸谱的大小而不同，大号200元人民币，中号和小号分别是150元人民币和100元人民币。
- Do you want to have a set or just one piece? 您是要买一套还是一个？
- We just look around. 我们随便逛逛。
- Enjoy your time. If there is anything I can do for you, please tell me. 请便。如果您有什么需要，请告诉我。
- Is this a facial cleanser? 这是洗面奶吗？
- It is a famous Chinese skin care brand. 它是中国著名护肤品牌。
- The facial cleanser is very mild and suitable for dry skin. 这款洗面奶非常温和，适合干性皮肤。
- It works very well for oily skin. It has good oil control effect and is kind to skin. 它非常适合油性皮肤，有很好的控油效果，又不刺激。
- Do you want to pay the bill together or separately? 您要一起付款还是分开付款？
- China is famous for tea planting, producing and export. 中国是茶叶种植、生产和出口大国。
- There are so many kinds of tea in China, and they can be classified into four major kinds according to the processing methods, such as green tea, black tea, oolong tea, and scented tea. 中国的茶叶有很多种类，按照加工方式可分为四大类：绿茶、红茶、乌龙茶和花茶。
- Usually people prefer to have scented tea in spring, green tea in summer, oolong tea in autumn and black tea in winter. 通常，人们喜欢春天喝花茶，夏天喝绿茶，秋天喝乌龙茶，冬天喝红茶。

Knowledge Extension

- **The Way of Treating Guests While Serving Them**

Greet guests nicely. Acknowledge the guests nicely with eye contact saying "hello" and smile.

Apologize to guests for any wait. Usually guests don't understand the reason why they need to wait. An apology with a smile can make them ensure that you are trying your best.

Ask the guests whether they have found everything that they are looking for. Perhaps some guests might automatically say "yes" but it is a part of good hotel shopping service.

Offer a bag with guests' purchase. If these bags are requested to pay additional charges, please let the guests know because some guests like to reuse the shopping bags.

Ask the guests the way they would like to pay for their purchase, which is always considerate. When the guests are prepared with their debit cards, credit cards or cash, this question is not always needed.

Be thankful. Your salary might be the highest each time the guests enter your store, and their purchase can increase your store overall sales.

Say "goodbye". It is simple and as important as your greeting.

You have been prepared well for your next guest.

- **Prices of Goods**

Compared with the people in most countries in the world, Americans do not usually bargain over prices. What they do is go around and try to find the shop where the quality of the goods is the best and the prices of that are the lowest. Almost everything sold in the United States varies in prices with stores and the time of year. For example, just before Christmas, the prices are often highest. On the contrary, after Christmas, the prices are the lowest and at times, the price can be different according to state or local taxes.

Section Summary

- Know about the working procedures of hotel shopping service.
- Learn about the way of treating guests while serving them.
- Know about prices of goods.

Practice

Part One Dialogue

1. Choose the correct sentences to fill in the blanks according to the context.

S: Salesgirl   G: Guest

S: Good afternoon. Can I help you?

G: Yes. _____ You know, it is really cold here.

S: Yes, the weather is changing recently and the temperature declines sharply.

G: _____

S: Yes. How about this one? It is imported from Paris. The gray color and the texture of the cloth make it formal and fashionable. _____

G: Yes.

S: _____

G: Medium size.

S: OK, Here you are.

G: Good, I like it. _____

S: RMB980 *yuan*.

A. Do you have a coat for formal situation?

B. How much is it?

C. Would you like to have a try?

D. What size do you need?

E. I want to buy a coat.

2. Act in pairs to finish the following role-play activities.

(1) Student A: Act as a guest staying in the hotel. Go to the shopping center to buy souvenirs for your kids.

Student B: Act as the salesperson working in the shopping center. Respond to the request of the guest.

(2) Student A: Act as a guest staying in the hotel. Go to the shopping center to buy cosmetics.

Student B: Act as the salesperson working in the shopping center. Respond to the request of the guest.

(3) Student A: Act as a guest staying in the hotel. Go to the shopping center to buy an overcoat for yourself. Ask for discount.

Student B: Act as the salesperson working in the shopping center. Respond to the request of the guest.

(4) Student A: Act as a guest staying in the hotel. Go to the shopping center to buy some paintings for your friends.

Student B: Act as the salesperson working in the shopping center. Respond to the request of the guest.

3. Look at the following words and translate them into English.

(1) 折扣

(2) 纪念品

(3) 国画

(4) 首饰

(5) 茶具

(6) 化妆品

(7) 口红

(8) 睫毛膏

(9) 眼影

(10) 内衣

4. Discussion:

(1) How would you recommend cosmetics to the guests if you were the salesperson in the hotel shop?

(2) What should you say if a guest asked you to give a discount for an item he or she bought?

5. Translate the following sentences.

(1) 请您随意看看。

(2) 我们这儿的茶叶种类齐全，价格合理。

(3) 您可以看看我们的手工艺品，非常受欢迎。

(4) 它们非常适合赠送亲友。

(5) 您觉得灰色的这款怎么样？

(6) 这是纯手工做的。

(7) 抱歉，这款产品目前没有折扣。

(8) 这是中国著名茶叶品牌。

(9) 您是要一起付款还是分开付款？

(10) 这是收据和找您的零钱。

Part Two　Knowledge Extension

According to the part of Knowledge Extension, write the answers to the following questions on the sheet of paper by using your own words, not simply copying the sentences. When you have completed the test, ask your lecturer for the answers.

The Way of Treating Guests While Serving Them

_____
_____
_____
_____
_____
_____

Prices of Goods

_____
_____

Appendices

Appendix I　Additional Material, Resources and References

Steffi Feldhaus，2009. 酒店英语 [M]. 上海：上海外语教育出版社.
编写组，2017. 宾馆英语 [M]. 北京：高等教育出版社.
丁国声，2015. 酒店英语 [M]. 上海：上海交通大学出版社.
高文知，2017. 酒店情景英语 [M]. 2 版. 北京：北京大学出版社.
姜文宏，李玉娟，2015. 饭店服务英语 [M]. 3 版. 北京：高等教育出版社.
李培娥，2013. 酒店英语阅读教程 [M]. 上海：上海外语教育出版社.
李永生，2015. 酒店英语会话 [M]. 3 版. 北京：高等教育出版社.
唐羽，2016. 酒店商务英语 [M]. 北京：北京交通大学出版社.
王丽华，王金茹，李艳，2012. 酒店服务英语 [M]. 北京：北京理工大学出版社.
朱华，2014. 酒店英语视听说教程 [M]. 北京：高等教育出版社.

Appendix II Contest Problems for Technical Competence

2017年全国职业院校技能大赛
高职组中餐主题宴会设计赛项
（英语口语测试题库及参考答案）

题型一　中译英

1. 我想确认一下，您公司在我们餐厅预订了两个宴会。
I'd like to confirm that your company has made two banquet bookings in our restaurant.

2. 请问有多少人来参加宴会？
May I know how many people will be at the banquet?

3. 您要预订几桌饭菜？
How many tables would you like?

4. 您想尝尝我们的招牌菜吗？
Would you like to try our house specialty?

5. 请问以谁的名字预订？
In whose name was the reservation made?

6. 我们晚餐营业时间是下午5点到晚上10点。
The dinner is served from 5 p.m. to 10 p.m..

7. 对不起，我们餐厅14日晚餐的餐位已经订满了。
I am sorry, sir. Our restaurant is fully booked on the evening of 14th.

8. 餐食通常从左侧服务，酒水通常从右侧服务。
Food is usually served from the left and beverages are served from the right.

9. 订餐有人均100元、150元和180元人民币三种标准，您想要订哪一种？
For set menus, the expenses per head range from RMB100 *yuan*, RMB150 *yuan* to RMB180 *yuan*. Which would you prefer?

10. 三百人用餐的收费是15 000元人民币，不含酒水饮料。
The charge for a 300-person-dinner party is RMB15,000 *yuan*, excluding beverages.

11. 欢迎光临我们餐馆。您是来参加约翰先生婚宴的嘉宾吗？
Welcome to our restaurant. Are you here for the wedding banquet of Mr. John?

12. 现在可以上菜了吗？
May I serve the dishes now?

13. 希望您用餐愉快。
Please enjoy your meal.

14. 今天的特价菜是麻婆豆腐，6折优惠。
Today's special is Mapo Tofu with a 40% discount.

15. 您的这瓶葡萄酒已经喝完了，请问还需要一瓶吗？
This bottle of grape wine is finished. Would you like one more?

16. 您的菜需要分一下吗？

May I separate the dish for you?

17. 您要不要来点烈性酒呢？要是喜欢低度酒的话，我们这儿还有米酒。

Do you care for something a little stronger? If you prefer something milder, you may try some rice wine available here.

18. 先生，您对我们的饭菜还满意吗？

Are you satisfied with the meal, sir?

19. 打扰了，女士。我给您换一个骨碟好吗？

Excuse me, madam. Shall I change a new side plate for you?

20. 菜已经上齐了，还有甜点。

This is the complete course. There is dessert to follow.

21. 还需要再加一把椅子吗？

Would you like one more chair to your table, please?

22. 我会在客人入座前把开胃凉菜摆放在餐桌上。

I will place the cold appetizers on the table before the guests are seated.

23. 您需要把宴会厅装饰一下吗？

Would you like to have the banquet hall decorated?

24. 请问您需要一杯冰水吗？

Excuse me, would you like a glass of iced water?

25. 愿意为您效劳！

At your service!

26. 您需要含糖的还是不含糖的食物？

Would you like your food with sugar or not?

27. 这道菜色、香、味俱全。

The dish looks good, smells good and tastes good.

28. 这是我们赠送给您的果盘。

This is the complimentary fruit for you.

29. 我们已经在总费用里加收了 10% 的服务费。

The total includes a 10% service charge.

30. 您想要在炒茄子的调味品里放些辣椒吗？

Would you like some chilli as seasoning in the stir-fried eggplant?

31. 这是我们最新的价目表。

This is our latest price list.

32. 您使用维萨信用卡结账可以享受 9 折优惠。

You have got a 10% discount for your Visa Card.

33. 许多宾客对这款葡萄酒大加赞赏。

Many guests speak highly of the grape wine.

34. 这是我们厨师长的推荐菜。

This is our chef's recommendation.

35. 您对我们的服务有什么建议吗?

What do you think of our service?

36. 请不要遗忘您的东西。

Please don't leave anything behind.

37. 您能告诉我事情的详细经过吗?

Can you tell me/describe what happened in detail?

38. 抱歉,我上错汤了。

I do apologize for serving you the wrong soup.

39. 谢谢您提醒我们。

Thank you for bringing this matter to our attention.

40. 很抱歉给您带来了这么多麻烦,这是我们特意送给您的甜点。

To express our regret for all the trouble, we offer you the complimentary dessert.

41. 您用餐时需要喝点酒吗?

Would you like to have some wine with your dinner?

42. 餐厅的早餐供应时间是早上 7 点到 9 点。

Breakfast is served from 7:00 to 9:00 a.m. in the restaurant.

43. 这是您的账单,请签字。

Here is the bill. Please sign it.

44. 请问您是否喜欢坐靠窗的位子?

Would you like to sit by the window?

45. 医生认为我在饮食中应多摄入咖啡因。

The doctor thinks I need more caffeine in my diet.

46. 您觉得鱼这样做怎么样?

How do you like the fish cooked this way?

47. 自助餐在那边,请随意取用。

The buffet is over there. Please help yourself.

48. 洗手间现在不能用,因为正在维修。

The rest room is not available, and it is being repaired.

49. 送餐服务,有什么事需要我们吗?

Room service. Can I help you?

50. 太对不起了,先生。账单上出了一点错。

I'm terribly sorry, sir. There is a mistake on the bill.

51. 我需要您的签名和房间号。

I'll need your signature and room number.

52. 糖醋鱼是今晚的特别推荐菜,您是否试试?

The sweet and sour fish is particularly recommended tonight. Would you like to try?

53. 对不起,恐怕我们没有这道菜,我可以向您推荐别的菜吗?

I'm afraid we do not have time to prepare the dish unfortunately. May I suggest something else?

54. 对不起，先生。我们现在没有空餐桌，请您在酒吧稍等一下好吗？

I'm sorry, sir. We do not have a table free now. Would you like to have a drink in the bar?

55. 请这边走。我们为你们安排了一个单间。

This way, please. We've got a private room for you.

56. 我建议您尝尝四川菜。

I suggest you have a taste of Sichuan cuisine.

57. 200 人的宴会最低标准是 6 000 元人民币，不包括饮料。

The minimum charge for a dinner party of 200 people is 6,000 *yuan*, excluding drinks.

58. 如果您不喜欢这道菜，是否考虑换一道菜？

If you don't like this dish, how about getting you another one?

59. 相信下次您再来时，一切还会让您满意。

I'm sure everything will be satisfactory next time you come.

60. 我们饭店是不收小费的。

In our hotel we don't accept tips.

题型二　英译中

1. How many people is it for?

请问有多少位客人用餐？

2. At the dinner banquet, Chinese food will be served and the minimum charge of RMB120 *yuan* per head is required.

晚宴将提供中餐，最低消费标准是每位 120 元人民币。

3. What drinks are you going to have for the banquet?

宴会需要什么酒水？

4. We don't have any vacant tables by the windows at the moment.

目前靠窗的位子都已经订出去了。

5. There is an increasing interest and appreciation of Chinese food in the West.

在西方国家，人们对中餐的兴趣日益浓厚，对中餐的了解也逐渐加深。

6. I'd like to cancel my reservation for Saturday night.

我想要取消周六晚上的预订。

7. I'd like a private room for 15 people at eight thirty tomorrow evening.

我要预订一个 15 人的包房，时间是明晚八点半。

8. We can only hold your private room till 7:30 p.m. because it will be peak hours after that time.

您的预订我们只能为您保留到晚上 7 点 30 分，因为那段时间之后将是用餐高峰时段。

9. Is there anything I can do for you?

还有什么需要我帮您的吗？

10. We look forward to seeing you.

我们恭候您的光临。

11. Could you give me some more napkins?

请多拿一些餐巾纸给我。

12. Do you have any vegetarian dishes?

你们餐厅是否供应素餐？

13. What would you like to drink?

您想喝点什么？

14. Each server should take a clean napkin at all times so as to be able to wipe drips or spills immediately.

所有服务人员必须随身携带干净的餐巾纸，以便随时抹去溢出或泼洒的食物。

15. You might have a taste of Shaoxing wine.

您不妨尝尝绍兴黄酒。

16. We have squeezed fresh orange juice, apple juice and watermelon juice.

我们的鲜榨果汁有橙汁、苹果汁和西瓜汁。

17. May I bring any wine or liquor by myself?

我可以自带酒水吗？

18. Could you give me a baby highchair for my child?

可以给我的孩子拿一把儿童餐椅吗？

19. This dish is called "Mapo Tofu". Enjoy it, please.

这道菜叫"麻婆豆腐"，请慢用。

20. What size of birthday party are you going to order and how would you like us to arrange the tables?

您想在我们餐厅办一个多大规模的生日聚会？您希望我们怎样摆放桌椅？

21. Please hold the food/Please put our order on hold because we still have one more friend coming.

请稍后上菜，我们还有一个朋友没到。

22. What kind of tea would you prefer to begin/start with, black tea or green tea?

您要先喝什么茶，红茶还是绿茶？

23. Make it two, please.

请再给我来一杯。

24. A seating plan is often made in advance, and cards with guests' names should be placed where each individual will sit.

入座安排要事先确定好，每位客人的座位上都应放置客人席卡。

25. The Chinese cuisine has a long history, and is one of the Chinese cultural treasures.

中式菜历史悠久，是中国文化中的瑰宝之一。

26. Huaiyang cuisine is famous for its cutting technique. Sichuan dishes are spicy and hot.

淮扬菜以其精湛的刀工见长，四川菜则以麻辣著称。

27. How many steps are taken to cook these dishes?

做这些菜需要几道工序？

28. What is the specialty of the house?

餐厅的招牌菜是什么？

29. To cook Chinese food, cutting skills and matching of ingredients are of equal importance.

做中国菜，刀工和菜肴的原料搭配都很重要。

30. A deposit of RMB500 *yuan* is required to secure your booking.

您需要预付500元人民币作为押金，以保证您的预订。

31. Please feel free to contact us if you have any questions about the payment arrangements.

如果您对结账方式有任何疑问，欢迎随时与我们联系。

32. I could give you a special price.

我可以给您一个优惠价。

33. Tables in a banquet will be formally set with an array of cutlery, glasses and table linen and with a floral table decoration at the center.

宴会餐桌在正式摆台时，将会整齐摆放餐具、玻璃杯和餐巾，并在餐台中央摆放花坛。

34. Here are some complimentary vouchers for you. You can pay with them next time when you have meals in our restaurant.

我们有一些赠券给您，下次您在我们餐厅消费时可以拿赠券抵用。

35. At the end of the banquet and after all guests have left, clear wine glasses, cups and saucers, and remove napkins and table cloths.

宴会结束，等所有客人离开后，再清理葡萄酒杯、茶杯和碟子，撤下餐巾和台布。

36. It would be on the house.

那是送给您免费享用的。

37. Any jugs of liquid (hot or cold) that are carried on trays must have their spouts facing inward so they do not spill onto guests.

放在托盘上的壶装液体（不论冷热），其壶口必须向内，以防溅洒到客人身上。

38. Sorry to have kept you waiting. I'll see to it right away.

抱歉，让您久等了。我马上去处理此事。

39. Our manager will get in touch with you soon.

我们经理将会尽快与您取得联系．

40. When a guest complains, the server should listen to them attentively with a good judgment.

在客人投诉时，服务员需要认真倾听，并且要有较强的判断力。

41. This Chinese restaurant was closed for private event for now.

这家中餐馆因私事暂停营业。

42. I was just about to pour myself a brandy.

我正想给自己倒一杯白兰地。

43. You should drop by. We just put a chocolate cake on the dessert menu.

您应该过来看看。我们刚刚在菜单上加了一个巧克力蛋糕。

44. Always keep a smile and an ear to listen to any complaints, compliments or anything guests would like to share with us.

时刻保持微笑，时刻准备倾听客人与我们分享抱怨、恭维或任何事情。

45. Waiters required. Please contact Charles Edward, deputy manager.

招聘男服务员。请联系副经理查尔斯·爱德华。

46. I'm polite, organized and hardworking. I think I have all the attributes of a good waiter.

我有礼貌，做事有条不紊，努力上进。我认为我具备一名优秀服务员的所有品质。

47. As a banquet waiter, I am on call.

作为宴会服务生，我随叫随到。

48. The dish of Chinese cucumber salad looks fantastic and tastes even better.

凉拌黄瓜看起来好极了，吃起来更棒。

49. I strongly recommend the fried chicken. It's crispy on the outside and really juicy inside.

我特意推荐炸鸡，它外面酥脆，里面多汁。

50. It is glutinous rice wrapped in bamboo leaves stuffed with meat, beans, salted egg yolks and many other ingredients.

它是用竹叶包裹糯米，用肉、豆、咸鸭蛋黄和其他原料做馅。

51. The sausage is very greasy.

香肠太油腻了。

52. Are you a sweet or savory person?

您喜欢吃甜食吗？

53. What about some sticky rice balls stuffed with taro?

吃点香芋馅的汤圆怎么样？

54. I like spicy food and I like my vegetables really crispy. I don't want them overcooked or soggy.

我喜欢吃辣，喜欢吃炒的松脆的蔬菜。我不喜欢炒过了或炒得湿而不脆的菜。

55. The best chefs in our hotel have all ever attended national cooking contests.

我们酒店最好的主厨全部参加过全国烹饪比赛。

56. Hello Madam, are you expecting someone?

您好女士，您是在等人吗？

57. As for green vegetables, what about some stir-fried broccoli?

关于青菜，清炒西蓝花怎么样？

58. This is a 40-year-old Bordeaux.

这是一瓶 40 年的波尔多葡萄酒。

59. I just got done working a 20-hour shift.

我刚刚完成 20 小时轮班工作。

60. If you like, the cook can make you an omelet with ham and cheese.

如果您喜欢，厨师可以为您做一个煎蛋，搭配上火腿和奶酪。

题型三　情景对话

1. When a guest walks into the banquet department and wants to reserve a farewell banquet for his boss, what kind of information will you get from the customer?

Answer: I need to get the information such as the time for the banquet, the number of people, the expense for each table, the customer's name, the customer's telephone number and so on. As the hotel requires, a sum of money as deposit is to be collected from the customer.

2. Is the preparation work for a banquet important? Can you explain it with your own experience?

Answer: Yes. It is very important to make a full preparation for a banquet. To prepare for a banquet, the staff should be aware of the food requirements, table decorations, and service methods, and set the table accordingly for the banquet. That's a tough job. Banquet staff could not provide good table service without these preparations.

3. What are the ways of arranging the tables in a banquet for your customer?

Answer: The layout of the tables depends on the size of the room and the purpose of the function. For example, at weddings, there is usually a "head table" for the bride and groom as well as their immediate family, and the rest of the tables will be of the same size, for approximately 8-10 people each.

4. If a foreign guest comes to you for suggestions on Chinese food, and he/she would like something light and fresh, what will you recommend?

Answer: There are four major Chinese cuisine, or say, four styles. Each cuisine is distinctive and has its own style and flavor. As the guest prefers something light and fresh, I'd recommend Huaiyang dishes, which are famous for their cutting techniques and original flavor. Boiled beancurd shreds and Yangzhou fried rice are worth trying.

5. Which step in the table service is the most important in your opinion? Why?

Answer: I think waiting at the table, meeting all the needs of the diners is the most challenging. Firstly, the waiter/waitress should be very alert to the requests of the guests. Secondly, waiters and waitresses should be familiar with the dishes and environment of the restaurant. Thirdly, they should also be good at communicating with the guests as well as with the kitchen staff.

6. If a guest got drunk during a wedding banquet and he broke a wine glass, what would you do?

Answer: Firstly, I would try to ask the guest to stop drinking alcohol, and ask him if I can serve him a cup of tea. Then, I will inform the banquet host of the incident and of the charge for the damage. If the host refuses to pay for the damage or it's beyond my ability to handle the situation, I will ask the manager for help.

7. Can you give a definition for "banquet"?

Answer: A banquet is a very formal sit-down meal organized for special occasions such as weddings, fellowship reunions, business dinners, conventions or birthday parties. A banquet is usually attended by a large number of people.

8. Do you think serving a Chinese banquet is much simpler than serving a Western one? Why?

Answer: No, I don't think so. The Chinese are used to taking dining as a part of their culture, and while serving a Chinese banquet, we have to follow certain procedures. Although the working procedures for Chinese banquets are quite the same as those for Western ones, throughout the Chinese banquet, the working staff should observe the Chinese dining etiquettes and provide proper services. Sometimes, the job is really tough. For example, when receiving a wedding banquet, we have to serve hundreds of guests at the same time. It is really not an easy job.

9. What do you think the server should do at a banquet?

Answer: The server should always follow the banquet service rules, such as carrying a clean napkin all the time, serving ladies first, serving beverages from the right, serving the head table first, etc.

10. Which is more important for banquet service, skills or attitude? State your reasons.

Answer: Both of them are important. One cannot do a job without professional skills; on the other hand, the guest won't be satisfied if you treat him/her badly. Sometimes, I think, good attitude can make up for the lack of skills, and as I believe, if we show consideration and concerns, the guest may be moved. We should try to serve our guests professionally with a good attitude.

11. What is the most important element in the hospitality industry?

Answer: The success of the hospitality industry depends on the people-pleasers. Everyone can master the techniques of being nice to guests if they receive good training and plenty of practical experience. If pleased guests leave the hotel with a good memory, they are likely to visit the hotel again.

12. Some experts say that it is good to have an open kitchen. Do you agree with that?

Answer: I think it is a good idea to have an open kitchen. First, it can show the guest the cleanliness of the food. On the other hand, it may be a good way to attract guests, as people are usually very curious about how the delicious food is cooked. And cooking is also a kind of art for people to enjoy.

13. What are the proper procedures for handling complaints?

Answer: The proper procedures for handling complaints are: (1) listen to the guest carefully, (2) make an apology, (3) give explanations, (4) offer help, (5) take action, and (6) give feedback.

14. What attitude hotel staff should have when dealing with guests' complaints?

Answer: Some complaints are serious and some are quite trivial, but the hotel staff should investigate them carefully. No matter how the guests behave, the hotel staff should always try to be nice to them. Don't lose your temper on any occasion. Avoid arguing with the guests.

15. If your hotel wants to promote wedding banquet this month, what measures will you take?

Answer: Advertising is a good way to sell products, so I think we can put advertisements on TV, magazines, newspapers and the Internet. We can also provide some special services to attract customers, such as toastmaster service, wedding cakes, special floral decorations, and so on. If the hotel regulations permit, we can also provide the new couple with a honeymoon suite in the hotel for one night.

16. If a guest wants to order some wine, but it seems that he/she is under 18 years old, what will you do then?

Answer: According to the law, only adults are allowed to drink wine or dine in the bar. If I am not sure about his/her age, I'll ask in this way, "May I see your ID card?" If he/she is under eighteen, I'll advise him/her to order some soft drinks or juices instead.

17. What do you think of the sentence "The guest is always right"?

Answer: In my opinion, it means that when we provide service for the guest, we should stand in his shoes. Try all our best to make the guest satisfied. When handling misunderstandings and complaints, we'd better make good use of professional skills to respect our guest, save his face and make him stay in comfort. If the guest's requests are not rational, we should explain patiently why we can not meet his requests, and offer an apology to him.

18. What is your own opinion of receiving tips? Please state your idea in your own words.

Answer: I think tips mean that the guest is satisfied with my job and service. And I know it is quite common in Western countries to accept a tip from a guest. If the policy permits, I would accept a tip in case the guest feels embarrassed.

19. Have you had any training in dealing with emergencies? What steps do you follow to settle problems? Please give an example of how you would do that.

Answer: It is quite important to have some training in handling emergencies during the banquet service. For example, a guest may suffer stomachache or faint while attending a banquet or having dinner in the restaurant. In that case, a server should first keep calm, then call for the ambulance and wait for the doctor. A server shouldn't move the guest as he/she has no proper first aid knowledge or skills. When the doctor comes, as a server, I will assist the doctor and keep the food and drink unmoved on the table, in case there will be an examination of the food.

20. If you are going to attend a job interview for the position as a banquet server, what qualifications and personalities are you expected of?

Answer: To be a server in a banquet department, one should be helpful, cooperative, enthusiastic, patient and quick to learn. Meanwhile, one should have self-control, the ability to work under pressure and loyalty. If possible, I think, work experience is important, too.

21. As a head server, how do you offer your service to your customers with a reservation after they are seated?

Answer: I will reconfirm the items in their reservation, ask them what they would like to have for their dinner and show them the menu for them to order, but I will also ask them for pre-dinner drinks and make some suggestions if possible. After I fetch the drinks for them, I would leave for a while and return to take the order.

22. What might you explain to your customers while they ask questions about the bill after they finish their dinner?

Answer: I might have to show the bill to them and explain the total charge, the dish items, the drink items and the service charge on the bill.

23. Suppose you are the manager of F&B department. How do you handle the situation when a customer complains to you about a waitress who has spilt cheese sauce over him?

Answer: Firstly I would apologize to him politely and sincerely, and pay for his clothes to be cleaned immediately. Meanwhile I would offer a coffee on the house while he is waiting.

24. You are required to send breakfast to Mr. White's room. What should you do?

Answer: I would knock at the door and say, " Room Service. May I come in? " When I get in the room I would ask him where I should place the breakfast and ask him to sign the bill before I leave politely.

25. After the food is served, what would you do for your guests?

Answer: I would remind them that all the food is served, ask for their comments on the food and offer a plate of fruit as a gift to them.

26. Would you please list several don'ts in banquet serving?

Answer: (1) Never say "No". (2) Never give an excuse. (3) Never bring an incomplete order to the table. (4) Never lean or rest in front of the guest. (5) Never come to work in bad mood. (6) Never eat in the back of the house area.

27. Please tell me some responsibilities as a banquet server.

Answer: (1) Maintain personal hygiene, and uniform clean, neat and tidy. (2)Set up the banquet room as specified by the customers. (3) Be totally familiar with the composition of all menu items. (4) Serve food and beverages in accordance with the hotel standards, but above all in a professional, courteous manner. (5) Explain the food or beverages if necessary. (6) Issue or report damage, maintenance, or breakage promptly.

28. How do you serve beverages as a banquet server?

Answer: (1) Beverages are served according to the menu. (2) Service is proceeded always from the right side of the guest. (3) The bottle is kept in my right hand and the napkin in the left. (4) The bottle top is dried with the napkin after a guest is served. (5) The level of glasses is paid attention to accordingly.

29. How much do you know about F&B department?

Answer: As far as I know, it is one of the most interesting and challenging departments in a hotel. Since the beginning of the hotel industry, this department has been the main generator of profit as well as the most important in terms of the impression the guest leaves with.

30. What do you think of reservation service in a hotel?

Answer: Reservation is a sub-division of F&B department. It concerns with all the outlets. The success of it depends on how well the reservations department handles customer calls and whether or not it can convince guests to come to dine in the hotel restaurant.